Augustine Francis Hewit

Problems of the Age

Augustine Francis Hewit

Problems of the Age

ISBN/EAN: 9783744660822

Printed in Europe, USA, Canada, Australia, Japan

Cover: Foto ©Thomas Meinert / pixelio.de

More available books at **www.hansebooks.com**

Problems of the Age.

Problems of the Age;

WITH

Studies in St. Augustine

ON

KINDRED TOPICS.

BY THE

REV. AUGUSTINE F. HEWIT,

OF THE CONGREGATION OF ST. PAUL.

"*Fides quærens intellectum.*"
S. Anselm.

New York:
THE CATHOLIC PUBLICATION HOUSE,
126 NASSAU STREET.
1868.

Entered, according to Act of Congress, in the year 1868, by
AUGUSTINE F. HEWIT,
In the Clerk's Office of the District Court of the United States for the Southern District of New York.

JOHN A. GRAY & GREEN, PRINTERS, 16 AND 18 JACOB STREET, NEW YORK.

PREFACE.

THE volume herewith presented to the public contains two distinct essays, treating, however, of identical or closely connected topics; each of which has been already separately published in the pages of a periodical. The first essay is republished from *The Catholic World*. It is entitled as it is, because it professes to discuss questions of difficulty and moment which are subjects of much interest and inquiry in our own time. The special problems discussed relate to the harmony and analogy between natural or rational theology and certain doctrines of revealed or supernatural theology. After waiting for some time in order to reëxamine what I have written, and to profit by the criticisms of others, I have deemed it to be suitable for publication in a permanent form, with some few alterations from the original text. I have subtracted from the beginning of the essay that portion which treated of the pure philosophy of the idea, because the statements contained in it were too succinct and concise to be satisfactory in regard to a topic so important and so much controverted. I have also added to the chapter which treats of original sin some further explanations of the exposition I have given, derived from the works of standard theologians. With these exceptions, the alterations are but trivial. I have spared no pains to conform my explication of theological and philosophical doctrines to the authoritative standard of Catholic teaching. In regard to open questions, I have avoided all that might provoke controversy, except in so far as I have thought it necessary to my purpose to propose the opinions of a specific school; and in all cases I have endeavored to observe due respect toward those who maintain different opinions.

The essay on the doctrine of St. Augustine, originally published in *The New-York Tablet*, is added to the PROBLEMS OF THE AGE in this volume, on account of the intimate connection of the topics treated in it with those discussed in the latter. An explanation of its scope and design is given in the introductory chapter, and need not be repeated here. Some portions of it are a repetition of what has been said in another form in the PROBLEMS OF THE AGE, a circumstance due to the fact that it was written as an independent essay. These subjects are, however, so abstruse in themselves, that I have not thought this repetition of the same ideas in a distinct connection a fault requiring to be corrected, but rather, perhaps, an advantage. In my translations I have aimed only at a literal and intelligible rendering, without attempting elegance, and I have abstained from swelling the size of the volume with the Latin text, because it is so easily accessible to scholars. I have brought the most ancient and the most modern school of Catholic theology into juxtaposition in these two essays, in order to show both the identity of the dogmas of faith in all ages, from the remotest to the one actually present; and also the progress made in the evolution of the philosophy of the dogmas as time goes on. Having completed my task, I leave what I have written in the hands of the Author of all wisdom, hoping that it may promote the intellectual and spiritual profit of that class of readers for whose benefit it is intended.

A. F. H.

St. Paul's, New York, May 20, 1868.

PROBLEMS OF THE AGE.

CONTENTS.

CHAPTER I.
Introductory, - - - - - - - - - - 9

CHAPTER II.
Relation of the Credible Object to the Creditive Subject, - - 14

CHAPTER III.
The Being of God the first article of the Creed, - - - - 23

CHAPTER IV.
The Revelation of the Supernatural Order, and its relation to the primitive idea of Reason, - - - - - - - 45

CHAPTER V.
The Trinity of Persons included in the One Divine Essence, - 76

CHAPTER VI.
The dogma of Creation—The Principle, Archetype, and End of the Creative Act, - - - - - - - - - 101

CHAPTER VII.
The End of Creation metaphysically final—The ascending series of grades in existence—The summit of this series is a nature hypostatically united to the Divine Nature of the Word—The Incarnation, the creative act carried to the apex of possibility—The supernatural end to which the universe is destined completed in the Incarnation, - - - - - - - 112

Contents.

CHAPTER VIII.

                                                                           PAGE

A further explanation of the Supernatural Order, - - - 134

CHAPTER IX.

The State of Probation, Its reason and nature—The Trial of the Angels, - - - - - - - - - - - 168

CHAPTER X.

The Original State of the First Parents of Mankind—The relation of Adam to his posterity—The Fall of Man—Original Sin, 203

CHAPTER XI.

The Mystery of Redemption, - - - - - - - 250

CHAPTER XII.

The Catholic Church, as the instrument of the Sanctification of the Human Race, - - - - - - - - - 257

CHAPTER XIII.

The Final Destination of Angels and Men—Condition of the Unregenerate in the Future Life—Eternity of the Penalty of Sin—The State of Final Beatitude, - - - - - - 268

STUDIES IN ST. AUGUSTINE.

CONTENTS.

CHAPTER I.
                                                     PAGE

Introductory, - - - - - - - - - - - 3

CHAPTER II.

The problem of Moral Evil and its cause, - - - - - - 17

CHAPTER III.

The cause and nature of Sin, and the reason of its permission, - 25

CHAPTER IV.

St. Augustine's doctrine of Original Sin, - - - - - - 65

CHAPTER V.

Freedom of Will after the Fall, Necessity of Grace, Predestination, - - - - - - - - - - - - 91

CHAPTER VI.

Faith and the Catholic Church, - - - - - - - 108

CHAPTER VII.

Baptismal Regeneration, - - - - - - - - 128

CHAPTER VIII.

The Holy Eucharist —Invocation of Saints—Purgatory—Penance, - - - - - - - - - - - 142

Problems of the Age.

CHAPTER I.

INTRODUCTORY.

THE object of this work is to present a solution, derived from the principles of the Catholic faith, of certain problems with which the minds of many persons in the present age are occupied and perplexed. Those who are destitute of Catholic faith evidently possess no solution of these problems which satisfies themselves, wherefore they are always in a state of intellectual unrest, ever seeking and never able to come to a knowledge of the truth. On the contrary, those who have received the principles of Catholic faith in their early education, and have preserved them uncorrupted by scepticism, possess in these principles a solution for all these problems which is perfectly tranquillizing to the mind, and prevents it from being disquieted by an anxious and ineffectual search after a solution.* If they desire to investi-

---

* Vide *Questions of the Soul.* By Rev. I. T. Hecker.

gate these problems in a more scientific manner, the same principles of faith enable them to obtain results which satisfy the intellect and increase the limits of rational knowledge. If these principles are objectively true and certain, that is, founded in the order of being and eternal reality, they can be justified on rational grounds, they can be proved to have a root in the constitutive rational principles of the human mind, and they can, therefore, be so presented to a mind destitute of them that it will be logically able to accept them, and strictly bound by its own intrinsic laws to do so. In order to do this completely, it is necessary to exhibit both the extrinsic and intrinsic credibility and reasonableness of the Catholic faith. The first is done by a formal demonstration, beginning from the first principles of natural theology and proceeding through the evidences of revelation to the proof of the authority of the church, and of the fact that all the dogmas she proposes are actually revealed by God to be received as true on the divine veracity. There are many admirable works presenting these extrinsic evidences of the Catholic faith in the most complete manner. We do not propose to attempt the task of adding another to the number, nor do we cherish the smallest intention of attempting to supplant the method which they follow. We desire to present the intrinsic credibility and reasonableness of the Catholic faith, in order to remove certain difficulties in the way of apprehending and believing its extrinsic evidences. In doing so, we follow a method which seems to us the best suited to our special purpose. We begin by taking the Catholic believer or creditive subject, as he really is from the first dawn of reason, in actual contact with the credible object or the Catholic faith. If his undoubting certitude respecting that which the church proposes to his belief is a rational certitude based on rational and real objective verity, and not a mere subjective mode of his own mind, the rationality of this certitude can be made evident from principles of reason. The child truly and infallibly knows something, which is a sufficient motive and ground of his truly and infallibly believing something else. Therefore, if he grows up into a philosopher and theologian, the ultimatum of his knowledge and faith must be a mere explication of that which he knew and believed as a child. Its root must be in his reason itself, as elevated and enlightened by the gift of faith. The first complete act of his reason on divine truth, evoked and perfected by divine grace, must contain implicitly all that is evolved in the last and highest act of the same reason. If he were capable of explaining this first act at the time he made it, he would be able to justify it on rational grounds and prove its infallibility or unerring certitude, just as clearly as he justifies that which he affirms to be divine truth when he becomes a consummate theologian. The child cannot do it while he is a child, but we may attempt to do it for him; that is, to go back to the first constitutive principles of reason, to its most incipient and elementary acts, to find there the ground of the rationality of faith, and follow up its growth into the stage of complete development.

We invite the really earnest and candid reader, therefore, to permit us to propose to him the Catholic faith as a hypothesis supposed to be known from the beginning ; and we will endeavor to prove to him that, this hypothesis being given, it is in accordance with reason. We invite him to take the viewing point of a Catholic believer, and endeavor to get the perspective of one brought up in the church. We do not ask him to take anything for granted of which he is not already convinced. We will endeavor to show the internal coherence and symmetry of the Catholic doctrines, and their correspondence or analogy with rational truths. For extrinsic evidences of Christianity and the church we refer him elsewhere, or suppose him already partially or completely informed. If he is a Protestant, less or more conformed in his belief to the standard of Catholic orthodoxy, he will proceed with us a certain distance without questioning, and may find some considerations not without weight presented to his mind to induce him to go further ; if he is an unbeliever, he will find that the rational formula, out of whose charmed circle he cannot think, is made the basis of demonstration for the revealed or Christian formula, and a synthesis constructed which binds the two into one coherent whole. The Catholic reader will find that idea which he already possesses presented to his intellect, it is hoped, in such a way as to aid him in apprehending its conformity with all that is true and sublime in the conceptions of reason and the deductions of philosophy; to aid him not in believing more firmly, but in understanding more clearly the truths of the Catholic faith which are the precious heritage of his baptism.

CHAPTER II.

RELATION OF THE CREDIBLE OBJECT TO THE CREDITIVE SUBJECT.

LET us begin with a child, or a simple, uneducated adult, who is in a state of perpetual childhood as regards scientific knowledge. Let us take him as a creditive subject or Christian believer, with the credible object or Catholic faith in contact with his reason from its earliest dawn. Before proceeding formally to analyze his creditive act, we will illustrate it by a supposed case.

Let us suppose that, when our Lord Jesus Christ was upon earth, he went to visit a pagan in order to instruct him in the truths of religion. We will suppose him to be intelligent, upright, and sincere, with as much knowledge of religious truth as was ordinarily attainable through the heathen tradition. Let us suppose him to receive the instructions of Christ with faith, to be baptized, and to remain ever after a firm and undoubting believer in the Christian doctrine. Now, by what process does he attain a rational certitude of the truth of the revelation made by the lips of Christ?

In the first place, the human wisdom and virtue of

our Lord are intelligible to him by the human nature common to both, and in proportion to his own personal wisdom and goodness. Having in himself, by virtue of his human nature, the essential type of human goodness, he is able to recognize the excellence of one in whom it is carried to its highest possible perfection. The human perfection visible in Jesus Christ predisposes him to believe his testimony. The testimony that Jesus Christ bears of himself is that he is the Son of God. This declaration includes two propositions. The chief term of the first proposition is " God." The chief term of the second proposition is " Jesus Christ." The first term includes all that can be understood by the light of reason concerning the Creator and his creative act. The second term includes all that can be apprehended by the light of faith concerning the interior relations of God, the incarnation of the Son or Word, the entire supernatural order included in it, and the entire doctrine revealed by Christ. The idea expressed by the first term is already in the mind of the pagan, as the first and constitutive principle of his reason. His reflective consciousness of this idea and his ability to make a correct and complete explication of its contents are very imperfect. But, when the distinct affirmation and explication of the idea of God are made to him by one who possesses a perfect knowledge of God, he has an immediate and certain perception of the truth of the conception thus acquired by his intelligence. God has already affirmed himself to his reason, and Christ, in affirming God to his intellect, has only repeated and manifested by sensible images, and in distinct, unerring language, this original affirmation.

It is otherwise with the affirmation which Christ makes respecting the second term. God does not affirm to his reason by the creative act the internal relations of Father and Son, completed by the third, or Holy Spirit, and therefore, although the Trinity is a necessary truth, and in itself intelligible as such, it is not intelligible as a necessary truth to his intellect. The incarnation, redemption, and other mysteries affirmed to him by Christ are not in themselves necessary truths, but only necessary on the supposition that they have been decreed by God. The certitude of belief in all this second order of truths rests, therefore, entirely on the veracity of God, authenticating the affirmation of his own divine mission made by Jesus Christ. We must, therefore, suppose that this affirmation is made to the mind of the pagan with such clear and unmistakable evidence of the fact that the veracity of God is pledged to its truth, that it would be irrational to doubt it. Catholic doctrine also requires us to suppose that Christ imparts to him a supernatural grace, as the principle of a divine faith and a divine life based upon it. The nature and effect of this grace must be left for future consideration.

These truths received on the faith of the testimony of the Son of God by the pagan are not, however, entirely unintelligible to his natural reason. We can suppose our Lord removing his difficulties and misapprehensions, showing him that these truths do not contradict reason, but harmonize with it as far as it goes, and pointing out to him certain analogies in the natural order which render them partially apprehensible by his intellect. Thus, while his mind cannot penetrate into the substance of these mysteries, or grasp the intrinsic reason of them after the mode of natural knowledge, it can nevertheless see them indirectly, as reflected in the natural order, and by resemblance, and rests its undoubting belief of them on the revelation made by Jesus Christ, attested by the veracity of God.

In this supposed case, the pagan has the Son of God actually before his eyes, and with his own ears can hear his words. This is the credible object. He is made inwardly certain that he is the Son of God by convincing evidence and the illustration of divine grace. This is the creditive subject, in contact with the credible object. It exemplifies the process by which God has instructed the human race from the beginning, a process carried on in the most perfect and successful manner in the instance we are about to examine of a child brought up in the Catholic Church.

The mind of the child has no prejudices and no imperfect conceptions derived from a perverted and defective instruction to be rectified. Its soul is in the normal and natural condition. The grace of faith is imparted to it in baptism, so that the rational faculties unfold under its elevating and strengthening influence with a full capacity to elicit the creditive act as soon as they are brought in contact with the credible object. This credible object, in the case of the child, as in that of the pagan, is Christ revealing himself and the Father. He reveals himself, however, not by his visible form to the eye, or his audible word to the ear, but by his mystical body the church, which is a continuation and amplification of his incarnation. The church is visible and audible to the child as soon as his faculties begin to open. At first this is only in an imperfect way, as Jesus Christ was at first only known in an imperfect way to the pagan above described. As he merely knew Christ at first as a man, and in a purely human way, so the child receives the instruction of his parents, teachers, and pastors, in whom the church is represented, in regard to the truths of faith, just as he does in regard to common matters. He begins with a human faith, founded in the trusting instincts of nature, which incline the young to believe and obey their superiors. As soon as his reason is capable of understanding the instruction given him, he is able to discover the strong probability of its truth. He sees this dimly at first, but more and more clearly as his mind unfolds, and the conception of the Catholic Church comes before it more distinctly. Some will admit that even a probability furnishes a sufficient motive for eliciting an act of perfect faith. According to their theory, the undoubting firmness of the act of faith is caused by an imperate act of the will determining the intellect to adhere firmly to the doctrine proposed, as revealed by God. There are many, however, who will not be satisfied with this, and we acknowledge that we are of the number. It appears to us that the mind must have indubitable certitude that God has revealed the truth in order to a perfect act of faith. Therefore we believe that the mind of the child proceeds from the first apprehension of the probability that God has revealed the doctrines of faith to a certitude of the fact, and that, until it reaches that point, its faith is a human faith, or an inchoate faith, merely. The ground and nature of that certitude will be discussed hereafter. In the meantime, it is sufficient to remark that the child or other ignorant person apprehends the very same ground of certitude in faith with the mature and educated adult, only more implicitly and obscurely, and with less power to reflect on his own acts. Just as the child has the same certainty of facts in the natural order with an adult, so it has the same certainty of facts in the supernatural order. When we have once established the proper ground of human faith in testimony in general, and of the certitude of our rational judgments, we have no need of a particular application to the case of children. It is plain enough that, so soon as their rational powers are sufficiently developed, they must act according to this universal law. So in regard to faith. When we have established in general its constitutive principles, it is plain that the mind of the child, just as soon as it is capable of eliciting an act of faith, must do it according to these principles. We do not, however, deny that grace may enable the mind to apprehend that motives of assent which are merely probable to unaided reason are really certain.

The length of time, and the number of preparatory acts requisite, before the mind of a child is fully capable of eliciting a perfect act of faith, cannot be accurately determined, and may vary indefinitely. It may require years, months, or only a few weeks, days, or hours. Whenever it does elicit this perfect act, the intelligible basis of the creditive act may be expressed by the formula, *Christus creat ecclesiam.** In the church, which is the work of Christ and his medium or instrument for manifesting himself, the person and the doctrine of Christ are disclosed. In the first term of the formula, *Christus*, is included another proposition, namely, *Christus est Filius Dei.*† Finally, in the last term of the second proposition is included a third, *Deus est creator mundi.*‡ The whole may be combined into one formula, which is only the first one explicated, *Christus, Filius Dei, qui est creator mundi, creat ecclesiam.*§ In this formula we have the synthesis of reason and faith, of philosophy and theology, of nature and grace. It is the formula of the natural and supernatural worlds, or rather of the natural universe, elevated into a supernatural order and directed to a supernatural end. In the order of instruction, *Ecclesia* comes first, as the medium of teaching correct conceptions concerning God, Christ, and the relations in which they stand toward the human race. These

---

* Christ creates the church.
† Christ is the Son of God.
‡ God is the creator of the world.
§ Christ, the Son of God, who is the creator of the world, creates the church.

conceptions may be communicated in positive instruction in any order that is convenient. When they are arranged in their proper logical relation, the first in order is *Deus creat mundum*, including all our rational knowledge concerning God. The second is *Christus est Filius Dei*, which discloses God in a relation above our natural cognition, revealing himself in his Son, as the supernatural author and the term of final beatitude. Lastly comes *Christus creat ecclesiam*, in which the church, at first simply a medium for communicating the conceptions of God and Christ, is reflexively considered and explained, embracing all the means and institutions ordained by Christ for the instruction and sanctification of the human race, in order to the attainment of its final end. In the conception of God the Creator, we have the natural or intelligible order and the rational basis of revelation. In the conception of the Son, or Word, we have the superintelligible order in its connection with the intelligible, in which alone we can apprehend it. God reveals himself and his purposes by his Word, and we believe on the sole ground of his veracity. The remaining conceptions are but the complement of the second.

All this is expressed in the Apostles' Creed. In the first place, by its very nature, it is a symbol of instruction, presupposing a teacher. The same is expressed in the first word, "Credo," explicitly declaring the credence given to a message sent from God. The first article is a confession of God the Father, followed by the confession of the Son and the Holy Ghost. After this comes " Sanctam Ecclesiam Catholicam," with the other articles depending on it, and lastly the ultimate term of all the relations of God to man, expressed in the words "Vitam æternam."

Having described the actual attitude of the mind toward the Creed at the time when its reasoning faculty is developed, and the method by which instruction in religious doctrines is communicated to it, we will go over these doctrines in detail, in order to explain and verify them singly and as a whole. The doctrine first in order is that which relates to God, and this will accordingly be first treated of.

CHAPTER III.

THE BEING OF GOD—THE FIRST ARTICLE OF THE CREED.

THE first article of the Creed is, "Credo in Deum," "I believe in God." The Christian child receives this belief through instruction, and a natural faith in the word of its teachers, before it is capable of exercising a complete act of reason or divine faith. Afterward, when it is capable of apprehending the rational evidence of the being of God, and attains a more perfect conception of his attributes, it still receives the form of its conception from Christian theology, which is itself the offspring of a tradition dating from the original creation of man. The same is true of all the conceptions of God existing among mankind universally. All are received by a traditional instruction purporting to come originally from a divine revelation. This revelation, originally given to the founders of the race, has come down pure and uncorrupted through the line of patriarchs and prophets to Jesus Christ, who has promulgated it anew, in such a manner as to secure its preservation to the end of time. Indirectly, and subject to many corruptions and counterfeit additions, it has descended through human language, mythology, and literature. No doubt, reason has always been capable of correcting the false conceptions of heathen tradition, and attaining a more correct notion of God. The Greek philosophy did, in fact, by a purely rational method, evolve some very sublime conceptions in natural theology; nevertheless, it still fell short of the perfect notion of the divine being and attributes which is presented by revealed theology, and failed to indoctrinate the masses of the population with its pure monotheistic principles. The only way in which pure theistic conceptions have ever been made the common belief of the people has been through a sacred traditional instruction based on a divine revelation. Nevertheless, the criterion of the truth of these conceptions cannot be either the authority of the teachers who transmit and explain the traditional doctrine, or the common sense of mankind. The perfect formula expressing with precise exactitude the explicit conception of God and his attributes is derived from revelation, and presented before the mind by the instructor. But the criterion is in the mind itself, that is, in pure reason. The doctrines of natural theology, although proposed by revelation, are within the sphere of reason, and are accepted by reason only because they are either self-evident or deduced from self-evident principles; just as the truths of mathematics are proposed by the teacher, but become really known to the pupil only so far as he perceives their intrinsic certitude. What we desire to do, therefore, is to describe and demonstrate the circle of the divine attributes: to propose the theistic conception of the first article of the Creed, as contained in Christian theology, and show its objective reality by the first principles of pure reason.

It is evident that we have no immediate vision of God as he is in his essence. There is an infinite and impassable abyss between us and him. In the words of St. Augustine, "Videri autem divinitas humano visu nullo modo potest; sed eo visu videtur, quo jam qui vident, non homines sed ultra homines sunt." "The Godhead can in no way be seen by human vision; but it is seen by a vision of such a kind, that they who see by it are not men, but are more than men."* Moreover, that intellectual cognition of God by which reason is capable of knowing, not what God is, but that God is, *non quid sit Deus, sed ut Deus sit*, is not an immediate intuition in the sense of being the constitutive principle or intellectual light or primitive *a priori* judgment of reason. If it were, it would be in all minds, without exception; everywhere, and under all circumstances the same; and would present itself to the reason as soon as it came into exercise, without any need of argumentation; in the same way that any self-evident truth, such as this, that the whole is greater than a part, presents itself, or, as it were, *affirms* itself, to the intellect. The reason why this truth, that God is, which is the *a priori* truth in itself, and in itself in the most absolute sense self-evident, is not self-evident to the human intellect, is be-

---

* *De Trin.* lib. ii. c. 11.

cause everything is known by its essence, and we have no intuition of the essence of God. This is the argument of St. Thomas. We cannot know by intuition that God is, unless we intuitively know what is meant by the word God, or what God is. But we have no immediate intuition of what God is; we cannot directly behold by our intellectual vision his essence as it is itself. We know what is contained in the conception expressed by the name God only by a process of discursive reasoning and a species of mental composition or construction. That is, we know what God is mediately, indirectly, in a reflective and analogical manner. We do not know that he is until we know what he is, or what are his essential attributes; until the complex, composite conception of God as the subject of certain predicates is present to our reflective consciousness. This is an act of discursive reason, and consequently the knowledge of God is and always remains an act of the discursive, and not of the intuitive, intellect. Reason attains only to a speculative contemplation of the being or essence of God; that is, to a contemplation of God as most perfect being in the creation which is the mirror reflecting his essential attributes.

This doctrine is clearly stated by the great father of the fathers and founder of Christian theology, St. Paul:

"Quis enim hominum scit quæ sunt hominis, nisi spiritus hominis qui in ipso est? Ita, et quæ Dei sunt, nemo cognovit, nisi Spiritus Dei." "For what man knoweth the things of a man, but the spirit of man which is in him? So the things also that are of God no one knoweth, but the Spirit of God."*

We understand this to mean, that just as the human spirit apprehends itself as an intellectual subject, and apprehends the spiritual nature of other similar subjects, by its self-consciousness, so God alone has, by nature, the knowledge of his own essence and interior activity, as being infinitely above all other spiritual essences.

"Quod notum est Dei manifestum est in illis. Deus enim illis manifestavit. Invisibilia enim ipsius, a creatura mundi, per ea quæ facta sunt intellecta, conspiciuntur: sempiterna quoque ejus virtus et divinitas." "That which is known of God is manifest in them. For God hath manifested it to them. For the invisible things of him, from the creation of the world, are clearly seen, being understood by the things that are made: his eternal power also and divinity."†

That is, God affirms himself to reason by the creative act.

"Videmus nunc per speculum in enigmate." "We see now by means of a mirror in an enigma."‡ That is, we understand the attributes and perfections of God as these are made intelligible to us by analogies derived from created things, in which, as in a mirror, the image of God is reflected.

The doctrine of St. Paul is all comprised in this brief formula: that human reason, when its eye is fully open, and its intellectual vision is fully exercised,

* 1 Cor. ii. 11. † Rom. i. 19, 20. ‡ 1 Cor. xiii. 12.

becomes a spectator of the creation. The word *creation* is here used in its strict sense as denoting the terminus of the creative act, or the effect proceeding from the supreme and absolute cause—*causa altissima.* In the language of St. John of the Cross: "Creatures are, as it were, traces of the passage of God, revealing his greatness, power, and wisdom, and his other divine attributes."* Sensible objects, the intellect itself, which is the subject perceiving, other similar intelligent existences, internal and external metaphysical truths, are present to the developed and active reason, and are apprehended by it as objectively real. They are also apprehended, in so far as they are particular things or actual existences, as finite, limited, included in the relations of definite time and of definite space, or something equivalent to space; that is, of something which limits their extent or quantity of being. They are consequently apprehended as not possessing in themselves the cause or reason of their existing at all or existing as they are. They have a beginning, and, therefore, the reason of their existence is not in themselves, but out of themselves, in being which is without beginning, and, therefore, eternal; which has in itself the reason of all being, and is, therefore, *ens a se*, or self-existing, and the cause of everything which is *ens ab alio*, or mere derived existence. Moreover, as finite or limited in extent, they have not the reason of their limits or the cause of their definite quantity of being in themselves.

* *Spir. Cant.* stanza v.

Problems of the Age. 29

Because that which has being in itself is what it is by necessity of nature, and to conceive it greater or less than it is would imply a contradiction, which is not the case with any particular finite thing, since it may be conceived without contradiction as greater or less than it is, or as not existing at all. Contingent finite existences, therefore, must receive their being with its definite limits from necessary being, or that which is being in plenitude and infinite.

The notions of space and time give the same result. Space is the relation existing between things coexisting as coexisting. Real space, as being a definite relation between definite, really existing things, is a finite relation, contingent on the existence of the related objects, which would cease to exist if they were annihilated, and had no existence before they began to be. It has no entity in itself, either created or uncreated, and is neither identical with God or a necessary effect of God's existence, nor something distinct from the universe which God has created. Leibnitz has fully shown the absurdity of all these notions in his controversy with Clarke. Ideal space is the possibility of relations between possible existences. It cannot be limited in thought by any possible effort of the mind. Knowing, as we do, actual existences, and apprehending, as we must, that they have origin from infinite, necessary being as first cause, we are incapable of fixing any necessary limit to the possible number or extent of existences in the finite order, and therefore are unable to confine the notion of ideal space within any necessary limits. We cannot think of ideal space without thinking of the infinite. This infinite is the infinite possibility of creation, or the infinite creative fecundity of being, the infinite causative power of the first cause.

Time is the relation of things successive as successive. The first instant of real time corresponds to the beginning of contingent existence, and the whole extent of real time corresponds to the actual succession of events that have really taken place. Annihilate the contingent, finite universe, and time goes with it. Nevertheless, the notion of possible time, or of a relation of order and succession among possible finite events and acts, cannot be eliminated from the reason or included within any definite, necessary limits. Look backward or look forward, the line is interminable. That is to say, the notion of eternity presents itself as one that cannot be dissociated from the notion of time. There is a duration which is eternal, not capable of measurement by succession, but which is capable of coexisting to unlimited periods of succession. Knowing, as we do, that things existing in time have their origin from being which is not in time or is without beginning, we apprehend that this eternity which we conceive is an attribute of being, or that being is eternal.

Our notions of space and time have a sensible form, because they are suggested to us, like all other notions, by the sensible. Nevertheless, they are in the order of the intelligible, and must necessarily terminate at last in the idea of pure, infinite, and eternal being. They force us to make a continual effort to grasp infinity and eternity under an adequate mental representation, although we can never succeed in doing it. We imagine ideal time as a succession of moments, and ideal space as a kind of atmosphere, to neither of which any limits can be given. It is impossible, however, that actual infinity should be composed of coexisting points, or actual eternity of successive moments. We must necessarily, therefore, recognize behind these conceptions the idea of the infinite and eternal, and we can never really explicate them into an adequate form until we affirm infinite and eternal being as the cause and origin of all that is limited by space and time, with a power to be the cause and origin of existences limited by space and time which is itself not limited by either. The same idea of the infinite lies behind the notion that mathematical quantities are divisible without end. We can never reach the boundary of divisibility, which is only another form of the endless multiplicability of mathematical lines. The conception of ideal number and quantity is rooted in the idea of the infinite possibility of creating things which have mathematical relations, that is, in the idea of being as infinite cause.

All mathematical truths, and all metaphysical truths which are self-evident or demonstrated from self-evident principles, present themselves as true by necessity, true in eternity, true in all parts of the real or possible universe to all existing or possible intelligences. The intelligible, or the idea, is eternal, self-subsisting, and is what it is by its own absolute, intrinsic necessity. The mind, as intelligent subject, when it contemplates the intelligible, that is, necessary and eternal truths, by a reflex act of consciousness perceives that it is intelligent. It gains the conception of intelligent spirit. Reflecting that the first cause of its existence is the first cause of its mode of existence as intelligent spirit, and has given it the light of the intelligible, it sees clearly that the intelligible, or the idea, is in the first cause as the adequate object of intelligence. Eternal truth is the idea of eternal, infinite intelligence, the origin and cause of all created intelligence. First cause, infinite and eternal being, supreme reason, self-subsisting, intelligent spirit, are all one.

The order of the universe is a further manifestation of the infinite intelligence of its first cause, as is most amply and lucidly shown by the numerous and excellent works and treatises in which the arguments *a posteriori* for the existence and attributes of God are developed.

The beauty of the particular objects of the universe, and of the universe as a whole, is referred by reason to a standard of absolute beauty, an infinite, eternal principle of harmony, fitness, and order, an eternal ideal of that which is beauty by its own intrinsic being, and an adequate object of the infinite intelligence considered as contemplating the idea of beauty, or absolutely beautiful being. From that which is being in itself all existences receive their being, and therefore their beauty, from which we infer that all creation is only a copy after the ideal in the mind of the creator. All particular notions respecting those things which are good, respecting moral qualities, obligation, duty, virtue, merit, sanctity, law, responsibility, have invariably the idea as existing in the infinite mind behind them. Everything which is in the effect must be in the cause in a more eminent mode; therefore, everything which the mind can apprehend in creation as contingent and finite must exist in the creator as infinite, necessary, uncaused, self-subsisting, eternal. That is, the rational conception of the first cause is the conception of the most perfect possible being, or the conception of God.

The explication of the conception of God as most perfect being proceeds by analysis of the contents of necessary being, or *ens a se*, as possessing the plenitude of being. God is *ens simplicissimum*, most simple being, to the exclusion of every negation or limitation of being, and of all composition of being with that which is separable from it, or of modes of being which in themselves singly are incomplete, conditioned, or relative, in the sense of being essential component parts of a composite essence. The human intellect, being incapable of grasping the idea of being in its totality under one conception, is obliged to discriminate and distinguish notes, attributes, or qualities of being in God. This is not by the way of addition or the composition of attributes with the essence of God, but by the way of identification. The affirmation of most pure and simple being is the affirmation of the subject of every possible predicate which predicates that which is real or is perfection, that is, something included in the plenitude or infinitude of being.

That which is most radical and first in the logical order in the conception of God is, according to some of the best theologians, intelligence; although it matters little which note is taken as primary. The infinite intelligence is identical with the infinite intelligible, because, as it is intelligent in itself, by its own nature or intrinsic necessary being, it must have all that is necessary to intelligence in itself, or contain the infinite idea as the innate principle and object of intelligence. The infinite intelligence and the infinite intelligible are, therefore, identical, and we may call God either the self-comprehending intelligence, or the self-comprehended intelligible essence.

It follows from this that God is pure spirit. The idea which is the intelligible object of intellect is by its nature the most remote of all things from matter, and the intellect or intelligent subject is of the same nature. The infinite intelligence is also removed beyond all potentiality, or inert capacity reducible to act, which is an imperfection in finite intellects by which they are, in so far as they have in their essence anything not evolved into act, non-intelligent, or similar to material substance. God alone is in the most absolute sense most pure spirit, and is infinitely more spiritual than the highest created spirit. In the language of the schools, he is *actus purissimus*, most pure act; that is, intelligence in act, comprehending by one simple intuition his own infinite essence as the intelligible in its infinite intelligibility. He is not *das Werden*, or the becoming, as pantheists say, but *das Seyn*, the Eternal Being. There is no process, no increase, no endless movement toward the evolution of intelligence in the direction of the infinite, but the eternally explicated actual intelligence of the intelligible object also actually infinite. This is what is meant by *actus purissimus*. It is also the explication of *ens simplicissimum*. It is actual being in eternity, the total, simultaneous, perfect possession of interminable being to the utmost limit of the possibility of being which can be thought by infinite intelligence. It exhausts in one indivisible act the total comprehensibility of being as it is in the idea of the divine intellect.

The unity of God is demonstrated as included in the idea of most simple being and most pure act. Intelligence and idea cannot be divided or enter into composition. All the intelligent power that can possibly be actually is by an eternal necessity in one infinite intelligence to constitute it infinite, and make it equal to and identical with necessary being. Its unity is, therefore, a necessary note of its infinity. The infinite intelligence has its sole, adequate, infinite object within its own being, and in the identity of the same indivisible essence. There is, therefore, nothing intelligible beyond one most simple being subsisting in one most pure act or as one most perfect spiritual essence, at the same time self-comprehensible and self-comprehending.

God is infinitely good. For will and volition are in the essence of intelligent spirit, and in God must terminate upon his own being as the infinite, necessary, and adequate object of his infinite volition. But this is the very idea of good, namely, being as the adequate object of volition, if we consider good objectively, and volition considered as terminating in its adequate object, if we consider good subjectively.

God is all-powerful. That is, he is infinite cause, able to produce those effects which are contained in the idea of the intelligible, without limitation from any other power, or from defect of any degree of power in himself which is conceivable or possible.

God is infinitely holy. That is, his intelligence and will terminate upon the same object, infinite good, which is his own being, and therefore agree together; which is the definition of the divine sanctity.

God is unchangeable. For change implies increase or diminution in being, which is contradictory of the very conception of eternal plenitude of being.

God is infinite and eternal. He is without physical extension in space, yet omnipresent by his most simple being to every point of real space, and capable of being present to every point of ideal space without limit. He is, moreover, infinite in every attribute or perfection, as possessing being which corresponds to a series of finite existences ascending upward without end toward the perfect, and yet transcending all possible existences in such a way that no conceivable quantity of being in them is an aliquot part of his infinitude. He is without succession or duration measurable by epochs, yet corresponding equally in the same relation to all epochs of actual time, and to infinite periods of ideal time *a parte ante* and *a parte post.** His eternity is *tota, simul, ac perfecta possessio vitæ interminabilis;* total, insuccessive, and perfect possession of illimitable life. This is merely saying, in other words, that he is *actus purissimus.*

God is absolute truth. Truth is identical with his essence. It is not an abstraction, an external, independent idea, seen by God as extrinsic to his being; it is concrete and identical with the being of God. Prescinding God as *ens in actu*, there is no truth, and no possibility for a thought. For we have already identified the intelligible with intelligence, and both with being, in the essence of God. He is eternally self-contemplating, and is to himself his own adequate object of thought, all finite things being eminently contained in the idea of the divine intellect, which is identical with the divine essence.

God is absolute beauty. For beauty is the splendor of truth, and the essence of God being truth, it is also its splendor. His essence is the infinite idea, by conformity to which all beautiful things have their beauty in a degree corresponding to their conformity. "Created things exhibit the impress of his beauty and magnificence."†

God is infinite love. That is, the subject and object of an infinite, eternal act of love or complacency in his own being as the sum of perfection, the *amor entis*, from which the love of created existences proceeds.

---

* In the past and future.
† St. John of the Cross, *Spir. Cant.* stanza vi.

He is, therefore, infinitely lovable, deserving to be loved supremely by all intelligent creatures, and necessarily loved by them in so far as he is known or truly apprehended by their intelligence.

For the same reason he is infinite beatitude in himself, and the source from which all beatitude proceeds; for this is the same as to say that he possesses the plenitude of being, truth, goodness, beauty, intelligence, love, life, perfection, in himself, and is the infinite term of his own intelligence and will.

God is, moreover, distinct from all contingent existence, and is its cause as creator by his own volition. For, as he is most perfect spirit, most simple being, most pure act, all that is potential, imperfect, composite, or contingent, all that is not essential to constitute the idea of necessary being, must be excluded from the category of that which has being in itself. Existence is, by its very essential note, *ens ab alio*, and not *ens a se*. It proceeds from God as cause, and that not as necessary cause; for necessity has no place except in that which constitutes the essence of God. Moreover, the limits of the creation are not fixed by any eternal necessity, and may be conceived as greater or less; and any or every creature may be conceived as not existing; wherefore, there is no ultimate cause assignable for the actual existence of the creation with its actual existence except the volition of God. The volition of God can only place a reality outside of his own being, or extrinsecate his creative act, by causing something to exist in time which has not existed from eternity, or making the passage from nothing to existence, which is the proper notion of creation, and which alone distinguishes the contingent from the necessary, the finite from the infinite, the temporal from the eternal, *ens ab alio* or *existentia* from *ens a se* or *ens simpliciter*.

God is an ocean of boundless, unfathomable good and perfection, to whom everything must be attributed that can increase our conception of him as most perfect being. We can explicate indefinitely this conception of most perfect being, and every proposition we can make which contains any real intelligible affirmation is evident from its own terms, requiring no proof except verification as truly identifying something with the idea of being. "We shall say much, and yet shall want words : but the sum of our words is, HE IS ALL."* All that we see in the created universe is but a radiation of being, light, life, truth, beauty, happiness, from God the source of being. We see the architecture constructed from his eternal designs ; we behold the infinitely varied and shifting sculptures and pictures in which he embodies the typical forms copied from the infinite ideal of beauty in his own mind. We hear the harmonies that echo the rhythm of his own eternal blessedness ; a colossal machinery plays regularly, silently, and resistlessly around us by the force of his creative impact ; his signs, emblems, and hieroglyphics are presented to our senses ; the perpetual affirmation of his being is making itself always heard in the depth of our

* Ecclus. xliii. 29.

reason. The influx of his creative force is continually creating our body and giving life to our soul. We breathe in it, and see by it, and move by its energy. By its virtue we think and are conscious. It concurs with every intellectual act. "In God we live, and move, and have our being." The divine idea surrounds us like an atmosphere, and encompasses us on every side like an ocean. We cannot soar above it, dive beneath it, or sail in sight of its coasts. It is the rational element in which we were made to live, and its negation is our rational death.

The Creed, therefore, when it proposes its first article to a child who is capable of a complete rational act, only brings him face to face with himself, or with the idea of his own reason. It gives him a distinct image or reflection of that idea, a sign of it, a verbal expression for it, a formula by which his reflective faculty can work it out into a distinct conception. As soon as it is fairly apprehended, he perceives its truth with a rational certitude which reposes in the intimate depths of his own consciousness. It is true that he cannot arrange and express his conceptions, or distinctly analyze for himself the operations of his own mind, in the manner given above. This can only be done by one who is instructed in theology. But although he is no theologian or philosopher, he has nevertheless the substance of philosophy or *sapientia*, and of theology, in his intellect; deeper, broader, and more sublime than all the measurements and signs of metaphysicians can express. We have taken the child as creditive subject in this exposition, in order

Problems of the Age. 41

to exhibit the ultimate rational basis of faith in its simplest act, and, so to speak, to show its *genesis*. But we do not profess to stop with this simple act which initiates the reason in its childhood into the order of rational intelligence and faith; rather we take it as only the terminus of starting in the prosecution of a thorough investigation of the complete development which intelligent faith unfolds in the adult and instructed reason of a Christian fully educated in theological science. Hence we have given the conception of God in its scientific form, but as the scientific form of that which is certainly and indubitably apprehended in its essential substance by every mind capable of making an explicit and complete act of rational faith in God as the creator of the world. In the language of Wordsworth, "The child is father of the man." A complete rational act in a child has in it the germ of all science. He is as certain that two and two make four, as is the consummate mathematician. A complete act of faith in a child is as infallible as the faith of a theologian, and has in it the germ of all theology. He is able to say, "Credo in Deum," with a perfect rational certitude; and this conclusion is the goal toward which the whole preceding argument has been tending.

But here we are met with a difficulty. The principle of faith cannot itself fall under the dominion of faith, or be classed with the *credenda*, which we believed on the veracity of God. How then can *Credo* govern *Deum?* The necessity for an intelligible basis for faith has been established, and this basis located in the idea of God evolved into a conception demonstrable to reason from its own constitutive principles. It would therefore seem that, instead of saying, "I believe in God," we ought to say, "I know that God is, and is the infinite truth in himself, therefore I believe," etc.

This formula does really express a process of thought contained in the act of faith, and implied in the signification of *Credo*. *Credo* includes in itself *intelligo*. Divine faith presupposes, and incorporates into itself, human intelligence and human faith, on that side of them which is an inchoate capacity for receiving its divine, elevating influence. Hence the propriety of using the word *Credo*, leaving *intelligo* understood, but not expressed. The symbol of faith is not intended to express any object of our knowledge, except as united to the object of faith. For this reason it does not discriminate in the proposition of the verity of the being of God that which is the direct object of intelligence, but presents it under one term with those propositions concerning God which are only the indirect object of intelligence through the medium of divine revelation. When we say, *Credo in Deum*, if we consider in *Deum* only that which is demonstrable by reason concerning God, the full sense of *Credo* is suspended, until the revelation of the superintelligible is introduced in the succeeding articles. The term *Deum* terminates *Credo*, only inasmuch as it is qualified by the succeeding terms; that is, inasmuch as we profess our belief in God as the revealer of the truths contained in the subsequent articles.

The foregoing statement applies to the use of the word *Credo* in relation with *Deum* in the first article of the Creed, taking *Credo* in its strictest and most exclusive sense of belief in revealed truths which are above the sphere of natural reason. In addition to this, it can be shown that there is a secondary and subordinate reason on account of which the mental apprehension of that which is naturally intelligible in God is included under the term faith, taken in a wider and more extensive sense.

This intelligible order of truth, or natural theology, was actually communicated to mankind in the beginning, together with the primitive revelation. We are, therefore, instructed in it, by the way of faith. The conception of God, and the words which communicate to us that conception, and enable us to grasp it, come to us through tradition, and are received by the mind before its faculties are fully developed. We believe first, and understand afterward; and the greater part of men never actually attain to the full understanding of that which is in itself intelligible, but hold it confusedly, accepting with implicit trust in authority many truths which the wise possess as science. Moreover, the term faith is often used to denote belief in any reality which lies in an order superior to nature and removed from the sphere of the sensible, although that reality may be demonstrable from rational principles. In a certain sense, we may say that this region of truth is a common domain of faith and reason. But we have now approached that boundary line where the proper and peculiar empire of faith begins, and, like Dante, left by his human guide on the coasts of the celestial world, we must endeavor under heavenly protection to ascend to this higher sphere of thought.

CHAPTER IV.

THE REVELATION OF THE SUPERNATURAL ORDER, AND ITS RELATION TO THE PRIMITIVE IDEA OF REASON.

OUR reason in apprehending the intelligible is advertised at the same time of the existence of the superintelligible. It is necessary to explain here the sense in which this latter term is used. It is evident that it can be used only in a relative and not in an absolute sense. That which is absolutely without the domain of the intelligible is absolutely unintelligible, and therefore a nonentity. The superintelligible must therefore be something which is intelligible to God, but above the range either of all created reason, or of human reason in its present condition. It will suffice for the present to consider it under the latter category.

Our reason undoubtedly apprehends in its intelligible object the existence of something which is above the range of human intelligence in its present state. The intimate nature of material and spiritual substances is incomprehensible. Much more, the intimate nature or essence of the infinite divine being.

All science begins from and conducts to the incomprehensible. Any one who wishes to satisfy himself of this may peruse the first few chapters of Mr. Herbert Spencer's *Principles of Philosophy*. That portion of the first article of the Creed which reason can demonstrate ; namely, the being of God, the creator of the world, in which is included also the immortality of the soul, and the principle of moral obligation ; advertises, therefore, of an infinite sphere of truth which is above our comprehension. The natural suggests the supernatural, in which it has its first and final cause, its origin and ultimate end. The knowledge of the natural, therefore, gives us a kind of negative knowledge of the supernatural, by advertising us of its own incompleteness, and of the want of any principle of self-origination or metaphysical finality in itself. A system of pure naturalism which represents the idea of reason under a form which satisfies completely the intelligence without introducing the supernatural is impossible. What is nature, and what do we mean by the natural? Nature is simply the aggregate of finite entities, and the natural is what may be predicated of these entities. A system of pure naturalism would therefore give a complete account of this aggregate of finite entities, without going beyond the entities themselves, that is, without transcending the limits of space, time, the finite, and the contingent. Such a system is not only incapable of rational demonstration, but utterly unthinkable ; for, when the mind has gone to its utmost length in denying or excluding every positive affirmation of anything except nature, there remains always the abyss of the unknown from which nature came and to which it tends, even though the unknown may be declared to be unknowable. Those who deny the super-intelligible and the supernatural, therefore, are mere sceptics, and cannot construct a philosophy. Those who affirm a first cause, in which second causes and their effects are intelligible, affirm the supernatural; for the first and absolute cause cannot be included under the same generic term with the second causes and finite forces of nature. The more perfectly and clearly they evolve the full theistic conception of pure reason, the more distinctly do they affirm the supernatural, because the idea of God as the infinite, intelligible object of his own infinite intelligence is proportionately explicated and apprehended. It is explicated and apprehended by means of analogies derived from finite objects; but these analogies suggest that there is an infinite something behind them which they represent. By these analogies we learn in a measure the meaning of the affirmation *Ut Deus sit*. We do not learn *Quid sit Deus;* but still we cannot help asking the question, What is God, what is his essence? We know that he is the adequate object of his own intelligence and will, and therefore we cannot help asking the question, What is that object, what does God see and love in himself, in what does his most pure and infinite act consist, what is his beatitude? Our reason is advertised of an infinite truth, reality, or being, which it cannot comprehend, that is, of the super-intelligible. Those who base their philosophy on pure theism, or a modified rationalistic Christianity, are therefore entirely mistaken when they profess to be anti-supernaturalists, and to draw a distinctly marked line between themselves and the supernaturalists. The distinction is only between more or less consistent supernaturalists. Those who are at the remotest point from the Catholic idea, see that those who are a little nearer have no tenable standing-point, and these see it of those who are nearer than they are, and so on, until we come to the Anglicans and the Orientals. But the extremists themselves have no better standing-point than the intermediaries, and in their theistic conception have admitted a principle from which they can be driven by irresistible and invincible logic to the Catholic Church. For the present, we merely aim to show that they are compelled to admit the supernatural when they affirm God as the first and final cause of the world. In affirming this, they affirm that nature has its origin and final reason in the supernatural, or in an infinite object above itself, which human reason cannot comprehend; that is, they affirm superintelligible and supernatural relations, of man and the universe. These relations must be regulated and adjusted by some law. This law is either the simple continuity of the original creative act which explicates itself through concreative second causes in time and space, or it is this, and in addition to this, an immediate act of the creator completing his original creative act by subsequent acts of an equal or superior order, which concur with the first toward the final cause of the creation. Whoever takes the first horn of this dilemma is a pure naturalist in the only sense of the word which is intelligible ; that is, while he is a supernaturalist in maintaining that nature has its first and final cause in the supernatural, or in God, he is a naturalist in maintaining that man has no other tendency to his final cause except that given in the creative act which is essential to nature, and no other mode prescribed for returning to his final cause than the explication of this natural tendency, according to natural law. Consequently, reason is sufficient, without revelation ; the will, without grace ; humanity, without the incarnation ; society, or the race organized under law, without the church. It is precisely in the method of treating this thesis of naturalism that the divarication takes place between the great schools of Catholic theology and between the various systems of philosophy, whether orthodox or heterodox, which profess to base themselves on the Christian idea, or to ally themselves with it. It is not easy to find the clew which will lead us safely through this labyrinth, and preserve us from deviating either to the right hand or to the left, by denying too much on the one hand to the naturalists, or conceding too much to them on the other. Nevertheless, it is necessary to search for it, or to give up all effort to discuss the question before us, and to prove from principles furnished by nature and reason the necessity of accepting a supernatural revelation.

The true thesis of pure naturalism or rationalism is, that God, in educating the human race for the destiny in view of which he created it, merely explicates that which is contained in nature by virtue of the original creative act, without any subsequent interference of the divine, creative power. He develops nature by natural laws alone, in one invariable mode. The physical universe evolves by a rigid sequence the force of all the second causes which it contains. The rational world is governed by the same law, and so also is the moral and spiritual world. The intellectual and spiritual education of the human race develops nothing except natural reason, and the natural, spiritual capacity of the soul. Reason extends its conquests by a continual progress in the super-intelligible realm, reducing it to the intelligible, and eternally approaching to the comprehension of the infinite and absolute truth. The spiritual capacity advances constantly in the supernatural realm, reducing it to the natural, and eternally approaching the infinite and absolute good or being. All nature, all creation, is on the march, and its momentum is the impulsive force given it by the creative impact that launched it into existence and activity.

Planting themselves on this thesis, its advocates profess to have an *a priori* principle by which they prove the all-sufficiency of nature for the fulfilment of its own destiny, and reject as an unnecessary or even inconceivable intrusion the affirmation of another divine creative act, giving a new impact to nature, superadding a new force to natural law, subordinating the physical universe to a higher end, implanting a superior principle of intelligence and will in the human soul, and giving to the race a destina-

Problems of the Age. 51

tion above that to which it tends by its own proper momentum. They refuse to entertain the question of a supernatural order, or an order which educates the race according to a law superior to that of the evolution of the mere forces of nature ; and in consequence of this refusal, they logically refuse to entertain the question of a supernatural revelation disclosing this order, and of a supernatural religion in which the doctrines, laws, institutions, forces, and instruments of this order are organized, for the purpose of drawing the human race into itself.

This is the last fortress into which heterodox philosophy has fled. The open plains are no longer tenable. The only conflict of magnitude now raging in Christendom is between the champions of the Catholic faith and the tenants of this stronghold. It is a great advantage for the cause of truth that it is so. The controversy is simplified, the issues are clearly marked, the opportunity is favorable for an unimpeded and decisive collision between the forces of faith and unbelief, and the triumph of faith will open the way for Christianity to gain a new and mighty sway over the mind, the heart, and the life of the civilized world. This stronghold is no more tenable than any of the others which have been successively occupied and abandoned. Its tenants have gained only a momentary advantage by retreating to it. They escape certain of the inconsistencies of other parties, and evade the Catholic arguments levelled against these inconsistencies. But they can be driven by the irresistible force of reason from their position, and made to draw the Catholic conclusion from their own premises.

We do not say this in a boastful spirit, or as vaunting our own ability to effect a logical demolition of rationalism. Rather, we desire to express our confidence that the reason of its advocates themselves will drive them out of it, and that the common judgment of an age more enlightened than the present will demolish it. It is our opinion, formed after hearing the language used by a great number of men of all parties, and reading a still greater number of their published utterances, that the most enlightened intelligence of this age in Protestant Christendom has reached two conclusions: the first is, that the Catholic Church is the true and genuine church of Christianity; and the second, that it is necessary to have a positive religion which will embody the same idea that produced Christianity. The combination and evolution of these two intellectual convictions promise to result in a return to Catholicism. And there are to be seen even already, in the writings of those who have given up the positive Christianity of orthodox Protestantism, indications of the workings of a philosophy which tends to bring them round to the positive supernatural faith of the Catholic Church. It is by these grand, intellectual currents moving the general mind of an age that individual minds are chiefly influenced, more than by the thoughts of other individual minds. Individual thinkers can scarcely do more than to detect the subtle element which the common intellectual atmosphere holds in solution, to interpret to other thinkers their own thoughts, or give them a direction which will help them to discover for themselves some truth more integral and universal than they now possess. Therefore, while confiding in the power of the integral and universal truth embodied in the Catholic Creed to bear down all opposition and vanquish every philosophy which rises up against it, we do not arrogate the ability to grasp and wield this power, or to exhibit the Catholic idea in ·its full evidence as the integrating, all-embracing form of universal truth. This idea is proposed in an honorable and conciliatory spirit to those who love truth and are able to investigate it for themselves. Many things must necessarily be affirmed or suggested in a brief, unpretending series of essays, which admit of and require minute and elaborate proof, such as can only be given in an extensive work, but are merely sketched here after the manner of an outline engraving, which leaves out the filling up belonging to a finished picture.

To return from this digression. We have begun the task of indicating how that naturalism or pure rationalism which affirms the theistic conception logically demonstrable by pure reason, can only integrate itself and expand itself to a universal Theodicy, or doctrine of God, in a supernatural revelation.

If the opposite theory of pure naturalism were true, it ought to verify itself in the actual history of the human race, and in the actual process of its education. The idea of the supernatural ought to be entirely absent from the consciousness of the race.

For, on the supposition of that theory, it has no place in the human mind—and no business in the world. If unassisted nature and reason suffice for themselves, they ought to do their work alone, and to do it so thoroughly that there would be no room for any pretended supernatural revelation to creep in. The history of mankind ought to be a continuous, regular evolution of reason and nature, like the movements of the planets; the human race ought to have been conscious of this law from the beginning, and never to have dreamed of the supernatural, never to have desired it. Philosophy ought to have been, from the first, master of the situation, and to have domineered over the whole domain of thought.

The reverse of this is the fact. The history of the human race, and the whole world of human thought, is filled with the idea of the supernatural. The philosophy of naturalism is either a modification and recombination of principles learned from revelation, or a protest against revelation and an attempt to dethrone it from its sway. It has no pretence of being original and universal, but always presupposes revelation as having prior possession, and dating from time immemorial. Now, human nature and human reason are certainly competent to fulfil whatever task God has assigned them. They act according to fixed laws, and tend infallibly to the end for which they were created. The judgments of human reason and of the human race are valid in their proper sphere. And therefore the judgment of mankind that its law of evolution is in the line of the supernatural is a valid judgment. Revelation has the claim of prescription and of universal tradition. Naturalism must set aside this claim and establish a positive claim for itself based on demonstration, before it has any right even to a hearing. It can do neither. It cannot bring any conclusive argument against revelation, nor can it establish itself on any basis of demonstration which does not presuppose the instruction of reason by revelation.

It cannot conclusively object to revelation. The very principle of law, that is, of the invariable nexus between cause and effect, which is the ultimate axiom of naturalism, is based on the perpetual concurrence of the first cause with all secondary causes, that is, the perpetuity of the creative act by which God perpetually creates the creature. There is no reason why this creative act should explicate all its effects at once or merely conserve the existences it has produced, and not explicate successively in space and time the effects of its creative energy. The hypothesis that the creative power can never act directly in nature except at its origin, and must afterward merely act through the medium of previously created causes in a direct line, is the sheerest assumption. Some of the most eminent men in modern physical science maintain the theory of successive creations. There may be the same direct intervention of creative power in the moral and spiritual world. Miracles, revelations, supernatural interventions for the regeneration and elevation of the human race, are not improbable on any *a priori* principle. The artifice by which the entire tradition of the human race is set aside, and a demand made to prove the supernatural *de novo*, is unwarrantable and unfair. The supernatural has the title of prescription, and the burden of proof lies only upon particular systems, to show that they are genuine manifestations of it, and not its counterfeits. The existence of a reality which may be counterfeited is a fair postulate of reason, until the contrary is demonstrated, and something positive of a prior and more universal order is logically established from the first principles of reason. We are not to be put off with assurances, like a fraudulent debtor's promises of payment, that our doubts and uncertainties will be satisfied after two thousand or two hundred thousand years. Exclude the supernatural, and natural reason will have, and can have, nothing in the future, beyond the universal data and principles which we have now, and have had from the beginning, with which to solve its problems. The connection between mind and matter, the origin and destination of the soul, the future life, the state of other orders of intelligent beings, the condition of other worlds, will be as abstruse and incapable of satisfactory settlement then as now. If we are to gain any certain knowledge concerning them, it must be in a supernatural way. And what conclusive reason is there for deciding that we may not? Who can prove that some of that infinite truth which surrounds us may not break through the veil—that some of the intelligent spirits of other spheres may not be sent to enlighten and instruct us?

One of the ablest advocates of naturalism, Mr. William R. Alger, has admitted that it is possible, and even maintains that it has already taken place. In his crudite work on the *History of the Doctrine of a Future Life*, he maintains the opinion that Jesus Christ is a most perfect and exalted being, who was sent into this world by God to teach mankind, who wrought miracles, and really raised his body to life in attestation of his doctrine, although he supposes that he laid it aside again when he left the earth. He distinctly asserts the infallibility of Christ as a teacher, and of the doctrine which he actually taught with his own lips. Here is a most distinct and explicit concession of the principle of supernatural revelation. To those who heard him he was a supernatural and infallible teacher. In so far as his doctrine is really apprehended, it is for all generations a supernatural and infallible truth. It has regenerated mankind, and Mr. Alger believes it is destined, when better understood, to carry the work of regeneration to a higher point in the future. It is true, he does not acknowledge that the apostles were infallible in apprehending and teaching the doctrine of Christ. But he must admit that, in so far as they have apprehended and perpetuated it, and in so far as he himself and others of his school now apprehend it more perfectly than they did, they apprehend supernatural truth and appropriate a supernatural power. Besides, once admitting that Christ was an infallible teacher, it is impossible to show why he could not do what so many philosophers have done—communicate his doctrine in clear and intelligible terms, so that the substance of it would be correctly understood and perpetuated. Miss Frances Cobbe—admitted to be the best expositor of the doctrine of the celebrated Theodore Parker—in her *Broken Lights*, and other similar writers, give to the doctrine and institutions of Christ a power that is superhuman and that denotes the action of a superhuman intelligence. Those who prognosticate a new church, a new religion, a realization of ideal humanity on earth, cannot integrate their hypothesis in anything except the supernatural, and must suppose either a new outburst of supernatural life from the germ which Christ planted on the earth, or the advent of another superhuman Redeemer.

Dr. Brownson, while yet only a transcendental philosopher on his road to the church, exhibited this thought with great power and beauty, in a little book entitled *New Views*. The dream of a new redemption of mankind in the order of temporal perfection and felicity was never presented with greater argumentative ability or portrayed in more charming colors, at least in the English language ; and never was anything made more clear than the necessity of supernatural powers for the actual fulfilment of this bewitching dream.*

Whether we look backward or forward, we confront the idea of the supernatural. This is enough to

---

* That is, bewitching to those who do not believe in something far more sublime, the restoration of all things in Christ, foretold in the Scriptures.

prove its reality. There are no universal pseudo-ideas, deceits, or illusions. That which is universal is true. We have therefore only to inspect the idea of the supernatural, to examine and explicate its contents, to interrogate the universal belief and tradition of mankind, to study the history of the race, and unfold the wisdom of the ancients, and the result will be truth. We shall obtain true and just conceptions of the original, universal, eternal idea, in which all particular forms of science, belief, law, and human evolution in all directions, coalesce and integrate themselves, as in a complete whole including all the relations of the universe to God as first and final cause.

We must now go back to the point where we left off, after establishing as the first principle of all science and faith the pure theistic doctrine respecting the first and final cause, or the origin and end of all things in necessary being, that is, God. We have to show the position of this doctrine in the conception of supernatural revelation, and its connection with the other doctrines which express the supernatural relation of the human race and the universe to God.

The conception of the supernatural in its most simple and universal form, is the conception of somewhat distinct from and superior to the complete aggregate of created forces, or second causes. In this sense, it is identical with the conception of first and final cause. It may be proper here to explain the term final cause, which is not in common use among

English writers. It expresses the ultimate motive or reason for which the universe was created, the end to which all things are tending. When we say that God is necessarily the final cause, as well as the first cause, of all existing things, we mean that he could have had no motive or end in creating, extrinsic to his own being. All that proceeds from him as first cause must return to him as final cause. From this it appears that the conception of nature in any theistic system implies the supernatural; because it implies a cause and end for nature above itself. The supernatural can only be denied by the atheist, who maintains that there is nothing superior to what the theist calls second causes; or by the pantheist, who either identifies God with nature, or nature with God. A theist cannot form any conception of pure nature or a purely natural order, except as included in a supernatural plan, because his natural order originates in a cause and tends toward an end above and beyond itself, and is not, therefore, its own adequate reason. As we have already seen, reason, by virtue of its original intuition of the infinite, is advertised of something infinitely beyond all finite comprehension. By apprehending its own limitation, and the finite, relative, contingent existence of all things which are, it is advertised of an infinite unknown, and thus has a negative knowledge of the supernatural. By the light of the creative act in itself and in the universe, it apprehends the being of God as reflected in his works and made intelligible by the similitude of created existences to the creator. It apprehends that there is an infinite being, whose created similitude is in itself and in all things ; a primal uncreated light, the cause of the reflected light in which nature is intelligible. Therefore it apprehends the supernatural. But it does not directly and immediately perceive what this infinite being or uncreated light is, and cannot do so. That is, by explicating its own primitive idea, and bringing it more and clearly into the reflective consciousness, and by learning more and more of the universe of created existences, it may go on indefinitely, apprehending God by the reflected light of similitudes, "*per speculum, in ænigmate ;*" but it must progress always in the same line : it has no tendency toward an immediate vision of God as he is intelligible in his own essence and by uncreated light. Therefore, it has only a negative and not a positive apprehension of the supernatural. God dwells in a light inaccessible to created intelligence, as such. There is an infinite abyss between him and all finite reason, which cannot be crossed by any movement of reason, however accelerated or prolonged. Therefore, although there is no science or philosophy possible which does not proceed from the affirmation of the supernatural, that is, of the infinite first and final cause of nature, yet it is not properly called supernatural science so long as it is confined to the limits of that knowledge of causes above nature which is gained only through nature. Its domain is restricted to that intelligibility which God has given to second causes and created existences, and which only reflects himself indirectly. Therefore, theologians usually call it natural knowledge, and in its highest form natural theology, as being limited within the bounds above described. They call that the natural order, in which the mind is limited to the explication of that capacity of apprehending God, or of that intuitive idea, which constitutes it rational; and is therefore limited to a relation to God corresponding to the mode of apprehending him. The term supernatural is restricted to an order in which God reveals to the human mind the possibility of apprehending him by the uncreated light in which he is intelligible to himself, and coming into a relation to him corresponding therewith; giving at the same time an elevation to the power of intelligence and volition which enables it to realize that possibility. This elevation includes the disclosure of truths not discoverable otherwise, as well as the faculty of apprehending them in such a vivid manner that they can have an efficacious action on the will, and give it a supernatural direction.

In this sense, rationalists have no conception of the supernatural. None have it, except Catholics, or those who have retained it from Catholic tradition. When we ascribe to rationalists a recognition of the supernatural, we merely intend to say that they recognize in part that immediate interference of God to instruct mankind and lead it to its destiny which is really and ultimately, although not in their apprehension, directed to the elevation of man to a sphere above that which is naturally possible. Therefore they cannot object to revelation on the ground of its being an interference with the course of nature or not in harmony with it, and cannot make an *a priori* principle by virtue of which they can prejudge and condemn the contents of revelation. But we do not mean to say that they possess the conception of that which constitutes the supernaturalness of the revelation, in the scientific sense of the term as used by Catholic theologians. Even orthodox Protestants possess it very confusedly. And here lies the source of most of the misconceptions of several abstruse Catholic dogmas.

It is in the restricted sense that we shall use the term supernatural hereafter, unless we make it plain that we use it in the general signification.

We are now prepared to state in a few words the relation of the conception of God which is intelligible to reason, to the revealed truths concerning his interior relations which are received by faith on the authority of his divine veracity. How does the mind pass through the knowledge of God to belief in God; through *Cognosco Deum* to *Credo in Deum?**

We have already said that *Cognosco* is included in *Credo*. The Creed begins by setting before the mind that which is self-evident and demonstrable concerning God, in which is included his veracity. It then discloses certain truths concerning God which are not self-evident or demonstrable from their own intrinsic reason, but which are proposed as credible, on the authority of God. The word *Credo* expresses this. "I believe in God," means not

---

* "I know God." "I believe in God."

merely, "I affirm the being of God," but also, "I believe certain truths regarding God (whose being is made known to me by the light of reason) on the authority of his Word." These truths must have in them a certain obscurity impervious to the intellectual vision; otherwise, they would take their place among evident and known truths, and would no longer be believed on the simple motive of the veracity of God revealing them. That is, they are mysterious, intelligible so far as to enable the mind to apprehend what are the propositions to which it is required to assent, but superintelligible as to their intrinsic reason and ground in the necessary and eternal truth or the being of God.

In the Creed, these mysteries, foreshadowed by the word "Credo," and by the word "Deum" considered in its relation to "Credo," which indicates a revelation of mysterious truths concerning the Divine Being to follow in order after the affirmation of the being and unity of God, begin to be formally expressed by the word "Patrem." In this word there is implicitly contained the interior, personal relation of the Father to the Son and Holy Ghost in the blessed Trinity, and his exterior relation to man as the author of the supernatural order of grace, or the order in which man is affiliated to him in the Son, through the operation of the Holy Spirit. These relations of the three persons of the blessed Trinity to each other, and to man, include the entire substance of that which is strictly and properly the supernatural revelation of the Creed, and the direct object of faith. Before proceeding, however, to the consideration of the mysteries of faith in their order, it is necessary to inquire more closely into the process by which the intellect is brought to face its supernatural object, and made capable of eliciting an act of faith.

The chief difficulty in the case is to find the connection between the last act of reason and the first act of faith, the medium of transit from the natural to the supernatural. The Catholic doctrine teaches that the act of faith is above the natural power of the human mind. It is strictly supernatural, and possible only by the aid of supernatural grace. Yet it is a rational act, for the virtue of faith is seated in the intellect as its subject, according to the teaching of St. Thomas. It is justifiable and explicable on rational grounds, and even required by right reason. The truths of revelation are not only objectively certain, but the intellect has a subjective certitude of them which is absolute, and excludes all suspicion or fear of the contrary. Now, then, unless we adopt the hypothesis that we have lost our natural capacity for discerning divine truth by the fall, and are merely restored by divine grace to the natural use of reason, there are several very perplexing questions on this point which press for an answer. Rejecting this hypothesis of the total corruption of reason, which will hereafter be proved to be false and absurd, how can faith give the mind absolute certitude of the truth of its object, when that truth is neither self-evident nor demonstrable to reason from its own self-evident principles? Given, that the intellect has this certitude, how is it that we cannot attain to it by the natural operation of reason? Once more, what is the evidence of the fact of revelation to ordinary minds? Is it a demonstration founded on the arguments for credibility? If so, how are they capable of comprehending them, and what are they to do before they have gone through with the process of examination? If not, how have they a rational and certain ground for the judgment that God has really revealed the truths of Christianity? Suppose now the fact of revelation established, and that the mind apprehends that God requires its assent to certain truths on the virtue of his own veracity. The veracity of God being apprehended as one logical premise, and the revelation of certain truths as another, can reason draw the certain conclusion that the truth of these propositions is necessarily contained in the veracity of God or not? If it can, why is not the mind capable of giving them the firm, unwavering assent of faith by its own natural power, without the aid of grace? If not, how is it that the assent of the intellect to the truth of revealed propositions does not always necessarily contain in it a metaphysical doubt or a judgment that the contrary is more or less probable, or at least possible? If it is said that the will, inclined by the grace of God, determines to adhere positively to the proposed revelation as true, what is meant by this? Does the will merely determine to act practically as if these proposed truths were evident, in spite of the lesser probability of the contrary? Then the assent of the intellect is merely a judgment that revelation is probably true, and that it is safest to follow it, which does not satisfy the demand of faith; for faith excludes all fear or suspicion that the articles of faith may possibly be false. Does the will force the intellect to judge that those propositions are certain which it apprehends only as probable? How is this possible? The will is a blind faculty, which is directed by the intellect. "*Nil volitum nisi prius cognitum.*"* There is no act of will without a previous act of knowledge. The will cannot lawfully determine the intellect to give any stronger assent to a proposition than the evidence warrants.† In a word, it is difficult to show how the intellect has an absolute certitude of the object of faith, without representing the object of faith as coincident with the object of knowledge, or the intuitive idea of reason, and thus naturally apprehensible. It is also difficult to show that faith is not coincident with knowledge, and thus to bring out the conception of its supernaturalness, without destroying the connection between faith and reason, subverting its rational basis, and representing the grace of faith as either restoring a destroyed faculty, or adding a new one to the soul, whose object is completely invisible and unintelligible to the human understanding before it is elevated to the supernatural state. The difficulty lies, however, merely in a defective statement, or a defective

---

* "Nothing is willed unless previously known."
† This is the statement of an objection, not a proposition affirmed by the author.

apprehension of the statement of the Catholic doctrine, and not in the doctrine itself. In order to make this plain, it will be necessary to make one or two preliminary remarks concerning certitude and probability.

There is, first, a metaphysical certitude excluding all possibility to the contrary. Such is the certitude of mathematical truths. Such, also, is the certitude of self-evident and demonstrable truths of every kind. The sphere of this kind of certitude is diminished or extended accordingly as the mind has before it a greater or lesser number of truths of this order. Some of these truths present themselves to every mind so immediately and irresistibly that it cannot help regarding them just as they are, and thus seeing their truth; for instance, that two and two make four. Others require the mind to be in a certain state of aptitude for seeing them as they are, and to make an effort to bring them before it. There are some truths self-evident or demonstrably certain to some minds which are not so to others; yet these truths have all an intrinsic, metaphysical certitude which reason as such is capable of apprehending, and the failure of reason to apprehend them is due in individual cases merely to the defective operation of reason in the particular subject. The operation of reason can never be altogether deficient while it acts at all, for it acts only while contemplating its object or primitive idea. But its operation can be partially defective, inasmuch as the primitive idea or objective truth may be imperfectly brought into the reflective consciousness. And thus the intellect in individuals may fail to apprehend truths which can be demonstrated with metaphysical certitude, and which the intellect infallibly judges to be absolutely certain in those individuals who are capable of making a right judgment. In this operation of apprehending metaphysical truths there is no criterion taken from experience, or from the concurrent assent of all men, but the truth shines with its own intrinsic light, and reason judges by its inherent infallibility.

Next to metaphysical certitude comes moral demonstration, resulting from an accumulation of probabilities so great that no probability which can prudently be allowed any weight is left to the other side, but merely a metaphysical possibility. For instance, the Copernican theory.

Then comes moral certainty in a wider sense; where there is probable evidence on one side without any prudent reason to the contrary, but not such a complete knowledge of all the facts as to warrant the positive judgment that there is really no probability on the other side. This kind of certainty warrants a prudent, positive judgment, and furnishes a safe, practical motion for action; but it varies indefinitely according as the data on which the judgment is based are more or less complete, and the importance of the case is greater or less.

Then come the grades of probability, where there are reasons balancing each other on both sides, which the mind must weigh and estimate.

To apply these principles to the question in hand.

First, we affirm that the being and attributes of God are apprehended with a metaphysical certitude. Second, that the motives of credibility proving the Christian revelation are apprehended, when that revelation is sufficiently proposed, with a varying degree of probability, according to varying circumstances in which the mind may be placed, but capable of being increased to the highest kind of moral demonstration. Third, that the logical conclusion which reason can draw from these two premises, although hypothetically necessary and a perfect demonstration—that is, a necessary deduction from the veracity of God, on the supposition that he has really made the revelation—is really not above the order of probability, on account of the second premise. It is not above the order of probability, although, as we have already argued, it is capable of being brought to a moral demonstration by such an accumulation of proofs within that order, that reason is bound to judge that the opposite is altogether destitute of probability.

From this it appears, both how far reason with its own principles can go in denying, and how far it can go in assenting to, revealed truth. We see, first, how it is that the truth of revelation does not compel the assent of all minds by an overwhelming and irresistible evidence. The first premise, which affirms the being of God, although undeniable and indubitable in its ultimate idea, may be, in its distinct conception, so far denied or doubted by those whose reason is perverted by their own fault, or their misfortune, as to destroy all basis for a revelation. The second premise, much more, may be partially or completely swept away, by plausible explanations of its component probabilities in detail. And thus, revelation may be denied. The influence of the will on the judgment which is made by the mind on revealed truth is explicable in this relation, and must be taken into the account. It is certain that the moral dispositions by which voluntary acts are biassed, bias also the judgment. The self-determining power of the will which decides positively which of its different inclinations to follow, controls the judgment as well as the volition. This is an indirect control, which is exerted, not by imperiously commanding the judgment in a capricious manner to make a blind, irrational decision, but by turning it toward the consideration of that side toward which the volition of choice is inclined. This influence and control of volition over judgment increases as we descend in the order of truth from primary and self-evident principles, and diminishes as we approach to them. In the case of truth which is morally or physically demonstrable, its control is exerted by turning the intellect partially away from the consideration of the truth and hindering it from giving it that attention which is necessary in order to its apprehension. In the case of divine revelation, various passions, prejudices, interests, or at least intellectual impediments to a right operation of reason, act powerfully upon a multitude of minds in such a way that the mirror of the soul is too much obscured to receive the image of truth.

But, supposing that reason and will both operate with all the rectitude possible to them, without supernatural grace, how far can the mind proceed in assenting to divine revelation? As far as a moral demonstration can take it. It can assent to divine truth, and act upon it, so far as this truth is adapted to the perfecting of the intellect and will in the natural order. But it lacks capacity to apprehend the supernatural verities proposed to it, as they are related to its supernatural destiny.

The revelation contains an unknown quantity. The will cannot be moved toward an object which the intellect does not apprehend. Therefore, a supernatural grace must enlighten the intellect and elevate the will, in order that the revealed truth may come in contact with the soul. This supernatural grace gives a certain connaturality to the soul with the revealed object of faith, by virtue of which it apprehends that God speaks to it in a whisper, distinct from his whisper to reason, and catches the meaning of what he says in this whisper. It is this supernatural light, illuminating the probable evidence apprehended by the natural understanding, which makes the assent in the act of faith absolute, and gives the mind absolute certitude. It is, however, the certitude of God revealing, and not the certitude of science concerning the intrinsic reason of that which he reveals. This remains always inevident and obscure in itself, and the decisive motive of assent is always the veracity of God. It is not, however, altogether inevident and obscure, for, if it were, the terms in which it is conveyed would be unintelligible. It is so far inevident that the intellect cannot apprehend its certainty, aside from the declaration of God. But it is partially and obscurely evident, by its analogy with the known truth of the rational order. It is so far evident that it can be demonstrated from rational principles that it does not contradict the truths of reason. Further, that no other hypothesis can explain and account for that which is known concerning the universe. And, finally, that, so far as the analogy between the natural and the supernatural is apprehensible, there is a positive harmony and agreement between them. This is all that we intend to affirm, when we speak of demonstrating Christianity from the same principles from which scientific truths are demonstrated.

Let us now revert once more to Jesus Christ and the pagan philosopher. The pagan first perceives strong, probable reasons, which increase by degrees to a moral demonstration, for believing that Christ is the Son of God, and his doctrine the revelation of God. The supernatural grace which Christ imparts to him enables him to apprehend this with a permanent and infallible certitude as a fixed principle both of judgment and volition. He accepts as absolutely true all the mysteries which Christ teaches him, on the faith of his divine mission and the divine veracity. We may now suppose that Christ goes on to instruct him in the harmony of these divine-verities with all scientific truths, so far, that he apprehends all the analogies which human reason is capable of discerning between the two. He will then have attained the *ultimatum* possible for human reason elevated and enlightened by faith, in this present state. Science and faith will be coincident in his mind, as far as they can be. That is, faith will be coincident with science until it rises above its sphere of vision, and will then lose itself in an indirect and obscure apprehension of the mysteries, in the veracity of God.

In the case of the child brought up in the Catholic Church, the church, which is the medium of Christ, instructs the child through its various agents. The child's reason apprehends, through the same probable evidence by which it learns other facts and truths, that the truth presented to him comes through the church, and through Christ, from God, who is immediately apprehended in his primitive idea. The light of faith which precedes in him the development of reason, illuminates his mind from the beginning to apprehend with infallible certitude that divine truth which is proposed to him through the medium of probable evidence. This faith is a fixed principle of conscience, proceeding from an illuminated intellect, inclining him to submit his mind unreservedly to the instruction of the Catholic Church on the faith of the divine veracity. It rests there unwaveringly, without ever admitting a doubt to the contrary, or postponing a certain judgment until the evidence of revelation and the proofs of the divine commission of the church have been critically examined. It may rest there during life, and does so, with the greater number, to a greater or lesser degree ; or, it may afterward proceed to investigate to the utmost limits the *rationale* of the divine revelation, not in order to establish faith on a surer basis, but in order to apprehend more distinctly what it believes, and to advance in theological science.

Some one may say : " You admit that it is impossible to attain to a saving faith in supernatural truth without supernatural light ; why, then, do you attempt to convince unbelievers that the Catholic doctrine is the absolute truth by rational arguments ?" To this we reply, that we do not endeavor to lead them to faith by mere argument ; but to the " preamble of faith." We aim at removing difficulties and impediments which hinder them from attending to the rational evidence of the faith ; at removing its apparent incredibility. We rely on the grace of the Holy Spirit alone to make the effort successful, and to lead those who are worthy of grace beyond the preamble of faith to faith itself. This grace is in every human mind to which faith is proposed, in its initial stage; it is increased in proportion to the sincerity with which truth is sought for ; and is given in fulness to all who do not voluntarily turn their minds away from it. If we did not believe this, we would lay down our pen at once.

CHAPTER V.

THE TRINITY OF PERSONS INCLUDED IN THE ONE DIVINE ESSENCE.

THE full explication of the first article of the Creed requires us to anticipate two others, which are its complement and supply the two terms expressing distinctly the relations of the Second and Third Persons to the First Person or the Father, in the Trinity. "Credo in Unum Deum Patrem," gives us the doctrine of the Divine Unity, and the first term of the Trinity, namely: the person of the Father. "Et in Unum Dominum Jesum Christum Filium Dei Unigenitum, et ex Patre natum ante omnia sæcula; Deum de Deo, Lumen de Lumine; Deum Verum de Deo Vero; Genitum non Factum, consubstantialem Patri, per quem omnia facta sunt," gives us the second term or the person of the Son. "Et in Spiritum Sanctum, Dominum et Vivificantem, qui ex Patre Filioque procedit, qui cum Patre et Filio simul adoratur et conglorificatur," gives us the third term or the person of the Holy Spirit. Both these are necessary to the explanation of the term "Patrem." The proper order is, therefore, to begin with the eternal, necessary relations of the Three Persons to each other in the unity of the Divine Essence, and then to proceed with the operations of each of the Three Persons in the creation and consummation of the Universe.

Our purpose is not to make a directly theological explanation of all that is contained in this mystery, but only of so much of it as relates to its credibility, and its position in regard to the sphere of intelligible truth. With this mystery begins that which is properly the objective matter of revelation, or the series of truths belonging to a superintelligible order; that is, above the reach of our natural intelligence, proposed to our belief on the veracity of God. It is usually considered the most abstruse, mysterious, and incomprehensible of all the Christian dogmas, even by believers; though we may perhaps find that the dogma of the Incarnation is really further removed than it from the grasp of our understanding. Be that as it may, the fact that it relates to the very first principle and the primary truth of all religion, and appears to confuse our apprehension of it—namely, the Unity of God—causes us to reflect more distinctly upon its incomprehensibility. Many persons, both nominal Christians and avowed unbelievers, declare openly, that in their view it is an absurdity so manifestly contrary to reason that it is absolutely unthinkable, and, of course, utterly incredible. How, then, is the relation between this mystery and the self-evident or demonstrable truths of reason adjusted in the act of faith elicited by the believer? What answer can be

made to the rational objections of the unbeliever?
If the doctrine be really unthinkable, it is just as
really incredible, and there can be no act of faith terminated upon it as a revealed object. Of course,
then, no inquiry could be made as to its relation with
our knowledge; for that which is absurd and incapable of being intellectually conceived and apprehended
cannot have any relation to knowledge. It is impossible for the human mind to believe at one and the
same time that a proposition is directly contrary to
reason and also revealed by God. No amount of extrinsic evidence will ever convince it. Human reason cannot say beforehand what the truths of revelation are or ought to be; but it can say in certain respects what they cannot be. They cannot be contradictory to known truths and first principles of reason
and knowledge. Therefore, when they are presented
in such a way to the mind, or are by it apprehended
in such a way, as to involve a contradiction to these
first truths and principles, they cannot be received
until they are differently presented or apprehended,
so that this apparent contradiction is removed. This
is so constantly and clearly asserted by the ablest
Catholic writers, men above all suspicion for soundness in the faith, that we will not waste time in proving it to be sound Catholic doctrine.* Of course
all rationalists, and most Protestants, hold it as an
axiom already. If there are some Protestants who

---

* See among others, Archbishop Manning on the *Temporal Mission of the Holy Ghost*.

hold the contrary, they are beyond the reach of argument.

The Catholic believer in the Trinity apprehends the dogma in such a way that it presents no contradiction to his intellect between itself and the first principles of reason or the primary doctrine of the unity of the divine nature. God, who is the Creator and the Light of reason, as well as the author of revelation, is bound by his own attributes of truth and justice, when he proposes a doctrine as obligatory on faith, to propose it in such a way that the mind is able to apprehend and accept it in a reasonable manner. This is done by the instruction given by the Catholic Church, with which the supernatural illumination of the Holy Spirit concurs. The Catholic believer is therefore free from those crude misapprehensions and misconceptions which create the difficulty in the unbelieving mind. He apprehends in some degree, although it may be implicitly and confusedly, the real sense and meaning of the mystery, as it is apprehensible by analogy with truths of the natural order. What it is he apprehends, and what are the analogies by which it can be made intelligible, will be explained more fully hereafter. It is enough here to note the fact. This apprehension makes the mystery to him thinkable, or capable of being thought. That is, it causes the proposition of the mystery in certain definite terms to convey a meaning to his mind, and not to be a mere collocation of words without any sense to him. It makes him apprehend what he is required to assent to, and puts before him an object of thought upon which an intellectual act can be elicited. It presents no contradiction to reason, and therefore there is no obstacle to his giving the full assent of faith on the authority of God.

It is otherwise with one who has been brought up in Judaism, Unitarianism, or mere Rationalism; or whose merely traditional and imperfect apprehension of Christian dogmas has been so mixed up with heretical perversions that his mature reason has rejected it as absurd. There is an impediment in the way of his receiving the mystery of the Trinity as proposed by the Catholic Church, and believing it possible that God can have revealed it. He may conceive of the doctrine of the Trinity as affirming that an object can be one and three in the same identical sense, which destroys all mathematical truth. Or he may conceive of it, as dividing the divine substance into three parts, forming a unity of composition, and not a unity of simplicity. Or he may conceive of it as multiplying the divine essence, or making three coördinate deities, who concur and coöperate with each other by mutual agreement. These conceptions are equally absurd with the first, although it requires more thought to discern their absurdity. It is necessary, then, to remove the apparent absurdity of the doctrine, before any evidence of its being a revealed truth is admissible. The first misconception is so extremely crude, that it is easily removed by the simple explanation that unity and trinity are predicated of God in distinct and not identical senses. The second, which is hardly less crude, is disposed of by pointing out the explicit statements in which the simplicity and indivisibility of the divine substance in all of the Three Persons is invariably affirmed. The third is the only real difficulty, the only one which can remain long in an educated and instructed mind. The objection urged on theological or philosophical grounds by really learned men against the dogma of the Trinity is, that it implies Tritheism. The simplest and most ordinary method of removing this objection, is by presenting the explicit and positive affirmation of the church that there is but one eternal principle of self-existent, necessary being, one first cause, one infinite substance possessing all perfections. This is sufficient to show that the church denies and condemns Tritheism, and affirms the strict unity of God. But, the Unitarian replies, you hold a doctrine incompatible with this affirmation, namely, that there are three Divine Persons, really distinct and equal. This is met by putting forward the terms in which the church affirms that it is the one, eternal, and infinite essence of God which is in each of the Three Persons. The Unitarian is then obliged to demonstrate that this distinction of persons in the Godhead is unthinkable, and that unity of nature cannot be thought in connection with triplicity of person. This he cannot do. The relation of personality to nature is too abstruse—especially when we are reasoning about the infinite, which transcends all the analogies of our finite self-consciousness—to admit of a demonstration proving absolutely that unity of nature supposes unity of person, and *vice versa*, as its necessary correlative. The church affirms the unity of substance in the Godhead in the clearest manner, sweeping away all ground for gross misconceptions of a divided or multiplied deity; but affirms also trinity in the mode of subsistence, or the distinction of Three Persons, in each one of whom the same divine substance subsists completely. This affirmation is above the comprehension of reason, but not contrary to reason. Even Unitarians, in some instances, find no difficulty in accepting the statement of the doctrine of the trinity made by our great theologians, when it is distinctly presented to them; and in the beautiful Liturgical Book used in some Unitarian congregations, the orthodox doxology, " Glory be to the Father, and to the Son, and to the Holy Ghost," has been restored.

The absurd misconception of what the church means by the word Trinity being once removed, the evidence that her doctrine is revealed, or that God affirms to us the eternal, necessary distinction of three subsistences in his infinite being, becomes intelligible and credible. Reason cannot affirm the intrinsic incompatibility of the proposition, God reveals himself as subsisting in three persons, with the proposition, There is one God; and therefore cannot reject conclusive evidence that he does so reveal himself through the Catholic Church. For aught reason can say, he may have so revealed himself. If satisfactory evidence is presented that he has done so, reason is obliged, in consistency with its principles, to examine and judge of the evidence, and assent to the conclusion that the Trinity is a revealed truth. This is enough for all practical purposes, and as much as the majority of persons are capable of. But is this the *ultimatum* of reason ? Is it not possible to go further in showing the conformity of the revealed truth with rational truths ? Several eminent theologians have endeavored to take this further step, and to construct a metaphysical argument for the doctrine of the Trinity. Some of the great contemplatives of the church, who are really the most profound and sublime of her theologians and philosophers, have also through divine illumination appeared to gain an insight into the depths of this mystery. For instance, St. Ignatius and St. Francis de Sales both affirm that the truth and the mutual harmony of all the divine mysteries were made evident to their intelligence in contemplation. In modern times, Bossuet, Lacordaire, and Dr. Brownson have reasoned profoundly on the rational evidence of the Trinity, and a Roman priest, the Abbate Mastrofini, has published a work entitled *Metaphysica Sublimior*, in which he proposes as his thesis, Given divine revelation, to prove the truth of all its dogmas by reason. The learned and excellent German priest Günther attempted the same thing, but went too far, and fell into certain errors which were censured by the Roman tribunals, and which he himself retracted. It is necessary to tread cautiously and reverently, like Moses, for we are on holy ground, and near the burning bush. We will endeavor to do so, and, taking for our guide the decisions of the church and the judgment of her greatest and wisest men, to do our best to state briefly what has been attempted in the way of eliciting an eminent act of reason on this great mystery, without trenching on the domain of faith.

First, then, it is certain that reason cannot discover the Trinity of itself. It must be first proposed to it by revelation, before it can apprehend its terms or gain anything to reason upon. Secondly, when proposed, its intrinsic necessity or reason cannot be directly or immediately apprehended. If it can be apprehended at all, it must be mediately, or through analogies existing in the created universe. Are there such analogies, that is, are there any reflections or representations of this divine truth in the physical or intellectual world from which reason can construct a theorem parallel in its own order with this divine theorem? Creation is a copy of the divine idea. It represents God as a mirror. Does it represent him, that is, so far as the human intellect is capable of viewing it, not merely as he is one in essence, but also as he is three in persons? Assuming the Trinity as a hypothesis, which is all we can do in arguing with an unbeliever, can we point out analogies or representations in creation of which the Trinity is the ultimate reason and the infinite original? If we can, do these analogies simply accord and harmonize with the hypothesis that God must subsist in three persons, or do they indicate that this is the most adequate or the only conceivable hypothesis, or that it is the necessary, self-evident truth, without which the existence of these analogies would be unthinkable and impossible? Do these analogies, as we are able to discover them, represent an adequate image of the complete Catholic dogma of the Trinity, or only an inadequate image of a portion of it?

It is evident, in the first place, that some analogical representation of the Trinity must be made in order to give the mind any apprehension whatever of a real object of thought on which it can elicit an act of faith. The terms in which the doctrine is stated, as, for instance, Father, Son, Holy Spirit, eternal generation, procession or spiration, person, etc., are analogical terms, representing ideas, which are otherwise unspeakable, by images or symbols. It is impossible for the mind to perceive that a proposed idea is simply not absurd, without apprehending confusedly what the idea is, and possessing some positive apprehension of its conformity to the logical, that is, the real order. Every distinct act of belief in the Trinity, therefore, however rudimental and imperfectly evolved into reflective cognition, contains in it an apprehension of the analogy between it and creation. If we proceed, therefore, to explicate this confused, inchoate conception, we necessarily proceed by way of explicating the analogy spoken of, because we must proceed by explaining the terms in which the doctrine is stated, which are analogical; and by pointing out what the analogy is which the terms designate. What is meant by calling God Father, Son, and Holy Spirit? Why is the relation of the Son to the Father called filiation? Why is the relation of the Holy Spirit to both called procession? The Niceno-

Constantinopolitan and Athanasian Creeds, all the other definitions of the church respecting the Trinity and all Catholic theology deduced from these definitions and from Scripture and tradition by rational methods, are an explication of the significance of these analogical terms. The only question which can be raised, then, is in regard to the extent of the capacity of human reason to discern the analogy between inward necessary relations of the Godhead, and the outward manifestation of these relations in the creation. The hypothesis of the Trinity assumes that this analogy exists, and is to some extent apprehensible. We will now proceed to indicate the process by which Catholic theologians show this analogy, beginning with those terms of analogy which lie in the material order, and ascending to those which lie in the order of spirit and intelligence.

First, then, it is argued that the law of generation in the physical world, by which like produces like, represents some divine and eternal principle. Ascending from the lower manifestations of this law to man, we find this physical relation of generation the basis of a higher filiation in which the soul participates. Man generates the image of himself, in his son, who is not merely his bodily offspring, but similar and equal to himself in his rational nature. As St. Paul says, the principle of this paternity must be in God, and must therefore be in him essential and eternal. But this principle of eternal, essential paternity, within the necessary being of God, is the very principle of distinct personal relations.

Again, the multiplicity of creation indicates that there is some principle in the Divine Nature, corresponding in an eminent sense and mode to this multiplicity. The relations of number are eternal truths, and have some infinite transcendental type in God. If there were no principle in the Divine Nature except pure, abstract unity, there would be no original idea, from which God could proceed to create a universe; which is necessarily multiplex and constituted in an infinitude of distinct relations, yet all radically one, as proceeding from one principle and tending to one end. Here is an analogy indicating that unity and multiplicity imply and presuppose one the other.

These two arguments combine when we consider the law of generation and the principle of multiplicity as constituting human society and building up the human race. Society, love, mutual communion, reciprocal relations, kind offices, diversity in equality, constitute the happiness and well-being of man; they are an image and a participation of the divine beatitude. All the good of the creature, all the perfections of derived, contingent existences, have an eminent, transcendental type in God. Love, friendship, society, represent something in the divine nature. If there were no personal relations in God, but a mere solitude of being existing in a unity and singularity exclusive of all plurality and society, it would seem that, supposing creation possible, the rational creature would copy his archetype, be single of his kind, and find his happiness in absolute solitude. It is otherwise, however, with the human race. The human individual is not single and solitary. Human nature is one in respect of origin and kind, derived from one principle which is communicated by generation and exists in plurality of persons. Society is necessary to the perpetuation, perfection, and happiness of the human race. This society is constituted primarily in a threefold relation between the father, the mother, and the child, which makes the family; and the family repeated and multiplied makes the tribe, the nation, and the race. Taking now the hypothesis of three persons in one nature as constituting the Godhead, it is plain that we have a clearer idea of that in God which is represented and imitated in human society, and which is the archetype of the life, the happiness, the love, existing in the communion of distinct persons in one common nature, than we can have in the hypothesis of an absolute singularity of person in the deity. That good which man enjoys by fellowship with his equal and his like, is a participation in the supreme good, that is in God. In that supreme good, this participated good must exist in an eminent manner. God must have in himself infinite, all-sufficing society, fellowship, love. He must have it in his necessary and eternal being, for he cannot be dependent on that which is contingent and created. Supposing therefore that it is consistent with the unity of his nature to exist in three distinct and equal persons, not only is the analogy of his creation to himself more manifest, but the conception we can form of the perfection of his being is more complete and intelligible.

There is another analogy in the intellectual operation of the human mind. The intellective faculty generates what may be called the interior word, or image of the mind, the archetype of that which is outwardly expressed in a philosophical theory, a poem, a picture, a statue, or a work of architecture. Through this word, the great creative mind lives and attains to the completion and happiness of intellectual existence. It loves it as proceeding from and identical with itself. Through it, it acts upon other minds, controls and influences their thought and life; and thus the spirit proceeding from the creative mind, through its generated word, is the completion of its inward and outward operation. Thus, argue the theologians, the Father contemplating the infinitude of his divine essence generates by an infinite thought, the Word, or Son. Being infinite and uncreated, his necessary act is infinite and uncreated, in all respects equal to himself, and therefore the Word is equal to the Father; possesses the plenitude of the divine essence, intelligence and personality. The divine act of generation is not a purely intellectual cognition, but a contemplation in which love is joined with knowledge. The Father beholds the Son, and the Son looks back upon the Father, with infinite love, which is the spiration of the divine life. This spiration or Spirit, proceeding from the Father and the Son, is the consummating, completing term of their unity, and contains the divine being which is in the Father and the Son in all its plenitude; constituting a third person, equal to the first and second. The operation of a limited, finite, created soul, presents only a faint, imperfect analogy of the Trinity, because it is itself limited, as being the operation of a soul participating in being only to a limited extent. Individual existences possess each one a limited participation in being. But in God, it is not so. There is no division in his nature, because the eternal, self-existing cause and principle of its unity is a simultaneous cause of the absolute plenitude, by which it exhausts all possible being. This plenitude of being is in the eternal generation of the second person, and the eternal spiration of the third person, in the Godhead, on account of the necessary perfection of the most pure act in which the being of God consists; wherefore personality is predicable, as one of the perfections of being, of each of the three terms of relation in God. The word of human reason and its spirit, are not equal to itself, or personal, because of the limited and imperfect nature of human reason and its operations. The Word or Son of the Eternal Father, and the Holy Spirit, are equal to him and personal, because the Father is God, and his act is infinite.

This prepares the way for a different method of presenting the argument from analogy, based on the conception of God as *actus purissimus*, or most pure act. This is clearly and succinctly stated by Dr. Brownson as follows:

"The one, or naked and empty unity, even in the Unitarian mind, is not the equivalent of God. When he says one, he still asks, one what? The answer is, one God, which implies even with him something more than unity. It implies unity and its real and necessary contents as living or actual being. Unity is an abstract conception formed by the mind operating on the intuition of the concrete, and as abstract, has no existence out of the mind conceiving. Like all abstractions, it is in itself dead, unreal, null. God is not an abstraction, not a mere generalization, a creature, or a theorem of the human mind, but one living and true God, existing from and in himself, *a se et in se*. He is real being, being in its plenitude, eternal, independent, self-living, and complete in himself. To live is to act. To be eternally and infinitely living is to be eternally and infinitely acting, is to be all act; and hence philosophers and theologians term God, in scholastic language, most pure act, *actus purissimus*. But act, all act demands, as its essential conditions, principle, medium, and end. Unity, then, to be actual being, to be eternally and purely act in itself, must have in itself the three relations of principle, medium, and end, precisely the three relations termed in Christian theology Father, Son, and Holy Ghost—the Father as principle, the Son as medium, and the Holy Ghost as end or consummation of the divine life. These three interior relations are essential to the conception of unity as one living and true God. Hence the radical conception of God as triune is essential to the conception of God as one God, or real, self-living, self-sufficing unity. There is nothing in this view of the Trinity that asserts that one is three, or that three are one; nor is there anything that breaks the divine unity, for the triplicity asserted is not three Gods, or three divine beings, but a threefold interior relation in the interior essence of the one God, by virtue of which he is one actual, living God. The relations are in the essence of the one God, and are, so to speak, the living contents of his unity, without which he would be an empty, unreal abstraction ; one—nothing."*

There is still another way of stating the argument, founded on the necessary relation between subject and object. In the rational order, subject is that which apprehends and object that which is apprehended. Intelligence is subject and the intelligible is object. The mere power or capacity of intelligence, if it is conceived of in an abstract manner as existing alone without relation to its object, must be conceived of as not in actual exercise. Intelligence in act implies something intelligible which terminates the act of intelligence. Even supposing that the object of the intelligence is identical with the subject, that is, that the rational mind contemplates itself as a really existing substance, nevertheless there is a distinction between the mind considered as the subject which contemplates, and the mind considered as the object which is contemplated. The reason contemplated must be projected before itself and regarded as an object distinct from the contemplating reason in the act of contemplation. The eye which sees objects external to itself, does not actually see or bring its

---

* *Brownson's Review*, July, 1863, pp. 266, 267.

visual power into act until an object is presented before it; and the individual does not become conscious that he can see or is possessed of a visual faculty, except in the act of seeing an object. The eye cannot see itself immediately by the mere fact that it is a visual organ, but only sees itself as reflected in a mirror and made objective to itself. God is the absolute intelligence and the absolute intelligible, as has been proved in a previous chapter. He contemplates and comprehends himself, and in this consists his active being and life. Thus in the divine being there is the distinction of subject and object. God considered as infinite intelligence is subject, and considered as the infinite intelligible is his own adequate object. The hypothesis of the Trinity presents to us God as subject, or intelligence, in the person of the Father, as object, or the intelligible, in the person of the Son. The Son is the image of the Father, as the reflection of a man's form in the mirror is the image of himself. The eternal generation of the Son is the eternal act of the Father contemplating his own being, and is terminated upon the person of the Son as its object. As this act is within the divine being, the image of the Father is not a merely phenomenal, apparent, unsubstantial reflection of his being, but real, living, and substantial. The Son is consubstantial with the Father. The being of God is in the act of intelligence or contemplation, whether we consider God as the subject or the object in this infinite act, that is, as intelligent and contemplating, or as intelligible and contemplated. The consummating principle of love, complacency, or beatitude, which completes this act, vivifies it, and unites the person of the Father with the person of the Son in one indivisible being, is the Holy Spirit, equal to the Father and the Son, and identical in being, because a necessary term of the most pure act in which the divine life and being consists. All that is within the circle of the necessary, essential being of God, as most pure, intelligent, living act, is uncaused, self-existent, infinite, eternal. By the hypothesis, we must conceive of God as subsisting in the three persons, Father, Son, and Holy Ghost, in order to conceive of him as *ens in actu*, or in the state of actual, living, concrete being, and not as a mere abstraction or possibility existing in thought only; as infinite intelligence, and the adequate object of his own intelligence, self-sufficing and infinitely blessed in himself. Therefore the Father is God, the Son is God, and the Holy Ghost is God. It is only by this triplicity of personal relations that the unity of God as a living, concrete unity, or the unity of one, absolute, perfect, infinite being, containing in himself the actual plenitude of all that is conceivable or possible, can subsist or be vividly apprehended. Therefore there cannot be, by the hypothesis, a separate and distinct Godhead in each of the three persons, since triplicity of person enters into the very essential idea of Godhead. The hypothesis of the Trinity, therefore, absolutely compels the mind to believe in the unity of God, and shuts out all possibility that there should be more Gods than one, because it shuts out all pos-

Problems of the Age. 95

sibility of imagining any mode or form of necessary being which is not included in the three personal relations of the one God. Unity and plurality, singularity and society, capacity of knowing, loving, and enjoying the true, the beautiful, and the good, and the adequate object of this capacity, or the true, beautiful, and good *in se*, the subject and the object of intelligent and spiritual life and activity, intelligence and the intelligible, love and the loved, blessedness and beatitude, subsist in him in actual being, which is infinite and exhausts in its most pure act all that is in the uncreated, necessary, self-existent principle of being and first cause. The adequate reason and type of all contingent and created existences is demonstrated also to be in the three personal relations of the one divine essence, in such a way, that the hypothesis of the Trinity, as a theorem, satisfactorily takes up, accounts for, and explains all discoverable truths as well in regard to the universe as in regard to God.

This last statement indicates the answer which we think is the most correct one to the question proposed in the beginning of this chapter, as to the full logical force of the rational argument for the Trinity. That is, we regard it as a hypothesis which in the first place is completely insusceptible of rational refutation. In the second place, contains certain truths which are established by very strong probable arguments and analogies. In the third place, suggests a conception of God which harmonizes with all the truth we know, or can see to be probable, and at the same time is more perfect and sublime than any which can be made, excluding the hypothesis. We do not claim for it the character of a strict demonstration. To certain minds it seems to approach very near a demonstration, probably because their intellectual power of vision is unusually acute. To others it appears nearly or quite unintelligible. Probably but few persons comparatively can grasp it in such a way as to attain a true intellectual insight into the relation between the doctrine of the Trinity and philosophy. Yet all those who have thought much on the doctrine, and who find their great difficulty in believing it to consist in a want of apparent connection with other truths, ought to be able to appreciate the philosophical argument by which the connection is shown. They must have an aptitude for apprehending arguments of this nature, otherwise they would not think on the subject so intently. All they can justly expect is that the impediment in their minds against believing that the doctrine is credible, or not incredible, supposing it revealed, should be removed. This is done by the arguments of Catholic theologians. If the doctrine be revealed, it is credible; that is, an intelligent person can in perfect consistency with the dictates of reason assent to the proposition that God has revealed it, and that it is therefore credible on his veracity. The ground of the positive and unwavering assent of the mind is in the veracity of God, and remains there, no matter how far the reasoning process may be carried; for, without the revelation of God, the conception of the Trinity, supposing it once obtained, would for ever remain a mere hypothesis, though the most probable of all which could be conceived.

As already explained, it is only by a supernatural grace that the mind is elevated to a state in which it clearly and habitually contemplates the object of faith as revealed by God. By divine faith, the intellect believes without doubting the mystery of the three persons in one divine nature, and incorporates this belief into its life, as a vivifying truth, and not a dead, inert, abstract speculation or theorem. When it is thus believed, and taken as a certain truth, the intellect, if it is capable of apprehending the argument from analogy, may be able to see that the Trinity is really that truth which is the archetype that has been copied in creation, and is indicated in the analogies already pointed out. It may see that one cannot think logically unless he is first instructed in the doctrine of the Trinity and proceeds from it as a given truth or datum of reasoning. Thus, he may by the light of faith attain an elevated kind of science, or eminent act of reason, which really rests on indubitable principles. Yet it will not be properly science or knowledge of the revealed mysteries, since one of these indubitable principles on which all the consequences depend, is revelation itself, which really constitutes the mind in a certitude of that which on merely rational principles remains always inevident. Probably this is what is meant by those who maintain that the Trinity can be rationally demonstrated. Given, that the Trinity is a revealed truth, it explains and harmonizes in the sphere of reason what is otherwise inexplicable. It is the same with other revealed truths, and to prove that it is so is the principal object of this essay. Presented in this light, the Catholic dogma of the Trinity vindicates its claim to be a necessary part of religious belief; an essential dogma of Christianity, revealed and made obligatory for an intelligible reason, and essential to the formation of a complete and adequate theology and philosophy. It is no longer regarded as a naked, speculative, isolated proposition, to which a merely intellectual assent is required by a precept of authority, and which has no living relation to other truths or to the practical, spiritual life of the soul. It is shown to be a universal and fundamental truth, the basis of all truth and of the entire real and logical order of the universe.

This can be shown much more easily, and to the majority of minds more intelligibly, in relation to the other truths of Christianity, than to those truths which are more recondite and metaphysical. It is necessary to an adequate explication of the creation, of the destiny of rational existences, of the supernatural order, of the character and mission of Christ, of the regeneration of man through him, and of his final end or supreme and eternal beatitude and glorification in the future life, as will be shown hereafter. Deprived of this dogma, Christianity is baseless, unmeaning, and worthless; and is infallibly disintegrated and reduced to nihilism, by the necessary laws of thought. This is true also of theism, or natural theology. And this suggests a powerful subsidiary argument in a different line of reasoning, proving that the doctrine of the Trinity is necessary to the perfection and perpetuity of the doctrine of the unity of God.

The same universal tradition which has handed down the pure, theistic conception, and has instructed mankind in the true, adequate knowledge of God, has handed down the Trinity; and traces of it are even found in heathen theosophy and the more profound heathen philosophy. Wherever the doctrine of the Trinity has been preserved, there the clear conception of the one God and his attributes has been preserved. And where this doctrine has been corrupted or lost, the conception of God as one living being of infinite perfection, the first and final cause of all things, has passed away into polytheism or pantheism or scepticism. Wherever God is apprehended as the supreme creator and sovereign, the supreme object of worship, obedience, and love, in intimate personal relations to man, he is apprehended in the personal relations which subsist in himself, that is, in the Trinity. His interior personal relations are the foundation of all external, personal relations to his creatures. This is even true of Unitarians, so long as they retain the Christian ethical and spiritual temper which connects them with the Christian world of thought and life, and do not slide into some form of infidelity. They retain some imperfect conception of the relations of Father, Son, and Holy Ghost, and in proportion as they become more positive in religion, they revive and renew this conception. The effort to make a system of living, practical theistic religion is feeble and futile; and what little consistency and force it has is derived from the conception of the fatherhood of God borrowed from Christian theology but imperfect without the two additional terms which constitute the complete conception of the Trinity. All this is a powerful argument for a theist or a Unitarian in favor of the divine origin and authority of the Catholic dogma. The instruction which completes the inward affirmation of God in the idea of reason, and is the complement of the creative act constituting the soul rational, must be from the creator. He alone can complete his own work. It is contrary to all rational conceptions of the wisdom of God to suppose that he has permitted that the same instruction which teaches mankind to know, to worship, to love, and to aspire after himself, should hand down in inseparable connection with the eternal truth of the unity of his essence, the doctrine of the threefold personal relations within this unity, if this were an error diametrically its opposite, and not a truth equally necessary and eternal.

CHAPTER VI.

THE DOGMA OF CREATION—THE PRINCIPLE, ARCHETYPE, AND END OF THE CREATIVE ACT.

THE next article of the Creed is, "*Creatorem cœli et terræ:*" "Creator of heaven and earth."

The mystery of the Trinity exhausts the idea of the activity of God within his own interior being, or *ad intra*. The dogma of the creation expresses the idea of the activity of God without his own interior being, or *ad extra*. It is an explication of the primitive idea of reason, which presents simultaneously to intelligence the absolute and the contingent in their necessary relation of the dependence of the contingent upon the absolute. Being an explication of the rational idea, it is rationally demonstrable, and does not, therefore, belong to the superintelligible part of the revelation, or that which is believed simply on the veracity of God. That portion of the dogma of creation which is superintelligible, or revealed truth in the highest sense, relates to the supernatural end to which the creation is determined by the decree of God. Nevertheless, although the idea of creation, once proposed, is demonstrable on purely rational principles, it is fairly and fully proposed to reason under an adequate and explicit conception adequately expressed, only by divine revelation. Wherever this adequate formula of revelation has been lost, the conception has been lost with it, and not even the highest philosophy has restored it. Plato's conception of the formation of the universe went no higher than the impression of divine ideas upon matter eternally self-existent. In all philosophy which is not regulated by the principles of revelation, the ideas of necessary being and contingent existence and of the relation between them are more or less confused, and the dogma of creation is corrupted.

The pure theistic conception gives at once the pure conception of creation.

Not that the idea of creation can be immediately perceived in the idea of God, which can be shown to be impossible; but that it can be perceived in the idea of God by the medium of the knowledge of finite existences given to the intellect together with the knowledge of infinite being, in the primitive intuition. When the idea of infinite being is fully explicated and demonstrated in the perfect conception of God; the existence of real entities which are not God, and therefore not included in necessary being, being known; the relation of these things extrinsic to the being of God, to the being of God itself, becomes evident in the idea of God. It is evident that they have no necessary self-existence either out of the divine being or in the divine being, and therefore have been brought out of nonentity into entity by the act of God.

This creative act of God is that by which he reduces possibility to actuality. It is evident that this possibility of creation, or creability of finite existences extrinsic to the divine essence, is necessary and eternal. For God could not think of doing that which he does not think as possible, and his thoughts are eternal. The thought or idea of creation is therefore eternal in the divine mind. It is a divine and eternal archetype or ideal, which the externized, concrete reality copies and represents.

The divine essence is the complete and adequate object of the divine contemplation. It is, therefore, in his own essence that God must have beheld the eternal possibility of creation and the ground or reason of creability. It is the divine essence itself, therefore, which contains the archetype or ideal of a possible creation. God's eternal knowledge of the possibility of creation is, therefore, his knowledge of his own essence as an archetype of existences, which he is capable of enduing with reality extrinsic to the reality of his own being by his omnipotent power. The eternal possibility of creation, therefore, exists necessarily in the being and omnipotence of God. It is the imitability of the divine essence as archetype, by finite essences which are its real and extrinsic similitudes, and which are extrinsecated by an act of the divine will. The ideal or archetype of creation is evidently as necessary, as eternal, as unchangeable, as God himself. God cannot create except according to this archetype; and in creating must necessarily copy himself, or give extrinsic existence to something which is a concrete expression of the divine ideal in his own intelligence. This ideal which creation copies being, therefore, eternal in the divine intelligence; and the interior activity of the divine intelligence, or its interior ideal life, not being explicable except in the relation of the three persons in God; creation is likewise inexplicable, except in relation to the distinct persons of the Trinity.

The Son, or Word, proceeds from the contemplation of the divine essence by the Father, who thus reproduces the perfect and coequal image of himself. In this act of contemplation, the knowledge of the archetype of creation, or of the creability of essences resembling the divine essence, is necessarily included. The expressed idea or archetype of all possible existences is therefore in the Word, as the personal image of the Father; and he contains, in himself, in an eminent and equivalent manner, infinite similitudes or images capable of being reduced to act, and made to reflect himself in a countless variety of ways. The Son thus communicates with the Father in creative omnipotence. The spiration of the Holy Spirit from the Father and the Son, consummating the act of contemplation by which the Son is generated, in love; and thus completing the interior, intelligent, or spiritual life of God within himself; is perfectly correlated to the eternal generation of the Son. The complete essence of God is communicated by the

Father and the Son to the Holy Spirit, and with it creative omnipotence as necessarily included in it. The object of volition in God is identical with the object of intelligence. The essence of God as being the archetype of a possible creation, that is, the ideal of creation, or the idea which creation copies, being included in the term of the divine intelligence, or in the Word, is also included in the term of the divine love, or the Holy Spirit. The idea of creation is therefore included in the object of the eternal, intelligent, living contemplation in which the three persons of the blessed Trinity are united. The power of illimitable creation according to the divine archetype in God is a necessary and eternal predicate of his divine being, which he contemplates with complacency. The idea of creation is therefore as eternal as God; it is coeval with him, and the object of the ineffable communications of the divine persons with each other from eternity. God has always been pleased with this idea, as the artist delights himself in the ideal of beauty to which he feels himself capable of giving outward form and expression, in sculpture, painting, or architecture.

The decree of God to reduce this possibility of creation to act, or the creative purpose, is likewise eternal; since all divine acts are in eternity, and there is no process of deliberation or progress from equilibrium to determination possible in the unchangeable God. God is *actus purissimus*, most pure act, and there is in him nothing potential or reducible to act which is not in act from eternity; since in him there is no past or future, and no succession, but *tota, simul ac perfecta possessio vitæ interminabilis*, a complete, simultaneous, and perfect possession of interminable life.

The necessity of his own self-existent being does not determine him to the creative act, but merely to the exercise of supreme omnipotence in choosing freely between the contemplation of creation in its ideal archetype alone, and of creation in its ideal archetype determined to outward actual expression. The inward life of God is necessary, and the interior act of beatific contemplation is of the essence of the divine being. Nothing beyond this, or outside of the interior essence of God, can be necessary, and the creation cannot therefore be necessary, or it would be included in the idea of God, and be identical with the essence of God. God does not create, therefore, by necessity of nature, but by voluntary choice. It is the only exercise of voluntary choice possible to him. It is a choice, however, which though free is determined from eternity. He might have eternally chosen the contrary, that is, to leave the possible creation unactualized, in its ideal archetype. He did eternally choose, however, to create.

The learned expositor of St. Thomas, F. Billuart, says that the purpose to create is communicated by the Father to the Word, concomitantly with the intelligence of the divine essence by which he is generated.* Creation is no afterthought, no capricious or

---

* *Tract. De Trin.*, Diss. V., Art. III.

sportive play of omnipotence, like the *jeu d'esprit* which a poet throws off from a sudden impulse of fancy. The creative purpose has been the theme of the mysterious communications of the three persons of the blessed Trinity, from all eternity. In God, purpose and act, consultation and decree, are one. The decree of creation and the creative act are identical. The creative act, therefore, *a parte Dei*, is eternal. It is an illusion of the imagination to conceive of time as having existed before creation. "In the beginning, God created the heavens and the earth." That beginning was the first moment of time, which St. Thomas says God created when he created the universe. Time is a mere relation of finite entities to each other and to infinite being, arising from their limitation. The procession of created existences is necessarily in time, and could not have begun *ab æterno* without a series actually infinite, which is impossible. Nevertheless, the first instant of created time had no created time behind it, and no series of instants behind it, intervening between it and eternity, but touched immediately on eternity.

The procession of created existences from God is a finite similitude of the procession of the Son and Holy Spirit from the Father. Creation is an expression in finite form of that archetype which is expressed in the infinite image of the Word. He is "the splendor of the glory, and the express image of the substance"* of the Father; and creation is a reflec-

---

* Heb. i. 3.

tion of this splendor, a reduplication in miniature of this image. It is an act of the same infinite intelligence by which the infinite Word is generated. For although finite itself, it is the similitude of an infinite archetype such as only infinite intelligence can possess within itself. It is also an act of the same infinite love whose spiration is the Holy Spirit. The sanctity of the divine nature consists in a perfect conformity of intelligence and volition. Volition is love, a complacency in good. Love must therefore concur with intelligence in every divine act, that it may be holy. The Holy Spirit, or impersonated love, must concur with the Father and the Son, as principle and medium, to consummate or bring to its final end the creative act. Creation is therefore essentially an act of love; proceeding from intelligence and ordained for beatitude; proceeding from God as first cause, and returning to him as final cause.

The final cause of creation must be God, just as necessarily as its first cause must be God. The creative decree being eternal, all that constitutes its perfection, including its end and consummation, must be eternal, and must therefore be in God. He is the principle and consummation of his own act *ad intra*, and of his act *ad extra*, which imitates it perfectly. God creates, because he freely chooses to please himself by conferring the good of existence through the creative act on subjects distinct from himself. The adequate object of this volition of God is himself as the author of created good, or the term of the relation which created existences have to him as their creator. The possession of good by the creature is inseparable in the volition of God from the complacency which he has in the exercise of the power of bestowing good by creation. Although he is necessarily his own final end in creating, yet this does not prevent creation from being an act of pure and free love; but, on the contrary, makes it to be so; because it is as infinite love that God is the end of his creative act. A charitable man, who confers good upon another, is moved by a principle of love in himself, which causes him to take delight in the happiness of his fellow-creatures. This movement originates in himself, and returns back to himself, being consummated in the pure happiness which the exercise of love produces. Yet the possession of good by another is the real object which elicits the act of love, and it is therefore pure, disinterested charity. Love makes the good as given, and the good as received, one identical object, and unites the giver and receiver in one good. Selfishness is inordinate self-love, or a love of others merely so far as they serve as instruments of our own pleasure and advantage, and not as themselves subjects of happiness. But the just love of self and of others is identical in principle, proceeding from the *amor entis*, or love of being. The benignant father, prelate, or sovereign, the generous benefactor of his fellow-men, is not less disinterested in his acts on account of the effect they produce in himself, filling his heart with the purest happiness of which it is capable. Thus in God; his complacency in his creative act, or sovereign pleasure in creating, is the purest and most perfect love to the creature. That which he delights in as creator is the bestowal of existence which participates in the infinite good of his own being.

The mode and degree in which existences participate in this infinite good which God distributes from the plenitude of his own being, specificates and determines their relation to him as final cause, and constitutes the ultimate term to which their creation is directed. This ultimate term or final end of creation as a whole, includes the ends for which each part taken singly is intended, and the common end to which these minor and less principal ends are all subordinated in the universal creative design. The end of a particular portion of the creation, taken singly, is attained, when it makes the final and complete explication of that similitude to the divine perfections which constitutes it in its own particular grade of existence. The end of the universe of existences is attained when they collectively reach the maximum of excellence which God proposed to himself in creating. That is, when the similitude of the perfections of God is expressed in the universe in that variety of distinct grades, and raised to that altitude in the series of possible states of existence, which God prefixed in the beginning as the ultimate term of the creative act. Whatever the maximum of created good may be, whatever may be the predetermined limits of the universe of existence, whatever may be the highest point of elevation to which it is destined, it is evident that the accomplishment of the creative act brings the creation back to God as final cause. It has its final end in God, wherever that finality may have been fixed by the eternal will of God. This is very plain and obvious. But it leads into one of the most abstruse, and, at the same time, one of the most unavoidable questions of philosophy, that which relates to the end of creation metaphysically final. What is the end of creation, or the relation of the universe of created existences to the final cause, which is metaphysically final? How far ought the actual end of created existences to coincide, and how far does it really coincide, with the end metaphysically final?

CHAPTER VII.

THE END OF CREATION METAPHYSICALLY FINAL—THE ASCENDING SERIES OF GRADES IN EXISTENCE—THE SUMMIT OF THIS SERIES IS A NATURE HYPOSTATICALLY UNITED TO THE DIVINE NATURE OF THE WORD—THE INCARNATION, THE CREATIVE ACT CARRIED TO THE APEX OF POSSIBILITY—THE SUPERNATURAL END TO WHICH THE UNIVERSE IS DESTINED COMPLETED IN THE INCARNATION.

BY the end of creation metaphysically final, is meant a relation of the universe to God as final cause, which is final in the divine idea, or the one which God beholds in his own infinite intelligence as the *ultimatum* to which his omnipotence can carry the creative act. It is a relation which brings the creature to the closest union and similitude to the creator in the good of being which the nature of the infinite and of the finite will admit.

We have already established the doctrine that God is by nature free to create or not to create, and eternally determines himself to creation by his own sovereign will to confer the pure boon of existence. We

Problems of the Age. 113

have also established that, since God determines himself from eternity to create, he necessarily creates in accordance with his own nature or essence, in accordance with the eternal archetype and idea reflected in the person of the Word; and for his own glory, or for an end in himself to which the creature is related, and which he must attain if he accomplishes his destiny. But we must inquire further, whether in determining himself to create according to the archetype contained in his own essence, he necessarily carries out this idea to the most perfect and complete actualization in the real universe? That is, does he necessarily create for an end metaphysically final, and carry the creative act to its apex, or the summit of possibility? Or is there any degree of existence or grade of resemblance and relation to God as archetype which must be supposed in order to conceive of an end accomplished by creation which is worthy of the divine wisdom and goodness? Or, on the contrary, is it just as free to God to determine any limit, however low, as the term of creation, as it is to abstain from creating? For instance, can we suppose it consistent with the divine wisdom to create only a grain of sand? On the one hand, it may be said that creation being a free act, the creation of a grain of sand does not take away the liberty of the divine will to abstain from creating anything else. On the other hand, God, as being in his very essence the infinite wisdom, must have an adequate end in view, even in creating a grain of sand. It may be said that the creation of a grain of sand is truly an infinite act, and that a grain of sand represents the omnipotence of God as truly as the universe itself. Yet, it is difficult to see any reason why Almighty God should make such a representation merely for his own contemplation. For the same reason, it is equally difficult to suppose any adequate motive for the creation of a merely material universe, however extensive. The wisdom and power of God are manifested, but manifested to himself alone. The very end of such a manifestation appears to be to manifest the attributes of God to intelligent minds capable of apprehending it. Suppose the material universe filled with sentient creatures, and, although its end is thus partially fulfilled, by the enjoyment which they are capable of receiving from it, its adaptation to the manifestation of the divine attributes to intelligence is still apparently without an object. The sentient creation itself manifests the wisdom and goodness of God in such a way that it seems to require an intelligent nature to apprehend it, in order that God may be glorified in his works, and that the love which is the essential consummating principle of the creative act may be reflected back from the creation to the creator, and thus furnish an adequate term of the divine complacency. This complacency of God in himself as creator, as we have seen, is complacency in the communication of good, or pure, disinterested love delighting in the distribution of its own infinite plenitude. The material creation can only be the recipient of this love *in transitu* or as the instrument and means of conveying it to a subject capable of apprehending it. The sentient creation can only be the recipient of it as its most imperfect term, and as an end most inadequate to the means employed. The wisdom and goodness of God in the creative act cannot therefore be made intelligible to us, except as we consider it as including the creation of intelligent natures, capable of sharing in the intelligent life of God. As soon as the mind makes this point, it is able to perceive an adequate motive for the creation, for it apprehends a good in the finite order resembling the infinite good which is necessary and uncreated. It is approaching to a finality, for it apprehends that the rational nature is that nature in which the finality must be situated, or in which the ultimate relation of the universe to the final cause must exist. In other words, it apprehends that God has created a *universe*, including all generic grades of existence explicated into a vast extent and variety of subordinate genera and species multiplied in a countless number of individuals, all subordinate to a common order, and culminating in intelligent life. It apprehends the correspondence of the actual creation to its ideal archetype ; or the realization in act of the highest possible nature which omnipotence can create after the resemblance of his own essence impersonated in the Word, and of every inferior nature necessary to the constitution of a *universe*, or a world of composite order and harmony comprising all the essential forms of existence whose infinite equivalent is in the divine idea.

It is evidently befitting the wisdom and grandeur of Almighty God, that the created universe should represent to created intelligence an adequate and universal similitude of his being and perfections; that its vast extent and variety, the multiplicity of distinct existences which it contains, its complicated relations and harmonies, the sublimity and beauty of its forms, the superabundance of its sentient life and enjoyment, the excellence and perfection of its intelligent creatures, should be adapted to overwhelm the mind with admiration of the might and majesty, the wisdom and glory, the goodness and love of the Creator; that, as far as possible, the procession of the divine persons within the essence of God should be copied in the procession of created existences; that the ineffable object of the divine contemplation, or the Word going forth from the infinite intelligence of the Father, and returning to him in the Holy Spirit, should be represented in created similitudes by the communication of being, life, and intelligence, in every possible grade, and the completion of these in the most sublime manner of union to God of which finite nature is capable. This consummation of the creative act is worthy of the wisdom of God; for it is the most perfect act of the divine intelligence *ad extra*, or extrinsic to the *actus purissimus*, by which the Word is generated in the unity of his eternal being, which is possible. It is worthy of the goodness of God; for it is the most perfect act of love *ad extra*, or extrinsic to the *actus purissimus* of the spiration of the Holy Spirit, consummating the interior life of God in eternal, self-sufficing beatitude, which omnipotence can produce.

Let us now analyze the composite order of the universe, and examine its component parts singly, in reference to the final end to which this order is determined. We will then proceed to examine more closely the mode by which the end of the universe is attained in the rational nature, and the relation of this rational nature to the end metaphysically final.

Theologians distinguish in the divine nature *esse*, *vivere*, and *intelligere*, or being, life, and intelligence, as constituting the archetype of the inanimate, animated, and rational orders of creation respectively.

The inanimate order, composed of the aggregate of material substances, imitates the divine *esse*, considered as concrete and real, simply; prescinding the idea of vital movement. It imitates the divine being in the lowest and most imperfect manner. The good that is in it can only be apprehended and made to contribute to the happiness of conscious existence when a higher order of existence is created. God loves it only as an artist loves an aqueduct, a building, or a statue, as the medium of contributing to the well-being or pleasure of his creatures. Its hidden essence is impervious to our intelligence. The utmost that we can distinctly conceive of its nature is that it is a *vis activa*, an active force, producing sensible effects or phenomena. This appears to be the opinion which is more common and gaining ground both among physical and metaphysical philosophers.*

---

* The philosophical works of Leibnitz may be consulted for a thorough exposition of this doctrine. The philosophical articles of Dr.

By active force is meant a simple, indivisible substance, which exists in perpetual activity. It is material substance, because its activity is blind, unconscious, and wholly mechanical, producing by physical necessity sensible effects, such as extension, resistance, etc. Though not manifest to intelligence in its hidden nature and operation, it is apprehensible by the intelligence through the effects which it operates, as something intelligible. Its sensible phenomena are not illusions, or mere subjective forms of the sensibility, but are objectively real. Nevertheless, our conception of them must be corrected and sublimated by pure reason, in order to correspond to the reality or substance which stands under them. Our imaginary conceptions* represent only the complex of phenomena presented to the senses. They represent matter as composite, because it is only through composition, or the interaction of distinct material substances upon each other, that the effects and phenomena are produced which the senses present to the imagination. The substance, or active force which stands under them, is concluded by a judgment of the reason. Reason cannot arrest itself at the composite as something ultimate. The common, crude concep-

---

Brownson in his *Review* contain some incidental arguments of great value on the same topic. F. Dalgairns, of the London Oratory, also treats, with the ability and clearness which characterize all his writings, of this subject, at considerable length, in his work on the *Holy Communion*.

* By "imaginary conceptions" is not meant fanciful, unreal conceptions, but conceptions of the imagination as an intellectual faculty which reflects the real.

tion of extended bulk as the ultimate material reality, is like the child's conception of the surface of the earth as the floor of the universe having nothing below it, and of the sky as its roof; or like the Indian conception of an elephant supporting the world, who stands himself on the back of a tortoise, who is on the absolute mud lying at the bottom of all things. It is the essential operation of reason to penetrate to the *altissima causa*, or deepest cause of things, and not to stop at anything as its term which implies something else as the reason or principle of its existence. It cannot therefore stop at anything short of the *altissima causa*, in the order of material second causes, any more than it can stop short of the cause of all causes, or the absolute first cause. That which is ultimate in the composite must be simple and indivisible in itself, and divided from everything else, or it cannot be an original and primary component. For, however far the analysis of a composite may be carried, it may be carried further, unless it has been analyzed to its simple constituent parts which are not themselves composite, and therefore simple. It is of no avail to take refuge in the notion of the infinite divisibility of matter. For, apart from the absurdity of the infinite series contained in this notion, one of these infinitesimal entities could certainly be divided from all others by the power of God and made intelligible to the human understanding. And the very question under discussion is, What is the intelligible essence of this ultimate entity?

Another proof that material substance is something

intelligible and not something sensible, is that it has a relation to spiritual substance, and therefore something cognate to spirit in its essence. The Abbé Branchereau defines relation: "Proprietatem quâ duo aut plura entia ita se habent ad invicem, ut unius conceptus conceptum alterius includat aut supponat." "A property by which two or more entities are so constituted in reference to one another, that the conception of one includes or supposes the conception of the other."*

The conception of spirit must contain the equivalent of the conception of matter, and the conception of matter must contain something the equivalent of which is contained in spirit. Else, they must be related as total opposites, which leads to the absurd conclusion that in the essence of God, which is the equivalent of all finite essences, total opposites and contradictions are contained. The same is affirmed by F. Billuart after the scholastic principles of the Thomists. "Supremum autem naturæ inferioris attingitur a natura superiori." "The summit of the inferior nature is touched by the superior nature."† Everything copies the essence of God and exists by its participation in his being. There is no reason therefore for any other distinction in creatures except the distinction of gradation in a series, or the distinction of a more or less intense grade of participation in being. God cannot create anything totally dissi-

---

* *Prælect. Philos. De Relat. Entis.* Num. 103, 3.
† *De Angelis.* Diss. II. Art. I.

milar to himself, because the sole archetype imitable in the creative act, whose similitude is externized in creation, is himself. All things therefore being similar to his essence are similar to the essence of one another, each to each, each grade in the ascending series containing the equivalent of all below it.

The material creation represents the real being of God, as distinguishable in thought from his life and intelligence, in an express and distinct manner. The being of God is the archetype of the material creation, and contains a reason why the material order was necessary to perfect the universe. All geometrical principles are intuitively seen by the reason to be eternal truths. As eternal and necessary they are included in the object of the divine contemplation. The complete and adequate object of the divine contemplation is the divine essence. It is therefore in his own essence that God sees these necessary geometrical truths, not as we see them, but as identical with the truth of his own being in some way above our human understanding. These eternal geometrical principles are the principles which lie at the basis of the structure of the material universe, which therefore represents something in the divine essence not immediately and distinctly represented by the spiritual world.

Without pretending to define precisely what the material universe represents as equivalently and eminently contained in the divine essence, we are only uttering a truism when we affirm that what man in his present state principally apprehends through it, is the idea of the immensity of the divine being. The material universe, which has a *quasi* infinitude to our feeble and limited imagination, is an image of God as possessing boundless infinitude, and including an immeasurable ocean of perfections. It is only when the mind becomes so overwhelmed with the magnitude of the creation as to forget its relation to the creator, that its judgment is erroneous. And the error of judgment does not consist in appreciating the material universe too highly, but in appreciating it too little, that is, in not appreciating its highest relation to the spiritual order, with which it is cognate in its essence. The physical, visible world is not to be despised. It is no illusion, no temporary phase of reality, no perishable substance, but real, indestructible, and of endless duration. Its essence and its relation to the final cause are incomprehensible. Its essence is, however, so far intelligible that we can understand it to be a real entity, bearing a similitude to the divine nature, endued with active force as a physical second cause, through which wonderful phenomena are produced in which the divine perfections are manifested. Its end is also intelligible as subordinated to the higher grades of existence and to the grand composite order of the universe.

The next grade of existence is that which represents the *vivere* of the divine essence, or presents an animated and living similitude of the life of God. The distinct type of this grade is in the animal world, but it is connected with the inanimate creation by an intermediate link, namely, that which is constituted by the world of vegetative life. This world of vegetative life represents the principle of life in an inchoate form, and ministers to the higher life of sentient existences, by furnishing them with the sustenance and food of their physical life, and contributing to their enjoyment by the beauty of its forms.

Thus far the creation is merely good as means to an end, or as the substratum of that order of existence which is capable of apprehending and enjoying good. In the sentient creation, existence becomes a good in itself, or a good capable of terminating the divine will. The countless multitudes of sentient creatures are created that they may enjoy life, and attain their particular end in this enjoyment. Nevertheless this particular end is a minor and less principal end in reference to the general end of the created universe. To this more general end the sentient order contributes, by increasing the beauty and perfection of the whole, and ministering to the happiness of the higher, intelligent order.

This third and highest grade of existence represents the divine *intelligere*. It includes all rational natures, or intelligent spirits, created after the similitude of that in the divine essence which is the highest archetype imitable in finite existences. According to the regular series of gradation, man comes next in order above the animal world, and should be first considered. There is a particular reason, however, which will appear hereafter, for considering the angels first.

The angels represent most perfectly the order of

pure intelligence, as distinct from the irrational creation. By their nature they are at the summit of existence, and participate in the most immediate and elevated mode which can be connatural to any created essence, in the divine perfections. The perfection of the universe requires that it should contain a grade of existence imitating that which is highest in the essence of God so far as it is an archetype of a possible creation. There is nothing conceivable in the divine essence higher than its intelligence or pure spirituality. The divine life is consummated in the most pure act of intelligent spirit, which is the procession of the Word and Holy Spirit from the Father. This divine procession within the divine essence being the archetype of the procession of created existences without it, the latter ought to imitate the former by producing that which represents the intelligent act of God as closely as possible. This intelligent act of God being consummated in love, or complacency in that infinite good which is the object of intelligence, creation, which imitates and represents it, ought to contain existences which are the recipients of love and are capable of its exercise in the highest possible manner which can be essential to a created nature. The creative act would therefore be most imperfect and incomplete if it stopped short with the material or even the sentient creation. Supposing that God determines to carry out his creative act by creating a universe or a world in which the potential is actualized in a universal manner by representing the *esse, vivere,* and *intelligere* of the divine essence in every generic mode, this universe must evidently contain intelligent spirits. Intelligent spirit alone can apprehend the image of God in creation, apprehend itself as made in the image of God, apprehend the infinite attributes of God by the intuition of reason, and become fully conscious of the good of existence, capable of enjoying it, and of returning to the creator an act of love, worship, and glorification, for his great boon of goodness conferred in creation. Creation is an overflow of the plenitude of good in the divine being proceeding from the complacency of God in the communication of this good. This communication can be made in a manner which appears to our reason in any way adequate to terminate the divine complacency, only by the communication of intelligence.

The type of intelligent nature is most perfectly actualized in the angels; whose essence and operation are purely spiritual, so far as created, finite nature and operation can be purely spiritual. Whatever is intelligible or conceivable of finite, intellectual activity as connatural, or intrinsically included in the essence of created spirit, is to be attributed to them.

The notion of any composition of nature in the angels, or hypostatic union of their pure, spiritual substance, with another material substance distinct from it, is wholly gratuitous. It destroys the distinctive type of the angelic nature and the specific difference between it and human nature. It has no foundation in reason except the baseless supposition that a distinct corporeal organization is necessary to the exercise of created intelligence. Nor has it any solid support from tradition or extrinsic authority.

Some of the fathers are cited as maintaining it. Their language is, however, for the most part explained by the best theologians as indicating, not the union of the angelic spirit to a distinct, subtle corporeity, but the existence of something analogous to matter in the angelic spirit itself. The angels are called corporeal existences, because their essence is extrinsic to the divine essence, and extrinsication attains its extreme limit in matter ; also because their potentiality is not completely reduced to act, and their operation is limited by time and space. This appears to be also the notion advocated by Leibnitz, and the exposition of the nature of material substance given above, in accordance with his philosophy, removes all difficulty from the subject.

The conception of the angelic essence as completely free from all composition with a distinct material substance, is also at least more evidently in harmony with the decree *Firmiter* of the Fourth Council of Lateran, than any other. "Firmiter credimus et simpliciter confitemur, quod unus est solus verus Deus æternus . . . . qui sua omnipotenti virtute simul ab initio temporis, utramque de nihilo condidit creaturam, spiritualem et corporalem, angelicam videlicet et mundanam : ac deinde humanam quasi communem ex spiritu et corpore constitutam."

"We firmly believe and confess with simplicity, that there is one only true eternal God . . . who by his own almighty power simultaneously from the beginning of time made out of nothing both parts of the creation, the spiritual and the corporeal, that is, the angelical and the mundane: and afterward the human creature, as it were of a nature in common with both, constituted from spirit and body."

Nevertheless, by the principle of the Thomist philosophy above cited, that the lowest point of any nature touches the highest of the nature beneath it, there may be something even in the spiritual operation of the angels cognate to material operation, and coming within the sphere of the sensible. We will venture to give a little sample of scholastic theology on this head from Billuart.

"It may be said with reason that the angels operate two things in the celestial empyrean. The first is the illumination by which the intrinsic splendor of the empyrean is perfected, according to St. Thomas and various testimonies of Holy Scripture in which certain places are said to have been sensibly illuminated by the angels. For although an angel cannot immediately produce alterative qualities, as heat or cold, he can produce light, because light is a celestial quality and the highest of corporeal qualities, and the summit of the inferior nature is touched by the superior nature.

"In the second place, the angels operate on the empyrean heaven, so that it may more perfectly and efficaciously communicate a suitable perpetuity and stability to all inferior things. For as the supreme angels who are permanently stationed there have an influence over the intermediate and lowest angels who are sent forth, although they themselves are not sent forth, so the empyrean heaven, although it is itself motionless, communicates to those things which are in motion the requisite stability and permanence in their being. And that this may be done more efficaciously and permanently the angels aid by their operation in it. For, the whole universe is one in unity of order; and this unity of order consists in this: that by a certain arrangement corporeal things are regulated by those which are spiritual, and inferior bodies by the superior; therefore, as this order demands that the empyrean sphere influence the inferior ones, it demands also that the angels influence the empyrean sphere."*

Whatever may be thought of this as philosophy, it is certainly brilliantly poetical, as is the whole treatise of the learned Dominican from which it is extracted. The physical theory of the universe maintained by the scholastics was a magnificent conception, although it has been supplanted by a sounder scientific hypothesis. There appears to be no reason, however, for rejecting the notion of angelic influence over the movement of the universe. The modern hypothesis of a central point of revolution for the universe being substituted for the ancient one of the empyrean, the entire scholastic theory of the influence of the angels upon the exterior order of the universe may remain untouched in its intrinsic probability.

The consideration of man has been reserved, be-

* *De Angelis.* Diss. II. Art. I.

cause, although he is inferior to the angels in intelligence, he sums up in himself the three grades of existence; and therefore the consideration of the three as distinct ought to precede the consideration of their composition in the complex human nature. The human nature includes in itself the material, vegetative, animal, and intelligent natures, which represent respectively the divine *esse*, *vivere*, and *intelligere*. For this reason man is called a microcosm, or universe in miniature. In certain special perfections of the material, sentient, and intelligent natures, he is inferior to each; but the combination of all gives him a peculiar excellence and completeness, and qualifies him to stand in the most immediate relation to the final cause of the universe, or to the consummation of its end.

What this end is, we must now more closely examine. It is plain at first sight that this end must be attained by creation through its intelligent portion, or through the angelic and human natures. As God is final cause as well as first cause; of necessity, these intelligent natures in themselves, and all inferior natures through them, must, in some way, terminate in God as their ultimate end. God is final cause as the supreme good participated in and attained to by the creation, through the overflow of the plenitude of the divine being. The divine complacency in this voluntary overflow of the fount of being and good was the ultimate and determining motive to the creative act. The good of being thus given is a similitude of the divine *esse*, *vivere*, and *intelligere*. As it is real, or existence in act, it must copy, as far as its grade of existence permits, the most pure act of God in the blessed Trinity. That is, the creature must reflect from its own essence an image of the divine essence, or a created similitude of the uncreated Word, in which its existence is completed and its act consummated. In the material world this is a mere dead image, like the representation of a living form made by a statue or picture. In the sentient world, so far as we can understand this most inscrutable and baffling of all parts of the creation, there is an apprehension by the sensitive soul of a kind of shadow of the intelligible object in sensible forms, and an imperfect resemblance of the life and felicity of an intelligent nature which corresponds to this imperfect apprehension. In the intelligent creature, its spiritual essence; by virtue of the rationality in which it is created, and which is its constitutive principle; reflects an image of the divine Word in the contemplation of which its intelligent life is completed. So far as intelligent nature is merely potential, it is potential to this act of intelligent life; and when its potentiality is reduced to act, so as to produce the nearest similitude to the divine intelligence in act which God has determined to create; intelligent nature, and in it all nature, has attained its finality. Intelligent nature has attained the highest good attainable; and, the different intelligent species and individuals existing together in due order and harmony in the participation of the common good, with all inferior grades of existence subordinated to them, the universe has unity and is determined to a common final end.

Thus, creation returns back to the principle from which it proceeded, by the consummation of the creative act. As the Father is united to the Word in the Holy Spirit, or in love and complacency, so the creation is united to God by the possession of good and the complacency of God in this good. This is actualized in the intelligent nature capable of knowing and loving God, and therefore having a similitude to the Son or Word. When it is ascertained what the highest union to the Father, or that approaching nearest to the union of the Son to him of which created nature is capable, is, it will be ascertained what is the end metaphysically final to which created nature can attain, if God wills to bring it to the summit of possibility. When it is ascertained what this summit of possibility is, it is ascertained what the end of creation is which is metaphysically final; and when it is ascertained how far toward this summit God has actually determined to elevate his creation, it is ascertained what is the end of creation actually final, and how far it coincides with the end metaphysically final.

This knowledge cannot be deduced from any first principle given to reason. It is communicated by revelation, and by this revelation we learn that God has determined to bring the creation to the end metaphysically final in the incarnation of the Word.

The revelation of the mystery of the Incarnation is concomitant with the revelation of the mystery of the Trinity; therefore, in the Creed, the same terms which propose the dogma that the Word is of God and is God, propose the dogma that the Word is incarnate in human nature. The name given to the Second Person in the Trinity, in the Creed, Jesus Christ, is the name which he assumed with his human nature. "Et in unum Dominum, Jesum Christum, Filium Dei unigenitum, Deum de Deo, Lumen de Lumine, Deum verum de Deo vero, genitum, non factum, consubstantialem Patri: per quem omnia facta sunt. Qui, propter nos homines, et propter nostram salutem, descendit de cœlis, et incarnatus est de Spiritu Sancto ex Maria Virgine, et homo factus est."

"And in one Lord, Jesus Christ, the only begotten Son of God, God of God, Light of Light, very God of very God, begotten, not made, consubstantial with the Father; by whom all things were made. Who, for us men, and for our salvation, descended from heaven, and was incarnate by the Holy Ghost of the Virgin Mary, and was made man."

The mystery of the incarnation presents to us the idea, that the Word has assumed human nature; not by assuming all the individuals of the race, but by assuming humanity individuated in one perfect soul and body into a union with his divine nature, in which it terminates upon his divine person as the final complement of its existence, without any confusion of its distinct essence with the divine essence to which it is united. By this union, the Word is a theandric person, or one divine person in two natures, divine and human, really distinct from each other in essence and existence, but with one common principle of imputability to which their attributes and operation are to be ascribed. This is the union, called in theological language hypostatic, of the creature to the creator, which is metaphysically final, or final to the divine intelligence and power; beyond which there is no idea in God of a possible act *ad extra*, and which is next in order to the procession of the divine persons *ad intra*. Through this hypostatic union, created nature participates with the uncreated nature impersonated in the Son in the relation to the Father as principle, and the Holy Spirit as consummation, of intelligence and love; that is, in the divine life and beatitude. The incarnation having been in the view and purpose of Almighty God from eternity, as the ultimatum of his wisdom and omnipotence, is the apex of the creative act, or the terminus at which the creative act reaches the summit of possibility. In it the creation returns to God as final cause, from whom it proceeds as first cause, in a mode which is metaphysically final. It is therefore certain that God, in his eternal, creative purpose, determined the universe to an end metaphysically final; and that this end is attained in the incarnation, or the union of created with uncreated nature in the person of the Word.

CHAPTER VIII.

A FURTHER EXPLANATION OF THE SUPERNATURAL ORDER.

IT has been already remarked, that the Incarnation is a more profound and inscrutable mystery than even the Trinity. The reason is that the trinity is a necessary truth, included in the very idea of God as most simple being and most pure act. The incarnation is not a truth necessary in itself, but only necessary on the supposition that it has been decreed by God. The trinity of persons proceeds from a necessity of nature in God, the incarnation from an act of free will. But the acts of the divine free will are more mysterious and inexplicable than those which proceed from necessity of nature.

Without revelation the incarnation would be inconceivable, and even when it is disclosed by revelation, the analogies by which it can be illustrated are faint and imperfect. The union between soul and body in animal nature and between the animal and spiritual natures in man furnish the only analogies of anything like a hypostatic union in the natural world. But these analogies do not illustrate the dark point in the mystery, to wit: the union of two *intelligent* natures in one *subsistence*, or one common personal principle of imputability to which the acts of both are referable. We have but little difficulty in apprehending that acts proceeding from two distinct natures in man, the animal and the spiritual, should be referred to one principle of imputability or one personality. These acts are so very distinct and different from each other, that they evidently have no tendency to become blended or confused, by the absorption of one nature into the other. But if we should try to conceive of a hypostatic union between the angelic and human natures in one person, it would be impossible to avoid imagining that one intelligent nature would be absorbed in the other. If there is but one principle of imputability, how can there be two distinct intelligent voluntary operations? Our opinion is, that a union of this kind between two finite natures is impossible. The possibility of assuming a distinct intelligent nature must then belong to a divine person only, and be included in the infinitude of the divine essence. The difficulty of understanding it lies then in the incomprehensibility of the divine essence. We apprehend nothing in the divine essence distinctly, except that which is apprehensible through the analogy which created essences bear to it. Evidently that in the divine essence which renders it totally dissimilar from all created essences cannot be represented by a similitude in created essences. And as the divine essence subsisting in the Second Person renders it capable of assuming human nature by an attribute which renders it totally dissimilar from all finite personality, there can be no analogy to it in finite things. In order to understand this it is necessary to recall to mind a principle laid down by St. Thomas, that we cannot affirm anything, whether being, intelligence, will, personality, or whatever other term of thought we may propose, of God and a creature, *univocally*, that is, in the same identical sense. The essence of God differs as really from the spiritual essence of angels and human souls as it does from the essence of animal souls and of matter. We apprehend what the intelligence and the will of God are only through the analogy of human intelligence and will, in a most imperfect and inadequate manner. In themselves they are incomprehensible to the human understanding. In the very essence of God as incomprehensible, or superintelligible, is situated that capacity of being the personality of created intelligent nature which constitutes the mystery of the hypostatic union. The only analogy therefore in created things which is appreciable by the human mind, is an analogy derived from the union of natures whose difference is intelligible to us, as the spiritual and animal. This analogy enables us to understand that the divine and human natures, not being intelligent natures in a univocal sense, but being dissimilar not only in degree of intelligence but in the very essence of intelligence, are capable of union in one personality. There is no analogy, however, which enables us to understand what this difference is, because it would be a contradiction in terms to suppose in the creature any analogy to that which is above all analogies and is peculiar to the divine nature as divine. The utmost that reason can do is to apprehend, when the mystery of the incarnation is proposed by revelation, that the incomprehensibility of the divine essence renders it impossible to judge that it cannot be hypostatically united to a created intelligent nature, and that it increases our conception of its infinitude or plenitude of being to suppose that a divine person can terminate a created nature as well as the nature which is self-existing. All that reason can do then is to demonstrate, after the mystery of the incarnation is proposed, that the impossibility of the incarnation cannot be demonstrated on the principles of reason, and that it is therefore credible on the authority of revelation; and, by the illumination of faith, to apprehend a certain degree of probability or verisimilitude in the mystery itself.

Once established, however, as a dogma or fundamental principle in theology, its reason and fitness in reference to the final cause of the universe, the harmony of all other facts and doctrines with it, and the grandeur which it gives to the divine economy, can be conclusively and abundantly proved by rational arguments.

We know that it must be fitting and worthy of the divine majesty to decree the incarnation, because he has done it. But we can also see that it is so, and why. We can see that it befits Almighty God to exhaust his omnipotence in producing a work which is the masterpiece of his intelligence and the equivalent of the archetype contained in his Word. To show his royal magnificence in bestowing the greatest possible boon on created nature. To pour forth his love in such a manner as to astound the intelligence of his rational creatures, by communicating all that is contained in filiation and the procession of the Spirit, so far as that is in itself possible. To glorify and deify the creature, by raising it as nearly as possible to an equality with himself in knowledge and beatitude.

The reason for selecting the human rather than the angelic nature for the hypostatic union is obvious from all that has preceded. Human nature is a microcosm, in which all grades of existence are summed up and represented. In taking human nature the Word assumes all created nature, from the lowest to the highest. For, although the angelic nature is superior to the human, it is only superior to it in certain respects, and not as a rational essence. Moreover, this superiority is in part only temporary, enduring while the human nature is in the process of explication; and as to the rest, the inferiority of the human nature is counterbalanced by the supernatural elevation given to it in the hypostatic union, which raises the natural, human operation of the soul of our Lord Jesus Christ far above that of the angelic nature. Although, therefore, in the series of grades in the natural order of existence, the angelic nature is above the human, it is subordinated to it in the supernatural order, or the order of the incarnation, and in relation to the final cause. For it is through the human nature united to the divine nature in the person of the Word that the angelic nature completes its return to God and union with him.

The elevation of created nature to the hypostatic union with God in the person of the Word introduces an entirely new principle of life into the intelligent universe. Hitherto, we have considered in the creative act a regular gradation in the nature of created existences, from the lowest to the highest. Each grade is determined to a certain participation in being superior in intensity to that of the one below it, and to a mode of activity corresponding to its essence. There can be no grade of existence in its essence superior to the rational or intelligent nature, which is created in the similitude of that which is highest in the divine essence. No doubt, the specific and minor grades included under the universal generic grade of rationality might be indefinitely multiplied. As the angels differ from man, and the various orders of the angelic hierarchy differ from each other, so God might continue to create *ad infinitum* new individuals or new species, each differing from all others, and all arranged in an ascending series, in which each grade should be superior in certain particulars to all below it. It is evidently possible that a created intelligence should be made to progress from the lowest stage of development continuously and for ever. Let us fix our thought upon the most distant and advanced limit in this progression which we are able to conceive. It is evident that God might have created an intelligent spirit in the beginning at that point, as the starting-point of his progression, and might have created at the same time other intelligent spirits at various distances from this point in a descending series. Suppose now that this is the case, and that the lowest in the scale progresses until he reaches the starting-point of the most advanced. The one who began at this advanced point will have progressed meanwhile to another point equally distant, and will preserve his relative superiority. But even at this point, God might have created him at first, with another series of intervening grades at all the intermediate points which he has passed over in his progressive movement. We may carry on this process as long as we please, without ever coming to a limit at which we are obliged to stop. For the creation being of necessity limited, and the creative power of God unlimited, it is impossible to equalize the two terms, or to conceive of a creation which is equal to God as creator. Nevertheless, all possible grades of rationality are like and equal to each other as respects the essential propriety of rationality, and never rise to a grade which is essentially higher than that of rational nature. The only difference possible is a difference in the mode in which the active force of the intellect is exercised, and in the number of objects to which it is applicable, or some other specific quality of the same kind. Whatever may be the increase which rational nature can be supposed to receive, it is only the evolution of the essential principle which constitutes it rational, and is therefore common to all species and individuals of the rational order. Although, therefore, God cannot create a spirit so perfect that it cannot be conceived to be more perfect in certain particulars, yet it is nevertheless true that God cannot create anything which is generically more perfect than spirit or intelligent substance. From this it follows as a necessary consequence, that God cannot create a nature which by its essential principles demands its last complement of being in a divine person, or naturally exists in a hypostatic union with the divine nature. For rational nature, which is the highest created genus, and the nearest possible to the nature of God, *Ipsius enim et genus sumus*,* developed to all eternity, would never rise above itself, or elicit an act which would cause it to terminate upon a divine person, and bring it into a hypostatic union with God. Produce a line, parallel to an infinite straight line, to infinity, and it will never meet it or come any nearer to it. The very essence of created spirit requires that it should be determined to a mode of apprehending God by an image reflected in the creation. The activity of the created intelligence must proceed for ever in this line, and has no tendency to coincide with the act of the divine intelligence in which God contemplates immediately his own essence. Increase as much as you will the perfection of the created image, it remains always infinitely dis-

---

* "For we are also his offspring," Acts xvii. 28.

tant from the uncreated, personal image of himself which the Father contemplates in the Word, and loves in the Holy Spirit, within the circle of the blessed Trinity. It has been proved in a previous chapter that infinite intelligence is identical with the infinite intelligible in God. If a being could be created which by its essence should be intelligent by the immediate vision of the divine essence, it would be intelligent *in se*, and therefore possess within its own essence its immediate, intelligible object, which, by the terms of the supposition, is the divine essence. It would possess in itself sanctity, immutability, and beatitude. It would be, in other words, beatified precisely because existing, that is, incapable of existing in any defective state, and therefore incapable of error, sin, or suffering. And as, by the terms, it is what it is, by its essence, its essence and existence are identical; it is essentially most pure act, essentially existing, therefore self-existent, necessary being, or identical with God. It is therefore impossible for God to create a rational nature which is constituted rational by the immediate intuition of the divine essence. For by the very terms it would be a creature and God at the same time. It would be one of the persons in the unity of the divine nature, and yet have a nature totally distinct. In the natural order, then, it is impossible that a created nature should either at its beginning, or in the progress of its evolution, demand as its due and necessary complement of being a divine personality. Personality is the last complement of rational nature. Divine nature demands divine personality. Finite nature demands only finite personality. It is evident, therefore, that there cannot be a finite nature, however exalted, which cannot come to its complete evolution within its own essence, or which can explicate out of the contents of its being an act which necessarily terminates upon a divine person, so as to bring it into a hypostatic union with the divine nature.

Let us go back a little in the scale of being, in order to develop this principle more fully. Lifeless matter is capable of indefinite increase in its own order, but this increase has no tendency to elevate it to the grade of vegetative life. A new and different principle of organization must be introduced, in order to construct from its simple elements a vegetative form, as, for instance, a flower. So, also, the explication of vegetative life has no tendency to generate a sentient principle. The plant may go on producing foliage, flowering, germinating, and reproducing its species for ever, but its vital activity can never produce a sentient soul, or proceed to that degree of perfection that it requires a sentient soul as its last complement or the proper form of its organic life. Suppose a plant or flower to receive a sentient soul; this soul must be immediately created by God, and it would be the principle or form of a new life, which, in relation to the natural, vegetative life of the flower, would be *super*-natural, elevating it to an order of life above that which constitutes it a flower.

A sentient creature, as a dog or a bird, has no tendency to explicate from the constitutive principle of its animal soul intelligence, or to attain a state of existence in which an intelligent personality is due to it as its last complement. If the animal soul could have an intelligent personality, it must be by a hypostatic union with an intelligent nature distinct from itself, which would then become the *suppositum*, or principle of imputability to the animal nature. The animal would then be elevated to a state which would be *super*-natural, relatively to the animal nature, or entirely above the plane of its natural development.

In like manner, the rational nature has no tendency or power to rise above itself, or to do more than explicate that principle which constitutes it rational. If it is elevated to a higher order, it must be by a direct act of omnipotence, an immediate intervention of the creator, producing in it an act which could never be produced by the explication of its rationality, even though it should progress to all eternity. This act is supernatural in the absolute sense. That is, it lies in an order above created nature as a totality, and above all nature which might be created; *supra omnem naturam creatam atque creabilem.*

It is beyond the power even of divine omnipotence to create a rational nature which, by its intrinsic, constitutive principle of intelligence, is affiliated to the Father through the Holy Spirit. Such a nature would be equal to the Word and another Word, and therefore equal to the Father, or, in other words, would be a divine nature although created; which would be absurd. The Father can have but one Son, eternally begotten, not made ; and the only possible way in which a created nature can be elevated to a strictly filial relation to the Father, is by a hypostatic union with the divine nature of the Son in one person, so that there is a communication of properties between the two natures, and but one principle of imputability to which all the divine and human attributes and acts can be referred. This union can be effected only by a direct intervention of God, or by the Word assuming to himself a created nature. For rational nature finds its last complement of personality, its *subsistentia*, or principle of imputability, within its own limits, which it never tends to transcend, even by infinite progression. The human nature individuated in the person of Jesus Christ, by its own intrinsic principles was capable of being completed in a finite personality, like every other individual human nature. The fact that the place of the human personality is supplied by a divine person, and the human nature thus completed only in the divine, is due to the direct, divine act of the Word, and is therefore supernatural. In this supernatural relation it becomes the recipient, so to speak, of the divine vital current, and participates in the act in which the divine life is consummated, which is the procession of the Son and Holy Spirit from the Father. This act consists radically and essentially in the immediate contemplation of the divine essence. Created intelligence, therefore, elevated to the hypostatic union, contemplates the essence of God directly, without any intervening medium, by the immediate intuition or beatific vision of God.

Thus, in the incarnation, the creation returns back to God and is united to him in the most perfect manner, by participating in the good of being in a way sublime above all human conception, exhausting even the infinite idea of God. Created intelligence is beatified, glorified, and deified. In Jesus Christ, man, in whose essence is included the equivalent of all creation, and God, meet in the unity of one person. The nature of God becomes the nature of man in the Second Person, who is truly man; and the nature of man becomes the nature of God in the same Person, who is truly God. Creation, therefore, attains its final end and returns to God as final cause in the incarnation; which is the most perfect work of God, the crown of the acts of his omnipotence, the summit of the creative act, the completion of all grades of existence, and the full realization of the divine archetype.

In Jesus Christ, the creative act is carried to the apex of possibility. In his human nature, therefore, he is the most preëminent of all creatures, and surpasses them all, not only singly but collectively. He has the primogeniture, and the dominion over all things, the entire universe of existences being subordinated to him. Nevertheless, his perfection is not completed merely by that which he possesses within the limits of his individual humanity. He is the summit of creation, the head of the intelligent universe, the link nearest to God in the chain of created existences. The universe, therefore, by virtue of the principle of order and unity which pervades it, ought to communicate with him through a supernatural order, so that the gradation in the works of God may be regular and perfect. The chasm between rational nature in its natural state and the same nature raised to the hypostatic union is too great, and demands to be filled up by some intermediate grades. Having taken created nature, which is by its very constitution adapted to fellowship between individuals of the same kind ; and, specifically, human nature, which is constituted in relations of race and family, the Son of God ought, in all congruity, to have brethren and companions capable of sharing with him in beatitude and glory. Being specifically human and of one blood with all mankind, it is fitting that he should elevate his own race to a share in his glory. Being generically of the same intellectual nature with the angels, it is also fitting that he should elevate them to the same glory. This can only be done by granting them a participation in that supernatural order of intelligence and life which he possesses by virtue of the hypostatic union ; that is, a participation in the immediate, beatific vision of the divine essence.

This supernatural order is denominated the order of regeneration and grace. It is cognate with the order of the hypostatic union, but not identical with it. The personality of the divine Word is communicated only to the individual human nature of Jesus Christ, who is not only the first-born but the only-begotten Son of God. God is incarnate in Christ alone. The union of his created substance with the divine substance, without any permixture or confusion, in one person, is something inscrutable to reason. The knowledge, sanctity, beatitude, and glory of his human nature are effects of this union, but are not it. These effects, which are due to the humanity of Christ as being the nature of a divine person, and are its rightful and necessary prerogatives, are communicable, as a matter of grace, to other individuals, personally distinct from Christ. That is to say, sanctity, beatitude, and glory do not require as the necessary condition of their communicability the communication of a divine personality, but are compatible with the existence of an indefinite number of distinct, finite personalities. All those rational creatures, however, who are the subject of this communicated grace, are thereby assimilated to the Son of God, and made partakers of an adoptive sonship. This adoptive sonship is an inchoate and imperfect state of co-filiation with the Son of God, which is completed and made perfect in the hypostatic union. The order of grace, therefore, though capable of subsisting without the incarnation, and not depending on it as a physical cause, can only subsist without it as an imperfect order, and cannot have in itself a metaphysical finality. The incarnation being absent, the universe does not attain an end metaphysically final, or actualize the perfection of the ideal archetype. The highest mode of the communication of the good of being, the most perfect reproduction of the operation of God *ad intra*, in his operation *ad extra*, which the Father contemplates in the Word as possible, remains unfulfilled.

Problems of the Age. 149

Those who hold, therefore, that the incarnation was not included in the original creative decree of God must maintain that in that decree God did not contemplate an end in creating metaphysically final. They are obliged to suppose another decree logically subsequent to the first, by virtue of which the universe is brought to an end metaphysically final in order to repair the partial failure of the angelic nature and the total failure of human nature to attain the inferior, prefixed end of the first decree. Nevertheless, as the decrees of God are eternal, God always had in view, even on this hypothesis, the incarnation as the completion of his creative act; and only took the occasion which the failure of his first plan through sin presented to introduce one more perfect. Billuart, therefore, as the interpreter of the Thomist school, maintains that God revealed the incarnation to Adam before his fall, though not the connection which the fulfilment of the divine purpose had with his sin as its *conditio sine quâ non*. If this latter view is adopted, it cannot be held that the angelic and human natures were created and endowed with supernatural grace in the express view of the incarnation, or that the angels hold, and that man originally held, the title to glorification from Jesus Christ as their head, and the meritorious cause of original grace. Nevertheless, as the incarnation introduces a new and higher order into the universe, elevating it to an end metaphysically final of which it previously fell short, all angels and all creatures of every grade are subordinated to Jesus Christ, who is the head of the creation, reuniting all things to the Father in his person.

This explanation is made in deference to the common opinion, although the author does not hold this opinion, and in order that those who do hold it may not feel themselves bound to reject the whole argument respecting the relation of the creative act to the incarnation.

It is in regard to the doctrine of original grace, or the elevation of the rational nature to that supernatural order whose apex is the hypostatic union, that Catholic theology comes into an irreconcilable conflict with Pelagianism, Calvinism, and Jansenism. These three systems agree in denying the doctrine of original grace. They maintain that rational nature contains in its own constituent principles the germ of development into the state which is the *ultimatum* of the creature, and the end for which God created it, and was bound to create it, if he created at all. They differ, however, fundamentally as to the principles actually constitutive of rational nature. The Pelagian takes human nature in its present condition as his type. The advocates of the other two systems take an ideal human nature, which has become essentially corrupted by the fall, as their type. Therefore the Pelagian says that human nature, as it now is, has in itself the principle of perfectibility by the explication and development of its essence. But the Calvinist and Jansenist say that human nature as it was first created, or as it is restored by grace to its primal condition, has the principle of perfectibility; but as it

Problems of the Age. 151

now is in those who have not been restored by grace, is entirely destitute of it. The conception which these opponents of Catholic doctrine have of the entity of that highest ideal state to which rational nature is determined, varies as the ratio of their distance from the Catholic idea. Those who are nearest to it retain the conception of the beatific union with God, which fades away in those who recede further, until it becomes changed into a mere conception of an idealized earthly felicity.

The Catholic doctrine takes as its point of departure the postulate, that rational nature of itself is incapable of attaining, or even initiating a movement toward that final end, which has been actually prefixed to it as its terminus. It needs, therefore, from the beginning, a superadded gift or grace, to place it in the plane of its destiny; which is supernatural, or above all that is possible to mere nature, explicated to any conceivable limit. At this point, however, two great schools of theology diverge from each other, each one of which is further subdivided as they proceed.

The radical conception of one school is, that nature is in itself an incomplete thing, constituted in the order of its genesis in a merely inchoate capacity for receiving regeneration in the supernatural order. Remaining in the order of genesis, it is in a state of merely inchoate, undeveloped, inexplicable existence, and therefore incapable of attaining its destination. There is, therefore, no end for which God could create rational existence, except a supernatural end. The natural demands the supernatural, the order of genesis demands the order of regeneration, and the wisdom and goodness of God require him to bestow on all rational creatures the grace cognate to the beatific vision and enabling them to attain it.

The radical conception of the other school is, that rational nature, *per se*, requires only the explication and perfection of its own constituent principles, and may be left to attain its finality in a purely natural order. The elevation of angels and men to the plane of a supernatural destiny was, therefore, a purely gratuitous concession of the supreme goodness of God, in view, as some would add, of the merit of the Incarnate Word.

These different theories are entangled and interlaced with each other, and with many difficult and intricate questions related to them, in such a way as to make a thicket through which it is not always easy to find a sure path. It is necessary, however, to try, or else to avoid the subject altogether.

The obscurity of the whole question is situated in the relation of created intelligence to the object which constitutes it in the intelligent or rational order. It is evident that a created substance is constituted an intelligent principle by receiving potentiality to the act connoted by this relation of the subject to its object, and is explicated by the reduction of this potentiality into act. The end of intelligent spirit is to attain to its intelligible object, by the act of intelligence. In the foresight of this, the exposition of the relation between intelligence and the intelligible, has been placed first in this discussion.

It is agreed among all Catholic theologians: 1. That created intelligence can, by the explication of its own constitutive principles, attain to the knowledge of God as *causa altissima;* or, that God is, *per se,* the ultimate object of reason. 2. That there is a mode of the relation of intelligence to its ultimate object, or to God, a permanent state of the intuition of God by a created spirit, called the intuitive, beatific vision of the divine essence, which can be attained only by a supernatural elevation and illumination of the intelligence.

The point of difference among theologians relates to the identity or difference of the relations just noted. Is that relation which intelligence has *per se* to God, as its ultimate object, the relation which is completed by supernatural elevation, or not? If not, what is the distinction between them? Establish their identity, and you have established the theory which was mentioned in the first place above. Establish their difference, and you have established the second theory.

If the first theory is established, rational creatures are *ipso facto* in a supernatural order. The natural order is merely the inchoation of the supernatural, cannot be completed without it, and cannot attain its end without a second immediate intervention of God, equal to the act of creation, by which God brings back to himself, as final cause, the creature which proceeded from him as first cause. This second act is regeneration; and creation, therefore, implies and demands regeneration. It follows from this, that reason is incapable of being developed or explicated by the mere concurrence of God with its principle of activity, or his concurrence with second causes acting upon it, that is, by the continuance and consummation of the creative, generative influx which originally gave it and other second causes existence. A regenerative influx is necessary, in order to bring its latent capacity into action, and make it capable of contemplating its proper object, which is God, as seen by an intuitive vision.

One great advantage of this theory is supposed to be, that it leaves the naturalists no ground to stand upon, by demonstrating the absolute necessity of the supernatural, that is, of revelation, grace, the church, etc. This presupposes that the theory can be demonstrated. If it cannot be, the attempt to do too much recoils upon the one who makes it, and injures his cause. Besides this, it may be said that the proposed advantage can be as effectually secured by proving that the natural order is actually subordinated in the scheme of divine Providence, as it really exists, to a supernatural end, without professing to prove that it must be so necessarily.

The great positive argument in favor of this hypothesis is, that rational nature necessarily seeks God as its ultimate object, and therefore longs for that clear, intellectual vision of him called the beatific. If this be true, the question is settled for ever. Those who seek to establish its truth state it under various forms. One way of stating it is, that reason seeks the universal, or the explanation of all particular effects, in the *causa altissima*. This is the doctrine of St. Thomas. God is the *causa altissima*, the universal principle, and therefore reason seeks for God.

Again, it is affirmed that there is a certain faculty of superintelligence, which apprehends the superintelligible order of being, not positively, but negatively, by apprehending the limitation of everything intelligible. Intelligence is therefore sensible of a want, a vacuum, an aimless, objectless yearning for something unknown and unattainable; showing that God has created it for the purpose of satisfying this want, and filling this void, by bringing intelligence into relation to himself as its immediate object, in a supernatural mode.

In a more popular mode, this same idea is presented under a countless variety of forms and expressions, in sermons, spiritual treatises, and poems, as a dissatisfaction of the soul with every kind of good attainable in this life, vague longing for an infinite and supreme good, a plaintive cry of human nature for the beatitude of the intuitive vision of God. "*Irrequietum est cor nostrum donec requiescat in te*," " Our heart is unrestful until it finds repose in thee," is the language of St. Augustine, which is echoed and reëchoed on every side.

These considerations are not without great weight; nevertheless, they do not appear to us sufficient to prove conclusively the hypothesis in support of which they are adduced, or to overbalance other weighty considerations on the opposite side.

Reason seeks for the *causa altissima*, but it remains to be proved that it seeks for any other knowledge of it but that which is attainable by a mode connatural to the created spirit.

Reason is conscious of its own limitation. But this does not prove that it aspires to transcend this limitation. Beatified spirits are conscious of their own limitation. Those who are in the lowest grade are aware of numerous grades above them, and the highest are aware of their inferiority to the exalted humanity of Jesus Christ, united to the divine nature in his person. All together, including Jesus Christ himself, as man, are aware of an infinite incomprehensibility in the divine nature. In the words of the greatest of all mystic theologians, St. John of the Cross: "They who know him most perfectly, perceive most clearly that he is infinitely incomprehensible. To know God best, is to know he is incomprehensible; for those who have the less clear vision do not perceive so distinctly as the others how greatly he transcends their vision."*

Beatified spirits do not feel any void within themselves, or any unsatisfied longing for the comprehension of the superintelligible. Neither do they aspire even to those degrees of clearer vision which are actually conceded to spirits of a higher order than their own. Why then should a rational creature necessa-

---

* *Spiritual Canticle*, stanza vii. Oblate Ed. vol. ii. p. 44.

rily desire to transcend its own proper and connatural mode of intelligence? The apprehension of the superintelligible shows that the intellect cannot be satisfied with a limitation of itself to a mere knowledge of second causes and the contingent—that it must think about God, and apprehend in some way the infinite, eternal, necessary being and attributes of the creator and first cause of all things. But it does not show that it must apprehend God in the most perfect way possible, much less in such a way that he does not remain always infinitely beyond its comprehension.

The dissatisfaction of the human heart may proceed in great measure from the fact that God purposely disquiets it by withholding from it the good it naturally seeks, in order to compel it to seek for supernatural good. Another cause of it is, that most persons have committed so many sins themselves, and are so much involved in the consequences of the sins of others, that they cannot possess the full measure even of that natural enjoyment of which human nature is capable. That the human heart in its misery and unhappiness turns longingly toward the hope of a supreme beatitude in the contemplation of God as he is revealed to the saints in heaven, may be owing to the fact that God, who proposes this beatitude to men, stirs up a longing for it in their souls by a supernatural grace.

The question, therefore, reverts to this, as has been repeatedly said already, What is the principle constitutive of the intelligent life and activity of a created spirit? When this principle is evolved into act, the created spirit fulfils its type, and realizes its ideal perfection in its own order. Now, according to the preliminary doctrine we have laid down, this is an active power to apprehend the image of God in the creation, or to contemplate a created image of God which is a finite similitude of the infinite, uncreated image of God, that is to say, the Word. Beatific contemplation is a contemplation of this infinite, uncreated image without any intervening medium. It is an intellectual operation of which God is both the object and the medium. It is not therefore the operation which perfects created intelligence in its own proper order, but one which elevates it above that order, giving it a participation in the divine intelligence itself. Created intelligence is perfected in its own proper order by its own natural operation; and although the intervention of God is necessary in order to conduct it to that perfection, so that it is strictly true that a supernatural force is necessary to the initiation, explication, and consummation of the natural order of intelligence, yet this does not elevate it to a supernatural mode and state of activity in the strict and theological sense of the word. Created intelligence is perfected by the contemplation of the creator through the creation, and has no tendency or aspiration to rise any higher. True, it has an essential capacity to become the subject of a divine operation elevating it to the immediate intuition of God, or it never could be so elevated. This is the really strong argument in favor of the hypothesis that God, if he creates at all, must create an intelligent order determined to the beatific union. It is equally strong in favor of the hypothesis, that he must complete his creative act in the incarnation, because created nature is essentially capable of the hypostatic union. For what purpose is this capacity? Does it not indicate a demand for the order of regeneration, and the completion of this order in the incarnation? It is not our purpose to answer this question definitely, but to leave it open, as it has no practical bearing upon the result we are desirous of obtaining. Presupposing, however, that God determines to adopt the system of absolute optimism in creating, and to bring the universe to an end metaphysically final, as he actually has determined to do, this question, as we have previously stated, must be answered in the affirmative. There is no metaphysical finality short of the hypostatic union of the created with the uncreated nature, which alone is the adequate, objective externization of the eternal idea in the mind of God. The metaphysical, generic perfection of the universe demands the incarnation, with its appropriate concomitants. But this demand is satisfied by the elevation of one individual nature to the hypostatic union, and the communication of the privileges due to this elevated nature to one or more orders of intelligent creatures containing each an adequate number of individuals. It does not require the elevation of all intelligent orders or all individuals, but admits of a selection from the entire number of created intelligences of a certain privileged class. It is only on the supposition that God cannot give an intelligent nature its due perfection and felicity without conceding to it the beatific vision, that we are compelled to believe that God cannot create intelligent spirits without giving them the opportunity of attaining supernatural beatitude. And it is merely this last supposition against which we have been contending.

The view we have taken, that rational nature, precisely as such, is not necessarily created merely in order to become the subject of elevating grace, but may be determined to an end which does not require it to transcend its natural condition, comports fully with the Catholic dogma of sanctifying grace. The church teaches that affiliation to God by grace is a pure boon or favor gratuitously conferred by God according to his good pleasure and sovereign will. It is not due to nature, or a necessary consequence of creation. The beginning, progress, and consummation of this adoptive affiliation, is from the grace of God, both in reference to angels and men. It was by grace that the angels and Adam were placed in the way of attaining the beatific vision, just as much as it is by grace that men are redeemed and saved since the fall. If rational nature cannot be explicated and brought to a term suitable for it which satisfies all its exigencies, without this grace, it is not easy to see how it can be called a grace at all, since grace signifies gratuitous favor.. Rather it would be something due to nature, which the goodness of God bound him to confer when he had created it. It would be the mere complement of creation, and an essential part of the continuity of the creative act as much as the act of conservation, by virtue of which the soul is constituted immortal. In this case, it would be very difficult to reconcile the doctrine of original sin, and the doom of those who die in it before the use of reason, with the justice and goodness of God. It would be difficult also to explain the whole series of doctrinal decisions which have emanated from the Holy See, and have been accepted by the universal church, in relation to the Jansenist errors, all of which easily harmonize with the view we have taken.

Moreover, the plain dogmatic teaching of the church, that man, as he is now born, is *saltem negativè aversatus a Deo*, "at least negatively averted from God," and absolutely incapable of even the first movement of the will to turn back to him without prevenient grace, cannot be explained on the theory we are opposing without resorting to the notion of a positive depravation of human nature by the fall, a notion completely irreconcilable with rational principles. If rational nature, as such, is borne by a certain impetus toward God as possessed in the beatific vision, it will spring toward him of itself and by its own intrinsic principles, as soon as he is extrinsically revealed to it, without grace. To say that it does so, is precisely the error of the Semipelagians, which is condemned by the church. It is certain that it does not; and therefore we must explain its inability to do so, either with the Calvinists and Jansenists by maintaining that its intrinsic principles are totally perverted and depraved, or by maintaining that rational nature, as such, is determined by its intrinsic impetus to an inferior mode of apprehending and loving God as its last end, which is below the plane of the supernatural.

This view accords fully with the teachings of the great mystic writers, who are the most profound of all philosophers and theologians. They all teach most distinctly, that, when God leads a soul into a state of supernatural contemplation, it has an almost unconquerable repugnance and reluctance to follow him, and is thrown into an obscure night, in which it undergoes untold struggles and sufferings, before it can become fit for even that dim and imperfect light of contemplation which it is capable of receiving in this life. Why is it that the human soul turns toward the supernatural good only when excited, illuminated, and attracted by the grace of God, and even then with so much difficulty? Why does it so easily and of preference turn away from it, unless it is that it naturally seeks to attain its object by a mode more connatural to its own intrinsic and constitutive principles?

The conclusion we draw is, that rational nature of itself is capable of attaining its proper perfection and felicity, without being elevated above its own order, by the mere explication of its rationality, and aspires no higher, but even prefers to remain where it is. The fact that it is in a state which in comparison with the state of elevation is merely inchoate existence, and is *in potentiâ* to a state not realized *in actu*, does not show that its felicity or the good order of the universe requires it to be elevated any higher, unless it is elected as a subject of elevating grace.* God alone is *actus purissimus* without any admixture of potentiality. The finite is always inchoate and potential, because finite. Its very nature implies what is called metaphysical evil, or a limitation of the possession of good in act. Every finite nature except that of the Incarnate Word is limited, not only in respect to the infinite, but also in respect to some other finite nature superior to itself. Its proper perfection consists in the possession of good, with that limitation which the will of God has prefixed to it as its term. The perfection and order of the universe, as a whole, are constituted by the subordination and harmony of all its parts in reference to the predetermined end. The individual felicity of a rational creature, and his due relation to the final cause of the universe, do not require his being elevated to the utmost summit of existence of which he is capable, unless God has predetermined him to that place. The mere inert capacity of receiving an augmentation or elevation of his intellectual and voluntary operation does not give him any tendency to exceed his actual limit, unless that inert capacity begins to be actualized, or unless the principle of a new development is implanted and vitalized. The inert capacity of being united to the

---

* This does not mean that any human being is at liberty to choose to decline proffered grace. The human race *en masse* is elected to grace, and at least all those to whom the faith is proposed have the proffer of grace, with a precept to accept it. Moreover, God has not provided any order except the supernatural for mankind in which the race can attain its proper perfection and felicity.

divine nature by the hypostatic union, is actualized only in Christ. If, therefore, rational nature could not attain its proper end and completion without the utmost actualization of its passive capacity, Christ alone would attain his final end. We must certainly admit, however, that the blessed in heaven all attain their final end and a perfect beatitude, each one in his own degree. We are not to understand, therefore, that the relation of the creation to God as final cause consists solely and purely in the return of the creature to God in the most sublime manner possible, and that everything which exists is created solely as a means to that end. If this were so, the hypostatic union of the human to the divine nature in the person of Jesus Christ would be the sole terminus of the creative act, the only end proposed by God in creating. Nothing else could or would have been created, except as a means to that end. The rest of creation, however, cannot contribute to that end. The union of the human nature to the divine in Christ, and its filiation to God, by which it is beatified, glorified, and deified, is completely fulfilled, within itself; and the rest of creation adds nothing to it. If God had no other end in view, in the reproduction of the immanent act within himself by a communication of himself *ad extra*, except the hypostatic union, he would have created only one perfect nature for that purpose. The beatification and glorification of the adopted brethren of Christ must be therefore included in the end of creation.

This is not all, however, that is included in it. The

supernatural order includes in itself a natural order which is not absorbed into it, but which has its own distinct existence. *Gratia supponit naturam*, grace supposes nature, but does not supersede or extinguish it. The inferior intellectual operations of our Lord are not superseded by his beatific contemplation, nor do they contribute to its clearness of intuition. The operation of his animal soul—that is, of the principle within his rational soul which contains in an eminent mode all the perfection that is in a soul purely animal, and adapts his rational soul to be the form of a body—continues also, together with the activity of the senses and of the active bodily life. This operation does not conduce to the perfection of the act of beatific contemplation, which does not require the mediation of the senses. The same is true of the inferior, natural operations of all beatified angels and men. If supernatural beatitude were the exclusive end of the creation, there would be no reason why these inferior operations should continue, any more than the exercise of faith, hope, patience, fortitude, or works of merit, which, being exclusively ordained as means for attaining beatitude, cease when the end is gained. The beatific act would swallow up the entire activity of the beatified, and all inferior life would cease. For the same reason, all corporeal and material organization would be swept out of the way as a useless scaffolding, and only beatified spirits, exclusively occupied in the immediate contemplation of God, would continue to exist for ever.

This is not so, however. The body is to rise again

and live for ever. The universe is to remain for ever, with all its various grades of existence, including even the lowest, or those which are purely material. There is therefore a natural order coexisting with the supernatural in a subordinate relation to it—a minor and less principal part, but still an integral part of the divine, creative plan. There is a *cognitio matutina* and a *cognitio vespertina*, a matutinal and vesperal knowledge, in the blessed; the one being the immediate intuition of the Trinity in unity, the other the mediate intuition of the idea or infinite archetype of creation in God, through his creative act. There is a natural intellectual life in the angels, and a natural intellectual and physical life in man, in the beatific state. The natural order is preserved and perfected in the supernatural order, with all its beauty and felicity—with its science, virtue, love, friendship, and society. The material world is everlasting, together with the spiritual. All orders together make up the universe; and it is the whole complex of diverse and multitudinous existences which completely expresses the divine idea and fulfils the divine purpose of the creator. The metaphysical finality or apex of the creative act is in the Incarnate Word, but the relation to the final cause exists in everything, and is fulfilled in the universe as a totality, which embraces in one harmonious plan all things that have been created, and culminates in Jesus Christ, through the hypostatic union of the divine and human natures in his person.

In this universe there may be an order of intelligent existences, touching at its lowest point the highest point of irrational existence, and at its highest point the lowest in the grade of the beatified spirits. That inferior order of knowledge and felicity may exist distinctly and separately which exists conjointly with supernatural beatitude in the kingdom of heaven. The perfection of the universe requires that there should be a beatified, glorified order at its summit. It may even be maintained that this consummation of created nature in the highest possible end is the only one which the divine wisdom could propose in creating. Yet this does not exclude the possibility of an inferior order of intelligence, upon which the grace elevating it to a supernatural state is not conferred.

We are prepared, therefore, to proceed to the consideration of the nature and conditions of that grace, as a pure, gratuitous gift of God, conferred upon angels and upon the human race through his free and sovereign goodness. From the point of view to which the previous reasoning has conducted us, the angels and mankind appear to us, not as mere species of rational creatures conducted by their creator along the path of rational development by natural law, but as the elect heirs of an entirely gratuitous inheritance of glory—candidates for a destiny entirely supernatural. The relation which they sustain to God in this supernatural scheme of grace will therefore be our topic next in order.

CHAPTER IX.

THE STATE OF PROBATION—ITS REASON AND NATURE
—THE TRIAL OF THE ANGELS.

IN the preceding chapter we have endeavored to show what is that order of regeneration or supernatural grace, in which rational nature, and through it all nature, attains the end of creation metaphysically final. The position we have taken is, that the creation returns to God as final cause through the hypostatic union of created nature with the divine nature in the person of the Incarnate Word, and the participation in this union by angels and men who are elevated through grace to the rank of sons of God.

We have now another problem to deal with. The Catholic doctrine teaches that angels and men are not brought to their destined end, in view of which they were created, by an immediate, indefectible operation of divine power alone; but by a concurrence of this divine operation with the spontaneous, contingent, and defectible operation of their own free-will. Moreover, that, in consequence of the contingent, defectible operation of the second cause which is concurrent with the first cause, a multitude of angels and men finally and irremediably fail to reach their destination.

This statement of the relation of the rational creature to God as final cause, involves a number of the most difficult and perplexing questions. The reason for placing creatures in a state of probation by which their eternal destiny is decided, the relation of divine foreknowledge to contingent events, the conciliation of the efficacy of grace with the liberty of the will, the nature of free-will itself, the reason for permitting the existence of evil, predestination, and similar vexed questions, start up at once to trouble and confound the feeble human intellect.

They are all summed up in the problem of probation. The creature is placed in a state where he is to decide in a certain brief space of time, by his own voluntary choice, his eternal destiny; this destiny including the alternative of the attainment or the forfeiture of supreme beatitude. What reason can be given for this? Why is the rational creature defectible or liable to fail of reaching his destination? Why does God place him in a state of probation, knowing his defectibility? Why is it that some fail and others do not fail to attain their destination?

A dechristianized and decatholicized philosophy cannot give even a plausible solution of this great problem, and the problems arising out of it. It must either deny the problem, or throw out some ingenious guesses which satisfy no one. It is wholly at fault, always has been, and always will be. With those who deny the whole problem, by denying the whole supernatural order, we have nothing to do at present; for we can not raise anew questions already discussed. We are concerned only with those who admit the moral order of the universe; and these admit the existence of a period of probation, although some of them may extend the limits of this probation indefinitely, and doubt or deny some of its consequences.

The very notion of probation springs from the notion of a free-will, permitted and even compelled to choose between good and evil. Now, why is the created will permitted and even compelled to exercise this prerogative which is too often the occasion of the greatest injury to its possessor?

A certain class of philosophers answer this question by asserting that it could not possibly be otherwise. They exaggerate beyond all measure this liberty of choice as something essential to all voluntary operation. They have no conception of any moral goodness, virtue, or sanctity, except that which is the product of this continual striving to make a right choice between two rival objects of desire, the good and the evil. They even extend their notion so far as to include God; as if he were in a kind of infinite state of moral probation, amenable to a standard or law above himself, and only preserving his holiness by a continual effort of will to choose among various possible determinations that which is most perfectly conformed to this standard. Of course, then, when he created intelligent spirits like himself, he was obliged to leave them to their liberty of choice. They could not become holy or happy in any other way. Indeed, according to this system, they must remain in this state of moral probation for ever. There is no conceivable way of determining them to good without destroying the liberty of will which is essential to a rational nature. The only immutability of will possible, is that which arises from a confirmed, long-continued habit of choice. Therefore God has not absolutely determined the wills of his rational creatures to good, because he could not. He has left them with the power and exposed to the risks of wrong choices because he could not help it.

This solution of the problem must be rejected as completely unsatisfactory. God is good, and is blessed, by his nature. The human nature of Christ is holy, impeccable, and beatified by its hypostatic union with the divine nature. The Blessed Virgin was impeccable from the instant of her immaculate conception. The holy angels and just men made perfect have finished their moral probation, and are in an unchangeable state. The perfection of intelligent nature, therefore, so far from implying, excludes liberty of choice between good and evil. If this be so, this liberty of choice is an imperfection. Why, therefore, did God create rational existences with this imperfection? Without doubt he could have given them impeccability. He could have elevated them to a state of perfection without requiring them to pass through any probation. He could have placed all rational creatures at once in the state of beatitude, and kept all sin and evil out of the universe. Why, then, is evil allowed to enter?

Moreover, *whence* and *what* is evil? How is it possible that there should be any evil? Extrinsic to the being of God which is the absolute good, nothing does or can exist, except that which God has created after the similitude of his own being, and which, therefore, participates according to its measure in his goodness. Besides, God has created all things in view of an end. Being infinitely wise, he knows how to attain this end through his works, and being infinitely powerful, he is able to do it. Being also infinitely good, only good can terminate his volition. Therefore, if evil were possible, he could not will to actualize it; and if, by an impossible supposition, it could come into actual existence without him, he must will to destroy it. The superficial theology and philosophy which dates from the Reformation, is tied up here in a Gordian knot which no skill can unravel. It contains two dogmas which are absolute contradictions: creation, and the substantive essence of evil. These two can never coexist in harmony. One or the other must be modified or given up. Either the dogma of creation must be so far given up as to admit of some eternal self-existent *materia* in which lies the essential principle of evil, or the substantive existence of evil must be denied. Those who deny or impair the first, have ceased to be theists in the strict and proper sense of the word, and are already moving toward pantheism. Those who deny the second, throw up with it the conception of a moral order in the universe, of a state of probation, strictly so called. There is no theistic, Christian philosophy of any depth or comprehensiveness on these topics, except that which is included in the theology of St. Augustine, St. Thomas, and other great Catholic writers.

It is well known how completely the ancient philosophers were befogged in regard to the nature and origin of evil. Plato taught that the *materia* out of which God formed the universe is eternal, and that, from an inherent intractability in its essence, it is incapable of perfectly receiving the impress of the divine ideas. The constructor of the universe was, therefore, hindered from realizing his ideal and fully executing his design by the defectiveness of his material. He was like an architect who has only soft, crumbling stone, or a sculptor with veined marble. From this source, according to Plato, is all the evil existing in the universe.

The Persians, whose great master was Zoroaster, resorted to the theory of two subordinate creators, both the offspring of the Supreme Being, one Ormusd, being good, and the other Ahriman, being evil. All that is good in the creation comes from the first, and all the evil from the second of these great master mechanics. Ahriman is destined, however, to be eventually converted, with all his liege subjects, his botched workmanship will be repaired, and the universe will come all right in the end. This ingenious theory left out, however, one essential point ; namely, how Ahriman came to have an evil nature, since he was created by the good God as well as Ormusd, and how he and his works could become good, if they were essentially evil.

Manes and the Manichæans carried their dualism to a point of more complete consistency, and more absolute absurdity. They taught the existence of two eternal, self-existing principles, one good, the other bad, who are engaged in perpetual warfare. Spiritual existences proceed from the good principle, corporeal existences from the evil one. Human souls, having been in some way allured into corporeal forms, are polluted by them and involved in evil. It is necessary for the soul to disengage itself from matter, and it will then be fit to return to the supremely good being from whom it proceeded.

Any system which teaches that evil has anything essential or substantive, must give up the pure dogma of creation. For it is inconsistent with that dogma to suppose that God can create anything essentially evil, or that any creature can create anything, or that any substance essentially good can become essentially evil by corruption; since corruption produces no new substance, but modifies substance already existing.

Whence, then, and *what* is evil? What can there be as an alternative of good before the intelligence and will of a rational creature to form the material for a dilemma, and oblige him to exercise a faculty of choice? Where is the substratum of a state of probation?

Metaphysical evil, or that evil which is included in the metaphysical essence of all created things, is merely the limitation of their possible good. Simple being, *ens simpliciter*, is alone the absolute good in possibility and in act. Jesus Christ has said, "There is one good, God."* In actual existences, evil is merely a recession from God. It is only relative, and negative, therefore, and expresses the absence of that good which exists in some other creature, or in God. In created existences, good is relative and positive, and evil, or the absence of good, is relative and privative. It is a mere deficiency, but nothing substantive, any more than darkness, cold, or vacuity is substantive.

If we can suppose, therefore, a certain good proposed to a rational creature as attainable by his free volition, with a power to the contrary, we have the necessary conditions of a state of moral probation. That is, the possibility is proved of a certain good being made contingent on the voluntary choice of rational creatures; and with it, the possibility of this good being forfeited by the deficiency of this choice. This answers the question whence and what is the possibility of evil as the concomitant risk annexed to a state of probation. It is only necessary, therefore, to show that we can make this supposition, by explaining how the will can be constituted in an equilibrium between this proffered good and some other object, with complete liberty to incline itself to either.

* St. Matt. xix. 17.

That other object cannot be an essentially evil object, for there is no such thing in existence. It must be, then, an inferior good. In the state of probation the will is inclined to all kinds of good indifferently, and capable of choosing any which the intellect judges to be best or most desirable. It is capable of making a false choice, because the intellect is capable of making a false judgment. Intelligent spirit has self-dominion where it is not determined by intrinsic necessity. It is lord over its own acts. It can determine its own judgments and volitions. And this makes it a proper subject of precept and moral obligation, capable of being placed in a state of probation.

It may appear very difficult to understand how this can be, but our own consciousness and practical experience give us an intimate sense of its truth. Let us take, then, a familiar example in illustration.

A child is capable of appreciating the good of delicious fruit, the good of approbation and reward, the good of play and amusement, and the good of knowledge. His parents allow him to eat peaches under certain restrictions, and forbid him to eat them without their permission. They allow him to play at certain times and under certain conditions, and forbid him all other amusement and recreation. They require him to devote a certain time to study, and to apply himself to this study with diligence. It is plain that the will of the child is in equilibrium toward all the various kinds of good in respect to which he receives precepts from his parents, and is thus placed in a state of probation, the issue of which is in great measure left to the arbitration of his own free choice. He can determine himself to obey his parents for the sake of their approbation and rewards, or to disobey them for the sake of eating forbidden fruit. He can determine himself to study for the sake of knowledge, or to neglect it for the sake of play. When he determines himself to the inferior, sensible good, he does so by a false judgment, that in the particular instance the present sensible enjoyment is best for him or most desirable. Yet he has power to the contrary, and both can and ought to make a right judgment. He is determined to neither side by any intrinsic necessity, but determines himself and destroys the equilibrium of his will by a free choice, by virtue of his self-dominion. The necessity of exercising this self-dominion proceeds from imperfection of nature. It is easily conceivable that his nature, if it were rendered more perfect, would determine him always to prefer the approbation of parents, and of his own conscience, to the pleasure of eating fruit, and the pleasure of knowledge to that of play.

This illustrates our present point, and shows how the imperfection of an intelligent creature, which makes him capable of false judgments in regard to the eligibility of different objects of volition, renders him a fit subject of probation.

But why is he created in this imperfect state, and obliged to run the risks of a difficult and dangerous probation? It is evident that God might easily pour such a flood of light upon his intelligence that he would be incapable of making a false judgment, and communicate to him such a degree of felicity in the enjoyment of the true good, that his will would be rapt away without effort beyond all possibility of attraction from any inferior objects. He might communicate the beatific vision simultaneously with the first act of reason, as he does to those infants who are translated to heaven in their infancy. Thus he might secure the eternal beatitude of all intelligent creatures without placing any of them in probation.

It is evident that God must have a reason for establishing a state of probation, and that this reason must involve some great good to be attained by it. This reason is, also, in part intelligible to us. So far as we can understand it, it is, that God and the creature are more glorified through the elevation of created nature to supernatural beatitude, when the created nature concurs with God as first cause, by its own activity, as second, concreative cause, in the highest manner possible. It is the will of God that beatitude should be the prize of merit, and merit implies liberty of choice. Supernatural beatitude is a pure boon from God to the creature, not due to him as simply existing. Therefore, God may bestow it on whom he pleases, and upon any conditions he pleases to establish. As probation implies imperfection, and the creature is created for his proper perfection, when he attains it probation must cease. The period of probation must therefore be limited. It must be also a real, *bonâ fide* probation; that is, the attainment of beatitude must really depend on the right use of the term of probation. Consequently, when the term of probation has expired, those who have failed in it must be left to the eternal consequences of their own voluntary error. That species of virtue which makes an intelligent creature capable of attaining supernatural beatitude is itself supernatural, and therefore impossible without divine grace. When this grace is lost, there is no natural power to regain it. Sin is therefore in itself irreparable. It can be repaired only by a second supernatural grace. If this grace is not conceded, there is no second probation, but the sinner must remain perpetually in that state to which his sin has reduced him. If this grace is conceded, and the limits of probation are extended, those who fail finally and pass out of the fixed period of probation must also remain perpetually in that state to which they have reduced themselves by their own free and voluntary election.

Another great difficulty here presents itself, namely: it appears that the fulfilment of the divine purpose is left to the contingencies of second causes, and at the mercy of the arbitrary wills of creatures. God appears to be like one who makes his plans in the dark, without being able to know what their success will be, or to take efficacious measures for securing their success. For how can he foresee future events that are purely contingent on the free choice of created wills? How can he predetermine an end, to be infallibly accomplished, when this accomplishment is contingent on the free arbitration of the creature? The Catholic doctrine teaches that a multitude of angels and men destined to supernatural beatitude finally fail of their destination. Does not this failure partially thwart the divine plan, mar the work of God, and deprive his universe of its perfection? Although the divine plan has a partial success, through the concurrence of a certain number of angels and men with the divine will, is not this success even due to hap-hazard? Must we not suppose that the divine plan ran the risk of a complete failure, so far as the coöperation of free-will is concerned?

It is evident that these suppositions are all incompatible with the essential attributes of God. He must necessarily have a perfect foreknowledge of all things that will ever come to pass. He must also have supreme dominion over his entire creation, and be able to accomplish all his purposes without any liability to be thwarted by his own creatures. He must have decreed from eternity whatsoever he does in time through his creative act.

Therefore some, overwhelmed by the difficulties which encompass the doctrine of the freedom of the created will, in its relation to the divine, have adopted the part of denying it altogether. The denial of free-will, however, makes the state of probation, and the entire moral order of the universe, with its retributions, completely illusory and fantastic. It is a denial of a fact of universal human consciousness. Whoever makes it ought to become a pantheist at once, and maintain that all individual existences are mere emanations of the divine substance.

The Catholic doctrine distinctly proclaims both the

divine foreknowledge and decrees, and also the liberty of choice in the created intelligent nature. A Catholic theologian, therefore, cannot dispose of the difficulty in the case, by summarily denying either side of the dogmatic truth. The school of St. Thomas Aquinas endeavor to resolve the difficulty by the hypothesis of a physical premovement of the will, or an efficacious grace, which has an infallible connection with a right choice, but yet leaves the will to make this choice freely and with power to the contrary. God has therefore predestined, by an infallible decree, all those to whom he gives this efficacious grace, to the attainment of beatitude. His foreknowledge is also explained as the knowledge of his own determination through which all events, even contingent, are made certain.

This system has a certain hypothetical finish and completeness about it, and it appears to vindicate the supreme dominion of God over all contingent existences, second causes, and events taking place in time, more effectually than any other. It fails, however, to reconcile with the attributes of God the freedom of the created will and the state of probation. For, according to this system, the will, although in equilibrium, and intrinsically capable of motion to either side, cannot put itself out of equilibrium by its own self-determining power, but needs a previous, efficacious concurrence of the divine will, in order to pass from the potentiality of choice to the act of choice. All acts of the created will are, therefore, determined by the will of God as efficient cause. If this is consistent with the liberty which is necessary to the created will, that it may be second and concreative cause in concurrence with the first cause to the effect of its own beatitude, God could infallibly determine all rational creatures to beatitude without infringing on their liberty. The creature could evolve into act all its causative activity, free-will could receive its fullest scope, the principle of merit and reward could be fully exemplified in the universe, without risking the eternal destiny of a single individual, or permitting even the smallest sin to be committed. It becomes very difficult, then, on this hypothesis, to explain the permission of sin, and the eternal loss of so many millions of rational creatures. The reason usually given, that sin is an evil incidentally necessary to a system of probation, permitted on account of the greater good attained through the probation of free-will, falls to the ground, and we have never yet seen any other satisfactory reason substituted for it.

It may be true that, without this hypothesis, the foreknowledge of God and his supreme dominion over his creation are more incomprehensible. This is no decisive argument, however, provided that these divine attributes can be shown to be intelligible without the said hypothesis.

First, in regard to the divine foreknowledge, it is argued that God cannot foresee that which is purely dependent on the created will, unless there is some cause or ground of certainty that the will shall actually place the effect which is foreseen. This cause or ground of certainty can only be the divine determination to concur efficaciously with the will, that it may infallibly place the foreseen act.

To this it is replied, that God foresees all contingent, future events, by a kind of knowledge called the supercomprehension of cause. Knowing completely all causes, he knows all their effects in them. This does not explain, however, his knowledge of the self-determining acts of the will, since in these the same cause is in equilibrium to opposite effects. It is better explained, we think, by the theory of Suarez, that God sees all things in their objective verity. He knows with certainty all that depends on the self-determining action of free-will, because he directly beholds the free-will determining itself. There is no succession in God. He coexists from eternity and in eternity to all the successive periods of created duration. What we call future is equally visible to God in eternity with the past. There is no more difficulty, therefore, in his knowing from all eternity all future contingent events, than there is in our knowing any one of these events in the time of its taking place, or after it has happened.

But, it is further argued, if God knows the acts of his creatures by an immediate vision of them in their objective verity, he is perfected by the creature, which is incompatible with his essence. God is the adequate object of his own intelligence; therefore, he knows all things in himself.

God is the adequate and sole object of his own intelligence in the act of simple intelligence in which his essential being in the Three Persons is constituted. Created existences are not included in this act, and the knowledge of them is not perfective of the being of God. God knows them in himself by the knowledge of vision, *scientiâ visionis*, and sees them in himself as in a mirror. This perfection of vision, by which God sees and knows all things which exist, is a perfection proceeding from his infinite intelligence, not given to him by the creature. The creature is its terminus, but the changes of the terminus affect itself alone, and do not make the essential attribute of God less immutable or infinite. The same objection might be made to the statement, that created existences are the terminus of the divine volition or love. The essential act of volition or love is completed in the act of God *ad intra*, or his infinite love of himself. Yet God loves the creature, delights in the love of the creature, wills the beatitude of the creature. That he may do this, the existence of the creature as the terminus of his volition is necessary as the *conditio sine quâ non*. It might be said, then, that the existence of the creature, and his act in loving God, is perfective of God. It is not. For it is altogether distinct from that which is the terminus of the divine act of love, in which the perfection of the being of God is constituted, namely, from the essence of God itself. God has the plenitude of love in himself, and it remains the same whether more or fewer created existences are its recipients. So the infinite power of vision in God is the same, whether more or fewer created existences or acts of existing agents come within its scope. There is no objection, therefore, to the theory respecting the science of God, which maintains that he knows all future contingents which depend entirely on his divine decree in that decree, all that depend on second causes determined of necessity to produce certain effects in his supercomprehension of cause, and all that depend on free-will in his foresight of the self-determination of free-will. The whole incomprehensibility of this foreknowledge is reduced to an identity with the essential incomprehensibility of God, as eternal and yet coexisting to all the successive periods of time.

Secondly, as regards the divine supremacy over creation, and the ability of the Sovereign Creative Spirit to bring the universe to an end predetermined by himself.

It is argued, that, if we reject the Thomist hypothesis, we reduce everything to the hap-hazard of capricious, eccentric, lawless free-will, which makes it impossible to suppose any plan regularly and infallibly carried out through the medium of second causes, in the universe.

This is not so. Free-will is not mere lawless caprice, directed by mere accident. It is directed by intelligence, and acts according to the law of motives. It must choose the good, and can never choose that which is evil, *ratione mali*. Since, by a law of its probation, the real chief good and the apparent chief good are presented before it in such a way as to leave it in equilibrium toward both, without any dominant or necessitating motive toward either, it makes the motive on one side preponderant by its exercise of self-dominion. This is not by chance or caprice. It is by the exercise of intellect, and through the impulse of powerful motives. Its circle of variability is restricted, and its determination is capable of being influenced by intellectual and moral considerations. It is perfectly evident that a man, even without the slightest power of exercising any determining influence on the wills of other men, can nevertheless, without infringing on their perfect liberty, reason them into a coöperation with himself in carrying out a plan, or persuade them into it by proving its advantages before them. Much more, then, is God able to bring a sufficient number of angels and men to a voluntary coöperation with himself, to secure the success of his great design. It is in this way that God manifests his infinite wisdom and divine art, by arranging all things with such consummate and complex skill and harmony, and directing all things from end to end by such a wise, far-reaching Providence, that he is able to bring out in the end the desired result, through the concurrence of free, concreative second causes. It may be said that, since all angels were free to reject the beatitude proffered to them, God, in creating them and giving them this freedom, exposed his plan to the risk of being completely thwarted by their unanimous refusal to comply with the terms of their probation. The same might also be said of mankind.

We must understand, however, that, although Almighty God does not deliberate, change, modify, watch for results, make experiments, profit by experience, devise new expedients, like a man of creative genius, and although his creative act is one, simple, and from eternity, yet it includes in itself in an eminent mode all these operations of the finite intelligence. If, by an impossible supposition, God had delegated creative wisdom and power to a created spirit, such as the Arians fancied the Logos, and others the Demiurgus, to be; and this mighty intelligence had proceeded to execute his task in the same manner, but on a grander scale, that men execute great undertakings, and we should endeavor to describe the way in which he accomplished his work, we should have a correct though imperfect representation of the actual operation of Almighty God in the execution of his works *ad extra*. The conceptions we are able to form of the operation of God are all analogical. We cannot transcend these analogies. And although we know them to be imperfect and inadequate, yet we know also that they have all the verisimilitude necessary to give us true conceptions. In this way we understand that God knew all the risks to which his plan was exposed, and made provision for them. Wherever it was necessary, he protected his designs from the risk of failure through the non-concurrence of second causes. For instance, having determined to create a heaven containing a multitude of beatified spirits, and foreseeing that a certain number of those who were destined to this high position would forfeit it by sin, he took this into the account in determining the number to be created, and the conditions of the trial through which they were to pass. A profound theologian who was of the strict Thomist school, the late Bishop of Philadelphia, expressed to the author on one occasion the opinion, that only the lower orders of angels were made liable to sin. He thought that the higher orders received a grace incompatible with sin, though not with merit, and that Lucifer was therefore the chief, not of the seraphim, but of the archangels. On this supposition, the risk of sin was confined within narrow limits, so far as the angels were concerned. Whether this be a well-grounded hypothesis or not, it is evident that these pure and exalted spirits, possessing the highest natural intelligence, being impelled to good by their nature, having received the gift of supernatural grace, and having the prospect of a still greater glory before them, were very likely, speaking after a human mode of thought, to make the requisite act of concurrence with the divine will and thus secure their confirmation in grace. In other words, there appears to be an *a priori* probability that at least a great number of them would do so. We know that, in point of fact, a great number of them did, and, according to the common opinion, much the largest portion of the whole number who were tried. Now, this to us apparent probability was a certainty to God, as clearly known before as after the fact. In view of this certainty, he created them and placed them in the state of probation. He foreknew, also, how many would fail, and therefore, if his purposes required it, could easily create such a multitude that the angels who fell would not be missed from their ranks. Those who fell did indeed thwart the benevolent designs of God, so far as their own particular persons were concerned. But these designs were conditional, as respecting individuals, and were made in full view of the actual event. God could not be thwarted or disappointed in regard to his grand design, because this did not depend on any particular individuals.

So in regard to men. Jesus Christ as man, and the Blessed Virgin, on whom the fulfilment of the divine plan absolutely depended, were absolutely predestined, and rendered impeccable; Jesus Christ by nature, and the Blessed Virgin by grace. If any other particular individuals were placed in a position which required it, they too received a grace which gave them immunity from any liability to fail in their necessary concurrence with the divine will as second causes. A vast multitude of human beings are elevated to beatitude without running any of the risks of probation. Adam, it is true, was able to thwart the first design of God in regard to the mode of bringing the race to its destination. But he could not thwart God's ultimate design, because he was able to accomplish it by another mode. Particular men, in vast numbers, are able to thwart the designs of God toward themselves. But they cannot thwart his designs toward the race. For he is able to regulate and order times, events, and circumstances, and to continue creating generation after generation, until, by moral means alone, he has completed the number of his saints and peopled heaven sufficiently to fulfil his purpose. Moreover, if necessary, he can always touch the springs of the will directly, and determine it to any act which he has positively decreed must be performed. He can also modify, restrict, alleviate, set aside, or shorten the risks of probation, according to his own good pleasure, in regard to any or all of men, with an infinite and infallible wisdom.

But it is again argued, that according to this view, God is not the absolute cause of all things, nor the absolute sovereign over all things. The created will has an independent sovereignty of its own, and God is dependent in certain things on his creatures, obliged to modify his plans and to condition his decrees to suit their determinations.

This is not a conclusive argument. It is a maxim of philosophy, that *causa causæ est causa causati;* the cause of a cause is the cause of that which is caused; that is, caused by this second cause. God is the creator of free-will, and his perpetual influx gives it always the power of choosing and acting. Free-will is not, therefore, an independent, but a delegated and dependent sovereign. God can deprive it of the opportunity of choosing, or frustrate its determinations. It is sovereign within a limited sphere, because God has chosen to create it and give it sovereignty.

If God is absolute sovereign, can he not concede to a creature the power to do his own will within a certain sphere, if it is his sovereign pleasure to do so? Can he not determine to do certain things on the condition that the creature uses his free-will in a certain way, if he pleases? He has pleased to do it. He has made his eternal decrees with a full view of all that his creatures would do, before him. All the incidental and partial evil resulting from the misuse of free-will in the universe he has foreseen, and determined to permit. He has decided on his great plan, notwithstanding the incidental evil, in view of a greater universal good. Not that sin and evil are necessary means of the greatest good, or directly conduce to a greater good than that which could exist in a universe without sin; but that the concession of liberty on a grand scale, the particular and incidental misuse of which occasions sin and evil, is the necessary means to that greater good. The greater good itself is the obedience, homage, love, service, and fidelity given to God by a multitude of creatures who have been left free to sin, and who have not sinned, or not sinned irremediably and finally.

We conclude, therefore, *pace tantorum virorum* who have maintained it, that the theory of the strict Thomists on this point is not conclusively established. To our mind, the theory which is in accordance with the philosophy of the great fathers before St. Thomas, with that of the Scotists in the middle ages, and with that of the most prevalent Catholic schools since the Jansenist controversy, is the more probable one. According to this theory, in a system of strict probation, a physical premovement or a grace efficacious *in se* and *ab intrinseco*, is not metaphysically necessary in order that free-will may actually concur with the divine will to secure the permanence of the creature in a supernatural state. Nothing is necessary beyond liberty of choice and the grace which gives power to elicit supernatural acts. When the angels passed through their probation, therefore, we cannot go behind the exercise of their liberty in choosing or rejecting the proffered boon of celestial glory, to seek a deeper cause, determining some to choose and not determining others. They were free to choose; and being free, some chose wisely and well, others foolishly and ill. So, also, with Adam. He might have stood, but he did not. He had the power to choose, and he chose wrongly. By the very same power he might have chosen rightly, without any additional grace. The *arbitrium mentis*, the exercise of free self-dominion, is the only reason that can be given. This prerogative is indeed mysterious and inscrutable. We do not pretend to have removed all difficulty of comprehending it. But it is incomprehensible to us in our present state of imperfect intelligence, because the soul itself is an inscrutable mystery. Its relation to the divine will and operation is a mystery full of inexplicable difficulties. But it is because of that grand mystery of mysteries, the coexistence of God and the creation, which was the insoluble enigma of all ancient philosophy. The great Aristotle saw the difficulty so clearly which is involved in the relation of a contingent world to the necessary being of God, that, unable to find an ideal formula which could unite the two terms by a dialectic relation, he denied all relation between them. He affirmed the existence of God and of the world. But he affirmed also, that the world exists independently of God, as self-existent, eternal, and necessary. Moreover, that God has or can have no knowledge of the world. For, he argued, God can have no knowledge of the world unless the world is the object or terminus of the divine intelligence. But if the world is the object of the divine intelligence, God is not perfect as intelligence in himself alone, but is conditioned and perfected by that which is inferior to his own being. Thus we see that the objection to the divine foreknowledge of the contingent in its objective verity which is found in scholastic theology, is one derived from Aristotle, and that the extremely subtle and acute reasonings of St. Thomas and the Thomists were directed toward a reconciliation of the Aristotelian philosophy with the Catholic dogmas. The difficulty lies in the creative act of God, which is a mystery not fully comprehensible by human reason, and, therefore, not fully to be explained by any hypothesis or theory of philosophy. The activity of free-will as concurrent, concreative cause with God, approaches the nearest of anything in creation to the creative act of God, and, therefore, is the most mysterious and incomprehensible fact of psychology. It is incomprehensible in itself, and it complicates still further the incomprehensibility of the creative act of God. It is not strange, therefore, that there should have been such a long and still unsettled controversy in the Catholic schools respecting this topic, since the church has hitherto abstained from deciding it. Still less can we wonder that non-Catholic schools, having no fixed dogmas or authoritative formulas of doctrine to check the spirit of private speculation, go round and round continually, involving themselves more hopelessly every day in entanglements from which they can never extricate themselves.

The explanation we have endeavored to set forth as the more probable will, we think, commend itself to the minds of most of our readers as the most intelligible and satisfactory which can be given. If a better one can be furnished by some one more competent to the task, we shall welcome it. Meanwhile, we leave what we have written to find what acceptance it may.

It will be seen at once, by those who are at all versed in these matters, that, according to the theory we have proposed, the predestination of those who attain eternal life as the term of a period of probation is consequent on the foresight of their fidelity and merit, at least as a general rule. It does not follow from this, however, that we reject the doctrine of efficacious grace. As this doctrine is immediately connected with the points we have been examining, we will give it a brief consideration now, in order to avoid returning to it hereafter.

In the Thomist theology, efficacious grace means a grace distinct in its own nature from sufficient grace. Sufficient grace gives the power to elicit a supernatural act: efficacious grace gives the act itself. It is, therefore, efficacious *in se* and *ab intrinseco*. This notion of efficacious grace is derived from the philosophical notion of the previous and efficacious concurrence of the will of God with every act of free-will, in the exercise of the faculty of choice. According to this philosophy, it is impossible for this faculty, as it is for every second cause *in potentiâ* to its proper act, to pass from potentiality into act without a special movement from the first cause.

The contrary hypothesis, sustained by Molina, the great body of the Jesuit theologians, Thomassinus, and the generality of modern Catholic authors, is, that the grace which is auxiliary to the will in eliciting free supernatural acts, is not efficacious *ab intrinseco*, but is made efficacious by the concurrence of free-will. This implies a different notion of divine concurrence from the one just stated, according to which the influx of divine power into free, spontaneous, active second causes gives merely an aid which is indeterminate, leaving free-will to its own election among two or more terms upon which it can direct this indeterminate aid. When an artilleryman sights his gun, the divine power which supports and gives efficiency to all natural laws and forces must propel the ball. But this divine power stands ready at his disposal, and will propel the ball in whatever direction, toward whatever point, he selects. So it is with the choice of free-will.

We have already indicated our adhesion to the latter hypothesis. It is far more in accordance with the doctrine of the fathers, Latin as well as Greek, including St. Augustine himself, than the other. The former one was wholly unknown to the Greek fathers, and does not appear in the Latin fathers before the Pelagian controversy. Even after this period it appears, in the writings of St. Augustine and others of his school, in an entirely different form from that which was given to it by St. Thomas. That is to say, it is applied to the case of fallen man, who is supposed to need an efficacious grace on account of the weakness of his will, and to receive it as a special gift of mercy through Christ. The perseverance of those angels who stood their trial successfully is attributed, not to a grace efficacious *ab intrinseco*, which was withheld from the other angels, but to a right use of the same grace which was equally conceded to all, and abused by some. So, also, the fall of Adam is attributed simply to his failure of concurrence with a grace which needed only his concurrence in order to become efficacious, but was frustrated of its effect by his abuse of his own free-will. Moreover, all that St. Augustine says about efficacious grace in fallen man is reconcilable with the doctrine of congruity, and sometimes directly favors it, as is proved by Antoine and others who have written in vindication of his theology from Jansenist perversions. This doctrine of congruity has been introduced in order to explain more satisfactorily the perfect liberty of the will, without denying the existence of efficacious grace differing *in actu primo*, or antecedently to the consent of the will, from grace merely sufficient. Although the opinion that the actual efficacy of divine grace is to be sought exclusively in the consent of the will has not been condemned, it has nevertheless been received with disfavor and generally rejected. It is commonly taught that God confers, whenever he pleases, upon men, a grace which infallibly secures their coöperation, and their final perseverance. In our view, this doctrine can be sustained by ample and certain proofs from Scripture and Tradition, and is the only one which can be completely developed in consonance with the decisions of the church, especially those of the Council of Trent respecting final perseverance.* The reason why certain graces are actually infallible in their effects is to be found in their congruity to the character, disposition, and circumstances of the subject, and in their multitude. The necessity for them is not a metaphysical but a moral necessity. The fragility of our nature is such, that, although a grace merely sufficient makes us metaphysically capable of persevering without sin, we are sure to become wearied, and through fickleness, weakness of purpose, changeableness, etc., to break down somewhere. Our own consciousness and experience teach us that we need a divine and protecting arm to encompass us continually and secure us against ourselves, and they incline us to utter that prayer of the divine Liturgy: "*Compelle, Domine, rebelles voluntates nostras:*" "Compel, O Lord! our rebellious wills." God, who knows human nature perfectly, can, in a thousand ways, by order-

---

* Si quis *magnum illud usque in finem perseverantiæ donum* se certo habiturum, absoluta et infallibili certitudine dixerit, etc., anathema sit.

If any one shall say that he will certainly have that *great gift of perseverance to the end*, with an absolute and infallible certitude, etc.

Si quis dixerit, justificatum vel sine *speciali auxilio Dei* in accepta justitia perseverare posse, vel cum eo non posse, anathema sit.

If any one shall say that the justified man either can, without a *special aid of God*, persevere in the justice he has received, or cannot persevere with it, let him be under the ban.—*De Justif.* Can. 16–22.

ing the circumstances of life, shortening or prolonging it, regulating the influences which act on the character, alluring or terrifying the heart, illuminating the mind, impelling without coercing the will, and adapting his influences with infinite wisdom to the special state of the soul, convert whom he will, sanctify whom he will, give perseverance to whom he will, and still gain his point with the free consent and concurrence of the creature. "*Non est volentis neque currentis, sed miserentis est Dei:*" "It is not of him who willeth or of him who runneth, but of God who showeth mercy." The difficulty may still be raised, that God withholds these graces of congruity and the gift of perseverance from those who do not in the first instance accept the proffered grace, or who do not finally persevere. But this is removed by the doctrine so ably and strenuously advocated by St. Alphonsus Liguori, that common grace is sufficient to enable one to pray fervently and do ordinary good acts; and that by prayer, with the use of other facile means, efficacious graces and the gift of perseverance may be infallibly obtained from God.

We may now return to our theme of the state of probation originally established by God for those who were made candidates for supernatural glory. We have endeavored to clear our track of difficulties impeding the clear view of the truth that God established this probation through goodness and love, or with the simple view of communicating the greatest good to the creature.

The principal questions respecting probation having been already discussed, there remains now but one, namely : what was the precise and specific nature of the trial to which rational nature was subjected? This divides itself again into two, one respecting the trial of the angels, and the other respecting the trial of man.

The angels, according to the doctrine of St. Thomas and theologians generally, were created at the summit of intelligent being, incapable of error or false judgment in their natural, intellectual operation, and therefore impeccable in the natural order. Supernatural grace was conferred upon them simultaneously with their creation, although, as F. Billuart holds, they may have concurred actively to the reception of this grace, by a spontaneous act preceding all deliberation. Grace made them capable of eliciting supernatural acts, but did not determine them to those acts without the free concurrence of their will. Their intelligence must have been, therefore, left in a certain obscurity as regards the supernatural object, in order that an error of judgment should be possible, or even an act of deliberation terminating in a free volition. What the precise object of deliberation and choice was cannot be certainly and precisely determined. It must in some way have presented the alternative of either eliciting a supernatural act by the aid of the obscure supernatural light, or of falling back on the free, natural operation of intelligence. God must have exacted some act of homage to his sovereign will, disclosed some condition as the indispensable prerequisite to obtaining the crown of supernatural glory, which the natural intelligence of the angels could not see to be just and right without the aid of a supernatural light. This light was given, clear enough to enable the will, by a strong voluntary effort, to determine itself to act by this light, in preference to its natural light; dim enough to allow the will to turn from it voluntarily, and find in its natural light a plausible reason for withholding its submission to the supreme will. Certain passages of Scripture, and the common traditional Catholic doctrine, indicate that the angels who fell, fell through pride, and that Lucifer, in particular, their chief spirit, in some way aspired to a resemblance with God. Some have thought that he desired to become God. St. Thomas, however, says that this is impossible, because his intelligence was too perfect to permit him to conceive such a thought. He explains the sin of the angels to have consisted in a refusal to accept supernatural glory as a pure boon from God, and a wish to attain beatitude by the exertion of their own natural powers.

The most plausible supposition, in our view, is one that may be said to be contained under the more generic statement just given. It is, namely, that the angels were tried by the revelation of the Incarnation. The union of the Second Person of the Trinity with human nature, the elevation of human nature to divine glory and honor, the obligation of doing homage to Jesus Christ as King, and to the Blessed Virgin, his mother, as Queen of Angels, was revealed, as the crucial test of the absolute obedience of the celestial spirits. According to their natural reason,

Problems of the Age. 201

and natural love of their own nature and kind, it would appear to them a violation of order and justice to pass them by, in order to assume an inferior nature partly corporeal and animal, into a hypostatic union with the Godhead; elevating this nature above their own, which was the highest in the natural order. Supernatural light suggested to them that God, as sovereign, had a right to bestow his supernatural gifts according to his own will, and, as infinitely wise, must have a secret reason for apparently inverting the order of nature in establishing the supernatural order of the universe. Those who voluntarily submitted themselves to the decree of God were rewarded by an illumination which disclosed to them the wisdom and goodness of the decree of the Incarnation, and the glory which they themselves as well as the whole universe would receive from it; and thus became incapable for ever of erring in their judgment respecting the highest good, and consequently of swerving from it through sin. Those who fell turned their minds away from the supernatural light toward the consideration of their own private good, and the glory of their own persons and their own order. They revolted at the idea of being subordinated to human nature, and desired that the angelic nature should be the subject of the hypostatic union. Lucifer, in particular, as their chief, desired that he himself might be assumed into union with the Word, exalted to the throne of the universe, and deified. He and his associates demanded this from God as a right due to their natural dignity, and thus rebelled against his sovereign majesty, were cast out of the celestial sphere, and forfeited for ever the crown of supernatural glory. Hence their enmity to the Incarnate Word, to the Blessed Virgin Mary, and to the human race. Hence their efforts to establish their own supremacy over man, and the continual conflict which the holy angels and the children of God on earth must wage against them in the sacred warfare for the triumph of Christ's kingdom upon earth. This brings us to the consideration of human probation.

CHAPTER X.

THE ORIGINAL STATE OF THE FIRST PARENTS OF MANKIND—THE RELATION OF ADAM TO HIS POSTERITY—THE FALL OF MAN—ORIGINAL SIN.

THE grand theatre of probation is this earth, and its chief subject the human race. The probation of the angels was completed almost instantaneously, and their transit to an immutable state followed almost immediately on their creation. The probation of the human race is long and complicated, diversified and extensive; and by it the most magnificent exhibition is made of the principle of merit. It has also this peculiarity, that mankind were created, not merely as individuals, each with his distinct probation, but also as a race; and that the whole race had a probation at its origin, in the person of its progenitor. It is our present task to unfold the Catholic doctrine concerning the nature and results of this original probation of the collective human race in the first epoch of its creation.

The Catholic doctrine teaches, in the first place,

that the entire human race, at present inhabiting the globe, is one ; not merely in being conformed to one archetype, but also in being descended by generation from one common progenitor, that is, from Adam.

That this is distinctly affirmed in the book of Genesis which the Catholic Church receives as a portion of the inspired Scripture, according to the obvious and literal sense of the words, is not questioned by any one. It is only necessary, therefore, to show that this obvious and literal sense is proposed by the authority of the Catholic Church as the true sense. That is, that it is an essential portion of Catholic doctrine, that God created at first one pair of human beings, Adam and Eve, from whom all mankind are descended.

It seems evident enough that the archaic records, in which the history of the creation of man is contained, were understood in this sense by those who transmitted them from the beginning of human history, and who first committed them to writing ; and by Moses, who incorporated them into the book of Genesis. This was the traditional sense universally received among the Jews, as is manifest from all the monuments of tradition. It is also the sense which is reaffirmed in the other sacred and canonical books which follow those of Moses, wherever they allude to the subject. For instance : " Who knoweth if the spirit of the *children of Adam* ascend upward ?"*
" Seth and Sem obtained glory among men: and

---

* Eccles. iii. 21.

above every soul Adam in the beginning." The similar traditions of heathen nations are well known. The sacred writers of the New Testament use the same explicit language. The genealogy of Jesus in St. Luke's gospel closes thus : " Who was of Henos, who was of Seth, *who was of Adam, who was of God."* St. Paul affirms repeatedly and emphatically: " By *one man* sin entered into this world, and by sin death:" " by *the offence of one* many have died :" " the judgment indeed was *by one* unto condemnation :" " by *one man's offence* death reigned through one :" " by the offence of *one*, unto *all men* to condemnation :" "for as *by the disobedience of one man, many were made sinners;* so also, by the obedience of one, many shall be made just."† These passages are plainly dogmatic, and teach the relation of all men to Adam, as an essential portion of the dogma of original sin. The whole force of the parallel between Adam and Christ depends, also, on the individual personality of the former, and his relation to all mankind without exception, as their head and representative. The same parallel reappears in another epistle : " For by a man came death, and by a man the resurrection of the dead. And as in Adam all die, so also in Christ all shall be made alive." " *The first man Adam* was made a living soul ; the last Adam a quickening spirit. But not first that which is spiritual, but that which is animal ; afterward that which is spiritual. The first man was of the earth, earthly ; the second

---

* Ecclus. xlix. 19.   † St. Luke, iii. 38 ; Rom. v. 12–19.

man from heaven, heavenly. Such as is the earthly, such also are the earthly; and such as is the heavenly, such also are they that are heavenly. Therefore as we have borne the image of the earthly, let us bear also the image of the heavenly."*

These passages all present the fact of the original creation of mankind in one pair from whom all men are descended, in an intimate and essential relation with Christian doctrine, especially with the dogma of original sin. It is, therefore, necessary to regard it as a dogmatic fact, or a fact pertaining to the essence of the revealed truth, which the sacred writers taught with infallibility under the influence of divine inspiration. So it has been always regarded in the church, and is now held by the unanimous consent of theologians. It is also incorporated into the solemn definitions of faith.

The canons of the second Council of Milevis, and of the Plenary Council of Carthage, A.D. 418, against the Pelagians, contain the following definitions:

"*Can.* 1. Placuit, ut quicunque dicit, *Adam primum hominem* mortalem factum, ita, ut sive peccaret, sive non peccaret, moreretur in corpore, hoc est de corpore exiret, non peccati merito, sed necessitate naturæ, anathema sit.

"*Can.* 2. Item placuit, ut quicumque parvulos recentes ab uteris matrum baptizandos negat, aut dicit in remissionem quidem peccatorum eos baptizari, sed nihil ex Adam trahere originalis peccati, quod

---

* 1 Cor. xv. 21, 22, 45-49.

regenerationis lavacro expietur, unde sit consequens, ut in eis forma baptismatis in remissionem peccatorum non vera, sed falsa intelligatur, anathema sit : quoniam non aliter intelligendum est quod ait apostolus : ' Per unum hominem peccatum intravit in mundum, et per peccatum mors, et ita in omnes homines pertransiit, in quo omnes peccaverunt :' nisi quemadmodum Ecclesia Catholica ubique diffusa semper intellexit."

"*Can.* 1. It was decreed, that whosoever says that *Adam, the first man*, was made mortal, so that, whether he sinned or did not sin, he should die in the body, that is, depart from the body, not by the merit of sin, but by the necessity of nature, should be under the ban.

"*Can.* 2. It was also decreed, that whosoever denies that new-born infants are to be baptized, or says that they are to be indeed baptized, for the remission of sins, but derive no original sin *from Adam*, which can be expiated in the laver of regeneration, whence it follows that in them the form of baptism is understood to be not true, but false, should be under the ban ; since that is not otherwise to be understood which the apostle says : ' By one man sin entered into the world, and death by sin, and so it passed upon all men, in whom all have sinned ;' *except as the Catholic Church everywhere diffused has always understood it.*"

These canons, although not enacted by ecumenical councils, were nevertheless approved by Popes Innocent I. and Zosimus, by them promulgated to the universal church, and ratified by the consent of the whole body of bishops ; so that they are justly included among the final and irreversible decisions of the Catholic Church. The second of these canons was also reënacted by the Council of Trent, which defined in the clearest terms the dogma of original sin as derived from the sin of Adam, the head of the human race.

"1. Si quis non confitetur, *primum hominem Adam*, cum mandatum Dei in paradiso fuisset transgressus, statim sanctitatem, etc., amisisse: A. S.

"2. Si quis Adæ prevaricationem sibi soli, et non ejus propagini, asserit nocuisse . . . . aut inquinatum illum per inobedientiæ peccatum, mortem et pœnas corporis tantum in omne genus humanum transfudisse, non autem et peccatum, quod est mors animæ: A. S. cum contradicit apostolo dicenti: 'Per unum hominem peccatum intravit in mundum,' etc.

"3. Si quis *hoc Adæ peccatum, quod origine unum est*, et propagatione, non imitatione, *transfusum omnibus*, inest cuique proprium . . . . per aliud remedium asserit tolli, etc.: A. S."

"1. If any one does not confess that *the first man Adam*, when he had transgressed the commandment of God in paradise, immediately lost sanctity, etc., let him be under the ban.

"2. If any one asserts that the prevarication of Adam injured himself alone, and not his posterity . . . . or that he, being defiled by the sin of disobedience, transmitted death and the pains of the body only to the whole human race, but not also sin, which is the death of the soul, let him be under the ban: since he contradicts the apostle, who says: 'By one man sin entered into the world,' etc.

"3. If any one asserts that *this sin of Adam, which in origin is one*, and being *transferred into all* by propagation, not by imitation, exists in each one as his own .... is taken away by any other remedy, etc., let him be under the ban."

All these decrees affirm positively that the whole human race without exception are involved in one common original sin, springing from one transgression committed by the first man Adam, and transmitted from him by generation. The dogma of original sin rests, therefore, on the fact that all mankind are descended from one first man Adam, and is subverted, if this fact is denied. An allegorical interpretation of the sacred history of Genesis, according to which Adam and Eve are taken to symbolize the progenitors of several distinct human species, cannot be admitted as tenable, in accordance with the Catholic faith. For, on this hypothesis, the different human races had each a distinct probation, a separate destiny, a separate fall, and are therefore not involved in one common original sin, but each one in the sin of its own progenitor. This doctrine of original sin, namely, that a number of Adams sinned, and that each one transmitted his sin to his own progeny, so that every man is born in an original sin derived from some one of the various primeval men, is essentially different from the Catholic doctrine as clearly taught by Scripture and tradition, and defined by the authority of the church. Moreover, the unity and individuality of Adam, as the sole progenitor of the human race, is distinctly affirmed in the decrees just cited, and in all the subsequent decrees concerning the primitive state of man which have emanated from the Holy See, and are received by the universal church. We must consider, therefore, the doctrine of the unity of the human race as pertaining to the faith. Perrone affirms this, in these words: "Prop. II. *Universum humanum genus ab Adam omnium protoparente propagatum est.* Hæc propositio spectat ad fidem ; huic enim innititur dogma de propagatione peccati originalis." "*The entire human race has been propagated from Adam the first parent of all.* This proposition pertains to faith; for upon it rests the dogma of the propagation of original sin."*

Bishop Lynch, of Charleston, who is not only one of the most learned of our theologians, but a man profoundly versed in the physical sciences, in a very able and interesting lecture recently delivered in New York, thus speaks on this matter :

"Some, nowadays, disregarding all that Holy Scripture teaches us concerning the origin of man, or treating it as a myth and fable, referring at most only to the Caucasian race, pretend that America had her own special Adam and Eve, or, as they think more probable, quite a number of them contemporaneously or successively in different localities.

"I shall not here undertake to discuss this last

---

* Perrone, *Præl. Theol. De Hom. Creat.*

opinion, *ventured certainly against the teachings of divine revelation*, and, as I conceive, no less against the soundest principles of philosophy, of comparative anatomy, of philology, and of natural history. I will assume it as an established and accepted truth, that God made all nations of one blood."*

The only point we have been endeavoring to make, that the doctrine of the unity of the race pertains to essential Catholic doctrine, is, we think, fairly made. The scientific refutation of the contrary hypothesis is a work most desirable, in our opinion, but one requiring a degree of scientific knowledge which the author does not possess. It is a work, also, which could be accomplished only by an extensive treatise. The judgment of the distinguished author just cited may be taken, however, as a summing up of the verdict of a great body of scientific men, given on scientific grounds, in favor of the doctrine of the unity of the race. The contrary doctrine is mere hypothesis, which no man can possibly pretend to demonstrate. It cannot, therefore, be brought out to oppose the revealed Catholic doctrine. Hypothesis, even when supported by a certain amount of scientific probability, is not science. Real science is indubitably certain. There cannot, therefore, ever arise a real contradiction between science and revelation. Science will never contradict revelation, and revelation does not contradict any part of science which is already

* Lecture by the Rt. Rev. P. N. Lynch, D.D., on *America before Columbus*. Reported in the *New York Tablet*.

known or ever will become known. We are not, however, to hold our belief in revealed truths in abeyance, until their perfect agreement with scientific truths is demonstrated. Nor are we to tolerate mere hypotheses and probable opinions in science, when they are contrary to truths known by revelation, because they cannot be demonstrated to be false on purely scientific grounds.

There are only two real difficulties to be encountered in the solution of the scientific problem. One is, the difficulty of accounting for the variations in type, language, etc., between different families of the human race within the commonly received historic period. The other is the difficulty of explaining certain discoveries in the historical monuments of Egypt, and certain geological discoveries of the remains of man or human works, in accordance with the same period. It has been justly and acutely remarked by a recent British writer on this subject, that the objections made under this second head, if they are sufficient to establish the necessity of admitting a longer chronology, destroy the objections under the first head. Given a longer time for these changes, and the difficulty of supposing them to be real variations from a unique type vanishes. The chronological difficulties under the second head are of two classes. One class relates to the history of well-known post-diluvian nations, whose historical records have been discovered, indicating a longer period than the one commonly reckoned between the age of Noah and that of Moses. The other relates to tribes or individuals about whom nothing is known historically, but to whom geological evidence assigns a higher antiquity than that commonly allowed to the epoch of the creation of man. Now, these difficulties in no way tend to impugn the doctrine of the unity of the race, but merely the chronology of the history of the race from the epoch of the creation of the first man, which has been commonly supposed to be established by the authority of Scripture. If this last supposition may be classed among theological opinions not pertaining to essential Catholic doctrine, and we may be permitted, *salvâ fide et auctoritate ecclesiæ*, to admit a chronology long enough to satisfy these claims of a higher antiquity for man, all difficulty vanishes. One thing is certain, that if the inspired books of Moses did originally contain an exact chronology of human history from Adam to the Exodus of Israel, we cannot now ascertain within fifteen hundred years what it was, since there is that amount of variation between the Hebrew and Greek copies. There is some probability in favor of the Septuagint, which gives the longer chronology. Yet, it is impossible to explain how the variation between the Septuagint and the Hebrew, and the variation of the Samaritan version from both, arose. The great essential facts pertaining to religious doctrine have been handed down by Scripture and tradition in their unimpaired integrity. We are bound to believe that the providence of God watched over their transmission, and protected them from any designed or accidental alteration. Some general principles and data of chronology are included in this essential history, which is guaranteed to us by inspiration and the authority of the church. Nevertheless, these chronological data are manifestly so incomplete and imperfect, that a precise and accurate chronological system cannot be deduced from them. So far as it is possible to form a chronological system at all, it must be done by the help of all the collateral evidence we can find. This evidence, so far as we are aware, does not tend to establish, with a high degree of probability, an epoch of creation more than a few thousand years earlier than the common one of 4000 years before Christ. This is certainly true of the historical records of Egypt, the principal source of new light on the ancient historical epochs. We are warranted by the Septuagint in adding fifteen hundred years to the common period. It is only, however, on critical and historical grounds that the Septuagint has greater authority on this point than the Hebrew, and not as having a higher sanction. For the Hebrew is the original and authentic Scripture, and the authorized Latin Version follows it, and not the Greek. If we can admit, then, a chronology longer by fifteen hundred years than the one contained in the received text, on historical grounds, why not one still longer, if sound historical evidence demands it? Supposing that the Scripture originally did contain a complete and infallible system of chronology, it is evident that the key to it was lost many ages ago; and we can just as easily suppose that the discrepancy between the Mosaic chronology as it now stands and the chronology of the Egyptian records has arisen by the same causes which produced the discrepancy of the Hebrew and Greek texts, as we can assign causes why so great a discrepancy should arise at all, and reconcile this with the reverence due to the sacred books.* This is a matter which needs to be more thoroughly discussed than it has been, by theologians who are fully acquainted with the subject, before we can lay down positively a principle upon which to solve the difficulty. We reject, however, as unprovable and untenable, all theories which throw the antiquity of man back to an epoch of vast remoteness, and assign hundreds or thousands of centuries to a prehistoric period, of which no records remain. It is on geological discoveries solely that this hypothesis is based. At present it is only a conjecture, founded on the fact that human remains have been found of a greater antiquity than those formerly known, whence it is concluded that they may hereafter be discovered of a greater antiquity still. We may safely wait for geology itself to clear up the obscurity at present existing in regard to this matter, and to set right, as science invariably does, the early and hasty conjectures of its own votaries.† Whichever way the matter may be

* Archbishop Manning says: "No system of chronology is laid down in the sacred books. There are at least three chronologies, probable and admissible, apparently given by Holy Scripture. It cannot be said, therefore, that there are chronological faults in Holy Scripture, forasmuch as no ascertained chronology is there declared."— *Temporal Mission of the Holy Ghost*, p. 171, American edition.

† See an article on the *Scientific Congress of Paris*, in 1867, in *The Catholic World* for February, 1868.

settled, the fossil remains of human skeletons or human works will be assignable either to a period not too remote to be included in the historic period, or to one so remote that it must be excluded from it. In the first case, there is no difficulty. In the second, nothing is established from which the falsity of our thesis can be demonstrated. Our thesis is, that the present human race now inhabiting the earth is descended from one man, Adam. When there is any very probable evidence presented that another and distinct species, having a physical organization like that of the human race, once existed on the earth, from which it has become extinct, it will be time to examine that theory. For the present we are concerned with Adam only and his race; to which both our readers and ourselves have but too conclusive evidence that we all belong.*

* *The Gentle Skeptic*, by Rev. C. A. Walworth, now pastor of St. Mary's church, Albany, treats of several topics, here noticed in a cursory manner. This work is the result of several years' close and accurate study in theology and science. It has, therefore, the solidity and elaborate finish of a work executed with care and diligence by one who is both a strong thinker and a sound scholar. In style it is a model of classic elegance and purity, and in every respect it deserves a place among the best works of English Catholic literature. The author has broke ground in a field of investigation which it is imperative on Catholic scientific men to work up thoroughly. The entire change which has taken place in the attitude of science toward revealed religion within a few years, and in the doctrines of science themselves, makes the old works written on the connection between religion and science to a great degree useless. The subject needs to be taken up afresh, and handled in a manner adequate to the present intellectual wants of the age.

We have now to consider what Catholic doctrine teaches of that state in which the first parents of the human race were constituted at their creation. Briefly, it is this: that this was a supernatural state of sanctity and justice, in which were contained, or with which were connected, the gift of integrity, or immunity from concupiscence, the gift of science, and the gift of corporeal immortality.

That man was constituted in sanctity and justice is affirmed as *de fide* by the decree of the Council of Trent, a part of which is cited above, in which Adam is declared "to have lost immediately the *sanctity and justice in which he had been constituted:*" "statim sanctitatem et justitiam in quo constitutus fuerat amisisse." That he possessed integrity is proved by the same decree, which declares that by the fall he was "changed *as to his body and soul into something worse:*" "secundum corpus et animam in deterius commutatum fuisse." That he possessed science is proved by the declaration of the book of Ecclesiasticus: "Disciplinâ intellectus replevit illos. Creavit illis scientiam spiritus:" "He filled them with the knowledge of understanding. He created in them the science of the spirit."* This is explained and corroborated by the traditional teaching of all the fathers and great theologians of the church. His immunity from death is proved by the decrees above cited and others familiar to all.

It is shown to be the Catholic doctrine that these

---

* Ecclus. xvii. 5, 6.

gifts were supernatural, by the condemnation of the contrary doctrine by the Holy See. The following theses of Baius, one of the precursors of Jansenism, were condemned by Pius V. and Gregory XIII.:

"21. Humanæ naturæ sublimatio et exaltatio in consortium divinæ naturæ, debita fuit integritati primæ conditionis, et proinde naturalis dicenda est, et non supernaturalis ; 26. Integritas primæ creationis non fuit indebita humanæ naturæ exaltatio, sed naturalis ejus conditio ; 55. Deus non potuisset ab initio talem creare hominem qualis nunc nascitur ; 78. Immortalitas primi hominis non erat gratiæ beneficium, sed naturalis ejus conditio ; 79. Falsa est doctorum sententia primum hominem potuisse a Deo creari et institui sine justitiâ naturali." Clement XI., in the Bull *Unigenitus*, also condemned the following proposition, the 33d of Quesnel : "Gratia Adami est sequela creationis et erat debita naturæ sanæ et integræ."

"21. The elevation and exaltation of human nature into the fellowship of the divine nature was due to the integrity of its first condition, and is therefore to be called natural and not supernatural ; 26. The integrity of the primal creation was not an exaltation of the human nature which was not due to it, but its natural condition ; 55. God could not have created man from the beginning such as he is now born ; 78. The immortality of the first man was not a benefit of grace, but his natural condition ; 79. The opinion of doctors is false, that the first man could have been created and instituted by God without natural justice, (righteousness.)" 33d of Quesnel: "The grace of Adam is a sequel of creation, and was due to sound and integral nature."

It is plain from the decisions which have been quoted, and from the consentient doctrine of all Catholic doctors, that the Catholic doctrine is: that the state of original sanctity and integrity did not flow from the intrinsic, essential principles of human nature, and was not due to it, but was a free gift of grace superadded to nature, that is, supernatural. We do not, however, censure the opinion held by some sound Catholic writers, that congruity, order, or the fitness of things, exacts that supernatural grace be always given to rational nature. It is our own opinion, already clearly enough insinuated, that, although the completion and perfection of the universe does exact that a supernatural order should be constituted, it does not exact the elevation of all rational species or individuals to this order. This opinion appears to be more in accordance with the obvious sense of the decrees just cited. It is also the opinion of St. Thomas, and, after him, of the more prevalent school of theology. St. Thomas thus expresses himself upon this point: " Poterat Deus, a principio quando hominem condidit, etiam alium hominem ex limo terræ formare, quem in conditione suæ naturæ relinqueret, ut scilicet mortalis et passibilis esset et pugnam concupiscentiæ ad rationem sentiens, in quo nihil humanæ naturæ derogaretur, quia hoc ex principiis naturæ consequitur; non tamen iste defectus in eo rationem culpæ et pœnæ habuisset, quia non per voluntatem iste defectus causatus esset." "God could have formed, from the beginning when he created man, also another man from the dust of the earth, whom he might have left in the condition of his own nature, that is, so that he would have been mortal and passible, and would have felt the conflict of concupiscence against reason, in which there would have been nothing derogatory to human nature, because this follows from the principles of nature; nevertheless this defect in him would not have had the quality of sin and punishment, because this defect would not have been caused by the will."*

The sanctifying grace conferred upon Adam is very clearly shown, according to this view, to have been a pure and perfectly gratuitous boon from God, to which human nature, as such, could have no claim whatever, even of congruity.

The nature of the probation of the father of mankind is now easily explained. He received a gratuitous gift on conditions, and these conditions were the matter of his probation. Our scope and limits do not admit of a minute discussion of the particular circumstances of the trial and fall of Adam in Paradise. The point to be considered is the relation in which Adam stood to all mankind his posterity in his trial, transgression, and condemnation. The Catholic dogma of faith on this head is clearly defined and unmistakable. The whole human race was tried, fell, and was condemned, in the trial, fall, and con-

---

* 2 *Sentent.*, Dist. 31, qu. 1, art. 2 ad 3.

demnation of Adam. It is needless to cite again the passages of Holy Scripture and the decisions of the church which establish this fundamental doctrine of Christianity. The only question to be discussed is, What is the real sense and meaning of the doctrine? How did all mankind sin in Adam, and by his transgression incur the condemnation of death? What is the nature of that original sin in which we are born?

One theory is, that the sin of Adam is arbitrarily imputed to his posterity. As a punishment for this imputed sin, they are born depraved, with an irresistible propensity to sin, and under the doom of eternal misery. The statement of this theory is its best refutation. Very few hold it now, and we may safely leave to Protestant writers the task of demonstrating its absurdity.

Another theory is, that all human wills were included in the will of Adam, so that they all concurred with his will in the original transgression.* We find some difficulty in comprehending this statement. Did we all have a distinct existence, and enjoy a deliberative and decisive vote when the important question of human destiny was decided? If so, the unanimity of the judgment, and the total oblivion which has fallen upon us all, respecting our share in it and our whole subsequent existence until a very recent period, are very remarkable phenomena which we

---

* We refer the reader to the arguments of Candace in Mrs. Stowe's *Minister's Wooing*, for a humorous but unanswerable refutation of the ancient Calvinistic doctrine of original sin.

have never seen adequately accounted for. The only other alternative is that of indistinct existence or virtual existence. That is, that the power of generating souls was in Adam, and that all human souls are actually derived from his soul by generation. Suppose they are. A father who has lost an organ or a limb does not necessarily transmit this defect to his posterity. Even if he does transmit some defect which he has contracted by his own fault to his son, that son is not to blame for it. If the principle of all souls was in Adam, virtually, their personality, which is the principle of imputability, commences only with their distinct existence. Personality is incommunicable. An individual soul cannot communicate with another in the principle of identity, from which all imputability of acts, all accountability, all possibility of moral relations, proceeds. This notion of the derivation of souls, one from another, or from a common soul-reservoir, is, however, one perfectly inconceivable, and contrary to the plainest principles of philosophy. Substance is simple and indivisible. Spirit, which is the most perfect substance, contains, therefore, in its essence the most manifest contradiction to all notion of composition, resolution, division, or separation of parts. The substance of Adam's soul was completely in his own individual intelligence and will. The notion of any other souls deriving their substance from his soul is therefore wholly without meaning. There is no conceivable way in which a spirit can produce spirit, except by creation, an act to which created spirit is incompetent.

There remains, therefore, only the doctrine, which is that of Catholic theology, that the human species is corporeally propagated by means of generation, and was, therefore, in this respect only, virtually in Adam; but that each individual soul is immediately created by God, and comes into the generic and specific relations of humanity through its union in one integral personality with the body.* How, then, can each individual soul become involved in original sin? Does God create it sinful? This cannot be; and if it could it would not be the sin of Adam, or the sin of the race, but its own personal sin. The soul as it comes from the hand of God cannot be sinful in act. The only possible supposition remaining is, that the soul contracts sin from contact or union with the body. Here the Calvinist, the Jansenist, or any other who maintains that original sin consists in positive depravation of the soul's essence, or in habitual moral perversity, or determination of the will to sin, is in a position where he cannot move a step forward. How can *soul* be corrupted by body? How has the innocent soul deserved to be thrust into a body by which it must be polluted? These questions will never receive an answer. Nor will any credible or rational method of vindicating the doctrine that all men are born totally and positively depraved, or with a nature in any respect essentially evil, on account

---

* "Cum sit anima immaterialis substantia, non potest causari per generationem, sed solum per creationem a Deo."—*St. Thom.* p. 1. qu. 118. art. 2.

of Adam's sin, ever be discovered. The doctrine is utterly incredible and unthinkable, and will no doubt ere long have a place only in the history of past errors.

The way is now clear for the exposition of the Catholic doctrine respecting the mutual relations of Adam and his posterity in the original probation, trial, and fall of the human race immediately after its creation. That probation of Adam, in which the human race was included, must not be understood as including the entire personal probation either of himself or of his descendants. His own probation lasted during his lifetime, and so does that of each individual man. Had he been faithful in that particular trial which is related in the first chapter of Genesis, it is probable that, although the special privileges whose perpetuation depended on it would certainly have been secured to the race, he himself would have had a longer personal trial. So, also, if the progeny of Adam had been confirmed in the perpetual possession of the privileges of the primeval state, each individual of the human race would have had a probation of his own, affecting his own personal destiny alone. Although each one of us would have been conceived and born in the state of original grace and integrity, as the Blessed Virgin was by a special privilege; as soon as the actual exercise of reason became completely developed, a period of probation would have commenced, in which we should have been liable to fail, as we are now after receiving grace through baptism.

The probation of the human race in Adam was, therefore, a special probation, on which the possession in perpetuity of certain supernatural privileges, freely and gratuitously conceded to the race, was alone dependent. The merely personal consequences of the sin of Adam and Eve affected themselves alone individually. That is, the guilt of an actual transgression with the necessary personal consequences following from it attached to them alone, and we have nothing to do with it, any more than with any other sins committed by our intermediate progenitors. The father of the human race did not act, however, in a merely individual capacity in this transaction. A trust was committed to him in behalf of all mankind, and this trust was the great gift of original sanctity and justice, the high dignity of supernatural affiliation to God, and the glorious title of the kingdom of heaven. By his sin he forfeited this gift in trust, both for himself as an individual, and also for his descendants who were to have inherited it from him. There is no ground for asking the question, why it followed that Adam, having fallen, should transmit a fallen nature by generation to his posterity. This question is only asked on the supposition that fallen nature is a nature essentially changed and depraved, whereas it is really a nature which has fallen from a supernatural height back to its own proper condition. With all due respect to the eminent writers who have attempted to answer this question, we must be allowed to say that we cannot attach any definite meaning to their answer. Adam, they say, having a fallen nature, could only transmit the nature which he had. All humanity was in him when he sinned, and therefore humanity as generic having fallen into sin, each individual who participates by conception in generic humanity participates in its sin, or is conceived in original sin. This language may be used and understood in a true sense; but in its literal sense, and as it is very generally understood, it has no meaning. It is derived from the extravagant and unintelligible realism of William of Champeaux,* and some other schoolmen, according to which humanity as a genus has a real and positive entity distinct from the individuals of the race, like the great animal *in se* of Plato, from whom all particular animals receive their entity. These notions have long since become obsolete, and it is useless to refute them. The human genus was completely in Adam, but it was not separate from his individuality; rather it was completely in his individuality, constituting it in its own generic grade of existence, as the individuality of a man. Humanity is also completely in every other human individual. This humanity, constituting the specific essence of Adam, as a man, was identical with his existence, for existence is only metaphysical essence reduced to act. It could not be essentially changed without destroying his human existence. Whatever is contained in *hu-*

---

* What is said supposes the account generally received of this author's philosophy to be correct. The author accepts the realism of St. Thomas, who defines universals to be mental conceptions with a foundation in reality.

manitas must have remained in him after the fall, otherwise he would no longer have remained a man, or indeed have continued to exist at all. It is only this *humanitas*, or specific essence of human nature, that Adam had any natural power to reproduce by generation. He could not have lost the power of transmitting it by the fall, except by losing altogether the power of reproducing his species. The immediate, physical effect of generation is merely the production of the life-germ, from which the body is developed under the formative action of a soul created immediately by God. The only depravation or corruption of nature, therefore, which is physically possible, or which can be supposed to follow by a necessary law from the corruption of nature in Adam, is a corruption or degeneracy in this life-germ, through which a defective or degenerate body is produced. This opinion has been long ago condemned by the church. It is, moreover, contrary to science. The human animal is perfect as an animal, and although there is accidental degeneracy in individuals, there is no generic degeneracy of the race from its essential type. But supposing that a defective body were the necessary consequence of Adam's sin, a defective soul could not be. The parent does not concur to the creation of the soul of his offspring, except as an occasional cause. God creates the soul, and he cannot create a human soul without creating it in conformity to the metaphysical archetype of soul in his own idea, and therefore having the essence of soul completely in itself. How, then, can the infusion of this soul into a body which is physically degenerate make it unworthy of that degree of the love of God and of that felicity, which it is worthy of intrinsically, and apart from its union with the body?

There is no law in nature by virtue of which Adam must or could transmit anything essentially more than human nature before the fall, or essentially less after the fall. The law by which he was entitled to transmit privileges or gifts additional to nature on condition of his fulfilling the terms of God's covenant with him was therefore a positive law; like those human laws which enable men to transmit with their blood property, titles of nobility, or the hereditary right to a crown. These privileges may be forfeited, by the crime of an individual in whom they are vested, for himself and for his posterity. They may be forfeited for posterity, because they are not natural rights. In the same manner, the supernatural gifts conferred on Adam were forfeited for the human race by his sin, because they were not natural rights or *debita naturæ*, but gratuitous gifts to which Adam's posterity had no hereditary right, except that derived from the sovereign concession of God, and conceded only in a conditional manner. This conditional right could only be perfected by the obedience of Adam to the precept of the Almighty forbidding him to eat of the fruit of the tree of knowledge of good and evil. As he failed to obey this precept, his posterity never acquired a perfect right to the gifts of supernatural grace through him. By virtue, therefore, of our descent from him, we possess nothing but human nature and those things which naturally belong to it; we are born in the state in which Adam would have been placed at the beginning if God had created him in the state of pure nature.

We do not stand, therefore, before God, by virtue of our conception and birth from the first parents of mankind, in the attitude of personal offenders, or voluntary transgressors of his law. Our essential relation to God as rational creatures is not broken. Our nature is essentially good, and capable of attaining all the good which can be evolved from its intrinsic principles; that is, all natural knowledge, virtue, and felicity. That which is immediately created by God must be essentially good. A spirit is essentially intelligence and will, and therefore good in respect to both, or capable of thinking the truth and willing the good. Moreover, it is a certain philosophical truth that when God creates a spirit he must create it in act, or that the activity of the spirit is coeval with its existence. The first act or state of a spirit, as it precedes all reflection, deliberation, or choice, and flows necessarily from the creative act of God himself, is determined by him, and must therefore be good. The acts which follow, either follow necessarily from the first, or are the product of free deliberation. In the first case they are necessarily good; and in the second they may be good, otherwise they would be necessarily evil, which is contrary to the supposition that they are free. The human soul being in its essence spirit, and incapable of being corrupted by the body, must therefore be essentially good at the moment when it attains the full exercise of reason and of the faculty of free choice. If so, it is capable of apprehending by its intelligence and choosing by its will that which is good, and cannot, therefore, come into the state of actual sin or become a personal transgressor except by a free and deliberate purpose to violate the eternal law, with full power to the contrary. It may exercise this power to the contrary by a correct judgment, a right volition, and thus attain the felicity which is the necessary consequence of acting rationally and conscientiously. So far as this is possible to mere unassisted nature, it may continue to put forth a series of acts of this kind during the whole period of its earthly existence.* That is to say, it is capable of attaining all the good which can be evolved from its intrinsic principles, or all natural knowledge, virtue, and felicity. This is equivalent to saying, that it can have a natural knowledge and love of God, as is affirmed by the best theologians with the sanction of the church. For Pius V. has condemned the following proposition, the 34th of Baius: "Distinctio illa duplicis amoris, naturalis videlicet quo Deus amatur ut auctor naturæ, et gratuiti quo Deus amatur ut beatificator, vana est et commentitia et ad illudendum sacris litteris et plurimis veterum testimoniis excogitata." "The distinction of a twofold love, namely, natural, by which God is loved as the author of nature, and gratuitous, by which

---

* It is understood, of course, that this cannot be done without the special aid of God.

God is loved as the beatifier, is vain and futile, and invented for the purpose of evading that which is taught by the Holy Scriptures and by many testimonies of the ancient writers."* It would be easy to multiply proofs that the doctrine of man's capability of moral virtue, from the intrinsic principles of his nature, is the genuine Catholic doctrine.† This is not necessary, however, at present.

We proceed to another point, namely, How it is that mankind can be said to be born in original sin, when they are innocent of all personal and actual sin at the time of birth? The state in which Adam's posterity are born, and which is denominated the state of original sin, considered subjectively, is a state of privation of supernatural grace and integrity. If man had been created for a natural destiny, this state of inability to the supernatural would not have been a state of sin. If he had been created in the state in which he is now born, as a preparatory state to the state of grace, to be endowed at a subsequent period with supernatural gifts, it would not have been a state of sin. Entitively it would have been the same state as that in which he is now born. It would not have been a state of sin, because the state of sin receives its denomination from a voluntary transgression which produces it. The particular notion of sin is an aversion from God as the supreme

---

* Denziger's *Enchirid.*, p. 305.
† See *Aspirations of Nature*, by Rev. I. T. Hecker, *passim*. That portion of this work which relates to original sin was read in manuscript to the late Archbishop Kenrick and approved by him.

good produced by the voluntary election of an inferior good in his place. The posterity of Adam are born in a state of habitual aversion from God as the supreme good in the supernatural order, which is the consequence of the original sin of Adam. Since they virtually possessed a right to be born in the state of grace and integrity, which was forfeited by his sin, the state of privation in which they are born, relatively to their original ideal condition and to the transgression by which they were degraded from it, is properly denominated a state of sin. This is incurred by each individual soul through its connection with the body which descends from our first parents by generation, because it is this infusion into a human body which constitutes it a member of the human race. As a member of the human race, and by virtue of his descent from Adam, each individual man participates in all the generic relations of the race. If Adam had not sinned, he would have received by inheritance from him a high dignity and great possessions, transmitted to him through the blood; as the case is, he is born disinherited. There is no injustice or unkindness in this; because the rights which have been forfeited were not rights involved in the concession of rational existence itself, but rights gratuitously conceded on certain conditions, and because no personal blame is imputed where none exists. The illustration so often employed by theologians of a nobleman who has suffered attainder is perfectly apt to the case. His posterity are born under an attainder, which in human law corresponds to original sin under the divine law, and are thus placed in a state of privation; relatively to that condition of nobility which was formerly hereditary in the family; but which in itself is an honest condition. In the eye of the law, their father's crime makes them incapable of the privileges of nobility, but it does not deprive them of the common rights of private subjects.

So the children of Adam, on account of his sin, inherit a disability to possess the nobility of the state of grace, and to inherit the kingdom of heaven. This disability is inherent in the person of each one, and therefore "*inest cuique proprium.*" It is a separation from God incurred by the transgression of Adam, who represented the human race in his trial, and therefore is truly and properly sin. It is a privation of grace which is the supernatural life of the soul, and is therefore properly called death, or "*mors animæ.*" The "*reatus culpæ*" is the obligation of being born in a state of relative degradation, and the "*reatus pœnæ*" the obligation of undergoing the conflicts, sufferings, and death which belong to the state of despoiled nature, as well as submitting to the sentence of exclusion from the kingdom of God. By it, human nature has been changed into something worse as to soul and body, "*in deterius mutatar quoad corpus et animam,*" because it is now deprived of integrity, immortality, and sanctifying grace. Nevertheless, this state is essentially the same with that which would have been the state of man if he had been created in the state of pure nature. Man in the state of lapsed nature differs from man in the state of pure nature, as Perrone says, only as *nudatus* from *nudo*, one denuded from one always nude. This is original sin, which consists formally, as St. Thomas teaches, in the privation of sanctifying grace and the other gratuitous gifts perfecting nature which depended on it. Mankind, therefore, by the sin of Adam, have simply fallen back on the state of pure nature, and are born with those attributes and qualities only which are contained in human nature by virtue of its intrinsic principles. To understand, therefore, the condition, capabilities, and ultimate destiny of man, apart from the grace which comes through the Redeemer, we have simply to inquire into the essence of these intrinsic principles, and ascertain what man is, simply as man, what he can do, and what is the end he can attain by his earthly life.

Man, as to his rational nature, is in the lowest grade of rational creatures. Except under very favorable circumstances, his intelligence is very imperfectly developed, and, so far as it is developed, it is chiefly employed in perfecting his merely exterior and social life. Under the most favorable circumstances his progress is slow, his capacity of contemplating purely intellectual and spiritual objects weak and limited. As to his body, he is also frail and delicate, and naturally liable to death. Moreover, there is in his constitution, as a being composed of soul and body, a certain contrariety of natural impulses, one set of influences inclining him to rational good, the other to sensible or animal good. Like the inferior animals, he is capable of an improvement of his species up to a certain point which cannot be fixed, and also liable to a degeneracy which brings him down to a state little above that of the brutes, and even to idiocy. There are indications enough in his soul of a latent capacity for a much higher and more exalted state, to make it certain that his present condition is one of merely inchoate existence, and that he is destined to a future life in which these latent capacities will be developed in a more perfect corporeal organization. The great difficulty of forming an ideal conception of the state in which he would have been constituted, had he been left to his merely natural development, consists in the fact that we have no human subject to study except man as he actually is, that is, under a supernatural providence from the beginning. The actual development of human nature has taken place under the influence of supernatural grace, and we cannot discriminate in human history the operation of natural causes from those which are supernatural. There are three principal hypotheses respecting the possible development of pure nature which may be sustained with more or less plausibility. The first is, that the human race, beginning in its perfection of type as a species, but without any revelation of language, or any instruction in natural theology, morals, or science, would have remained always in the same state in which it was created, without any intellectual or moral progress. According to this view, the present state of man on earth would have been a mere state of existence, which could have no ulterior end, except the production of a species destined to begin its higher life in a future state. The second hypothesis is, that the human race, beginning from the same point of departure, might have progressed slowly, through very long periods of time, to a high limit of civilization, knowledge, virtue, and natural religion. The third is, that a kind of natural revelation, including a positive system of religion, morals, and science, would have been requisite; in a word, that human society must have been placed at first, by the immediate intervention of the creator, in the state of civilization, and conducted in its course by a continuance of the same intervention. We have little room, however, for anything beyond conjecture in this matter. The only point we are anxious to establish is, that the state in which we are now born is not one intrinsically evil; that it is not one derogatory to human nature as such; that it is not one in which God might not create man in consistency with his sanctity and goodness.

This point is established on sound theological and philosophical principles; and from these principles it follows that all the phenomena of man which are referable to his original fall are the natural consequences of his human constitution, and not evidences of a positive, innate depravity. He is a weak, frail, inconstant creature, easily led away by the senses and passions, liable to fall into many errors and sins, but he is not an object of loathing and abhorrence to his creator, or an outcast from his love. He has in him all the primary elements of natural virtue, the germ from which a noble creature can be developed. Nevertheless, although his natural condition is one which is not derogatory to himself or his creator, it seems to cry out for the supernatural. Its actual weakness and imperfection, coupled with its latent capacities for a high development, mark it as being, what it is, the most fitting subject for the grace of God ; and indicate that it was created chiefly to exemplify in the most signal manner the gratuitous love and bounty of the creator. It is only in the idea of the supernatural order that we can find the adequate explication and solution of all the problems relating to the destiny of man. For that order he was created by an absolute, not a conditional decree of God. The fulfilment of that decree was not risked on the issue of Adam's probation. According to our view, the creation of man was only the inchoation of the incarnation of the Eternal Word in human nature ; and the decree of the incarnation being absolute, the elevation of human nature was necessary and must be efficaciously secured. The fall of man from original grace could not therefore hinder it. After the sin of Adam, the human race had still a supernatural destiny, and was under the supernatural order of Providence. The divine decree to confer grace on man was not abrogated, but only the form and mode under which the grace was to be conferred were changed. Moreover, by this change, the human race was, on the whole, a gainer, and came into a better and more favorable position for attaining its destiny. There was a reason both for the original constitution of man in the grace of Adam, and also for the change of that constitution which followed upon Adam's sin. By the original grant of grace, God showed to mankind his magnificent liberality and good-will. He gave them also an ideal which has remained imperishably in their memory of the state of perfection, and left a sweet odor of paradise to cheer them along their rugged road of labor and trial. By the withdrawal of that grace he brought them under a dispensation of mercy, in which their condition is more humble and painful, but safer and more advantageous for gaining the highest merit.

St. Francis de Sales says: " L'état de la rédemption vaut cent fois plus que l'état de la justice originelle:" " The state of redemption is a hundred times preferable to the state of original justice."* The church herself, in her sublime hymn *Exultet*, breaks out into the exclamation: "O certè necessarium Adæ peccatum ; O felix culpa! quæ tantum et talem habere meruit Redemptorem !" " O certainly necessary sin of Adam ; O happy fault! which merited to know such and so great a Redeemer !" We have no reason to lament our lost paradise, or to mourn over the fall of our first parents. Our new birth in Christ is far better than that ancient inheritance forfeited in Eden.

To the foregoing exposition of the doctrine of original sin we have thought it proper to add some brief statements of the theology of the question, in order

---

* This thought has been beautifully developed by Mr. Simpson in some Essays on Original Sin, published in *The Rambler*.

to elucidate and corroborate more fully the view we have advanced. We have not presented it as being throughout of a dogmatic character, or as in all respects the only theory either tenable or actually defended by orthodox writers. It is our aim throughout this treatise to propose a theory or philosophy which includes and justifies every Catholic dogma, rather than to define precisely the limits separating dogma from opinion, or to advocate the particular tenets of any school purely in a controversial spirit. The Augustinians and some others hold that man is not only despoiled of supernatural gifts through the fall, but also injured in his natural powers. We do not question the orthodoxy of those who follow either theory, or desire to stretch the censures of the Holy See against the Baian or Jansenistic propositions beyond the sense in which they are understood by a common consent of all respectable theologians. The doctrinal exposition we have given is presented as orthodox, but not as orthodox to the exclusion of every other; and as, in our opinion, both more manifestly consonant to the mind of the church and the spirit of her latest decisions, and also more rational and intelligible. As to the last points, we leave every one to form his opinion, with a perfect willingness that he should differ from ours if he sees cause to do so. The first point we think is unquestionable, and has been made sufficiently manifest already; but we will, nevertheless, endeavor to cite some proofs which may make it still more evident.

Archbishop Kenrick defines the limits of the dogmatic and theoretical portions of the doctrine in these words: "De theoriâ enim statuenda haud agitur, sed de re ipsâ: utrum scilicet, peccante Adamo, universi homines constituti sint peccatores, et idcirco morti obnoxii: non adhuc quæritur quomodo id contigerit, quâ ratione reatus ille transfundatur, quâve in re peccati hujus natura sit posita. Has quæstiones ad *theorias* relegari patimur libenter; sed dogma, rem, *factum*, negat, qui dicit homines Adæ posteros tunc primum peccatores constitui quando suis actibus deliquerunt; apostolus quippe docet omnes Adæ peccato peccatores constitutos." "We are not at present concerned with establishing a theory, but with the thing itself; to wit, whether, Adam sinning, all men are constituted sinners, and therefore obnoxious to death: it is not the question how that occurred, in what manner that guilt is transmitted, or in what the nature of this sin is constituted. These questions we freely permit to be classed as *theories;* but the dogma, the reality, the *fact*, is denied by one who says that men descended from Adam are then first constituted sinners when they have offended by their own acts; since the apostle teaches that all are constituted sinners by the sin of Adam."*

Cardinal Bellarmine states the common doctrine of the ancient and modern schools respecting the change or privation which human nature underwent through the fall, in these words:

"Non magis differt status hominis post lapsum

* *Theol. Dogm. Ed. Mechl. De Pecc. Orig.* § 98.

Adæ a statu ejusdem in puris naturalibus, quam differt spoliatus a nudo ; neque deterior est humana natura, si culpam naturalem detrahas, neque magis ignorantia et infirmitate laborat, quam esset atque laboraret in puris naturalibus condita. Proinde corruptio naturæ non ex alicujus doni naturalis carentiâ, neque ex alicujus malæ qualitatis accessu, sed ex solâ doni supernaturalis ob Adæ peccatum amissione profluxit. Quæ sententia communis est doctorum scholasticorum veterum et recentiorum."

" The state of man after the fall of Adam does not differ any more from the state of the same in a purely natural condition, than one who has been stripped differs from one who is naked ; nor is human nature worse, if you subtract the natural fault, nor does it any more labor under ignorance and infirmity, than would have been the case if it had been created in a state of pure nature. Wherefore, the corruption flowed not from the want of any natural gift, nor from the accession of any evil quality, but from the sole loss of a supernatural gift on account of the sin of Adam, which is the common opinion of the ancient and modern scholastic doctors."*

It is, therefore, a certain and Catholic doctrine, as we have above most conclusively proved, that the original sanctity and justice, with the other gifts flowing from them for the perfecting of nature, in which Adam was constituted, were supernatural, and were forfeited by the whole human race when Adam sinned. St. Thomas, with the whole Thomist school,

* *De Grat. Prim. Hom.* c. v. *Controv.* t. iv.

both ancient and modern, and the majority of theologians, maintain further, that the state of pure nature is possible, and that in that state man might have been destined to attain his final end without being elevated to the supernatural order. In the essay on St. Augustine's doctrine, we have shown that this idea is contained in the writings of this great doctor himself. In the sense of strict possibility, all Catholic theologians are obliged to admit this as a part of Catholic doctrine, a small number only denying that such a state could have been established in congruity with that perfection which is demanded in the works of God by his infinite wisdom. The distinction between the state of pure nature and of elevated nature being thus established, and the common scholastic doctrine shown to be that the state of original sin is the state of nature denuded or despoiled of gratuitous grace, it remains to inquire what is the *ratio peccati*, or sin, distinguishing fallen nature from the same nature unelevated. Archbishop Kenrick says upon this point: "De ejus naturâ variæ sunt theologorum sententiæ, inter quas ea nobis arridet, quæ peccatum illud in privatione justitiæ originalis constituit ; hæc enim quum sit animæ vita, ejus privatio mors est." "Concerning its nature, there are various opinions of theologians, among which we prefer the one which constitutes it in the privation of original justice; for as that is the life of the soul, the privation of it is death."* Perrone says: "Homo læsus est in natu-

---

* *Ubi supra*, § 100.

ralibus, id est gratuitis et respective ad statum naturæ integræ, *concedo;* in essentialibus et naturæ humanæ propriis, *nego.* Neque alia est mens Concilii Tridentini. Magna tamen inter theologos contentio viget, num deterior nunc homo sit, quam foret in puris naturalibus ; huc quidam, quidam alio in diversas sententias distrahuntur. S. Thomas, Bellarminus, Suarez, et communis scholasticorum sententia negant."* "I concede that man was injured in his natural gifts, that is, in those which were gratuitous, and relatively to the state of integral nature ; I deny it in regard to things essential and proper to human nature. Nor is the judgment of the Council of Trent otherwise. There exists, however, a great contention among theologians whether man is now worse than he would have been in the state of pure nature ; and they are divided among various opinions. St. Thomas, Bellarmine, Suarez, and the common sentiment of the scholastics are on the side of the negative."

It being, then, an orthodox and common opinion that the state of man as he is now born is no worse than the state in which God might have originally created him, it remains to be seen why this is called a state of sin. Archbishop Kenrick says : " Peccatum originis, quod Adæ posteris commune est, longe differre a peccato actuali, quod scilicet quisque patraverit, in confesso est." "It is an admitted fact that the sin of origin, which is common to the posterity of Adam, differs widely from actual sin, to wit, that

---

* *Prælat. De Protopar. Gratia,* 367.

which any one has committed." Once more: "*Objicitur.* Lex nequit obligare eos qui nondum existunt. Peccare nequit quis antequam nascatur. *Respondeo.* Nemo certè vel lege ligari, vel peccare potest antequam existat, directè scilicet, et suo actu. Sed legis datæ capiti humani generis sequelæ possunt ad omnes ejus posteros pertingere, ipsâ vi suâ et ordinatione divinâ. *Peccare idcirco hi dicuntur in latiori sensu,* nec enim suo peccârunt actu et voluntate; sed noxâ communi, quam unus admisit, omnium pater, tenentur." "It is objected that a law cannot bind those who do not yet exist, that one cannot sin before he is born. I answer, No one certainly can either be bound by a law, or sin, before he exists, that is, directly and by his own act. But the consequences of a law given to the head of the human race can extend to all his descendants, by its own inherent force and the divine ordination. Therefore *these are said to sin in a wider sense,* for they have not sinned by their own act and will; but they are held by a common fault which one, the father of all, admitted."*

What is this *wider sense* in which we are all constituted sinners by the sin of Adam? This is explained by Perrone in these words: " Quod si status ille, qui in alia hypothesi fuisset *conditio puræ naturæ* nunc habet rationem *naturæ peccatricis, lapsæ et depravatæ,* ideo est, quia a peccato personali Adæ seu

---

* *Ubi supra,* §§ 100, 120, 121. St. Thomas affirms and proves that we cannot have contrition for original sin, because it does not proceed from our own will. (*Supplem.* qu. 2, art. 2.)

primi parentis inductus est. Hinc in iis, qui nascuntur ex Adam, defectus gratiæ habet, ut diximus, rationem privationis rei debitæ, seu peccati, defectus vero integritatis habet rationem pœnæ, seu effectus peccati. Quare in præsenti conditione, nomina peccati et pœnæ sunt relativa ad statum elevationis et integritatis, et ideo sunt peccatum et pœna non in se, sed quia relationem habent ad peccatum Adami; contrarium autem damnatum fuit in propositione 47 Baii, quæ ita se habet: 'Peccatum originis verè habet rationem peccati sine ulla ratione et respectu ad voluntatem, a quâ originem habuit.'" "If that state, which, in another hypothesis, would have been the *condition of pure nature*, now has the character of a nature *sinful, fallen, and depraved*, it is so for this reason, because it was brought in by the personal sin of Adam, the first parent. Therefore, in those who are born of Adam the defect of grace has, as we have said, the character of a privation of something due, that is, of sin; moreover, the defect of integrity has the character of a punishment, that is, of an effect of sin. Wherefore, in the present condition of things, the denominations of sin and punishment are relative to the state of integrity and elevation, and are therefore sin and punishment not in themselves, but because they have relation to the sin of Adam; and the contrary statement was condemned in the 47th proposition of Baius, which is as follows: 'The sin of origin has truly the character of sin, without any relation or regard to the will from which it had its origin.'"*

* *De Peccat. Orig. Propag.* 467.

In accordance with this idea, Kenrick, Perrone, and a host of other standard authors answer the objection that it is unjust to condemn the whole human race for the sin of one. Kenrick says: "Rationi autem certè non repugnat, ut Deus homini rebelli dona gratis concessa subducat, ejusque posteros iis carere velit, quæ nullo suo jure possent sibi vindicare; . . . . nec enim illis denegabantur debita, sed quæ gratis concessa sunt ex summa donantis munificentia." "It is certainly not repugnant to reason, that God should withdraw from a rebellious man gifts gratuitously granted, and should will that his descendants should lack these gifts which they could not claim for themselves by any right of their own; . . . . for the things which were due to them were not denied to them, but those which were gratuitously conceded by the supreme munificence of the giver."* The definition of the sin of human nature as privation of a habit *due to it* must, therefore, be understood as presupposing that this habit is due to it only by the grant made to Adam on condition of his obedience. So, also, this privation is called a *macula*, stain, as depriving the soul of supernatural lustre, as Perrone says: "Privat ipsa præterea hominem seu animam candore et fulgore; unde *macula* est et labes animæ." "It deprives, moreover, man or the soul of lustre and splendor; whence it is a *stain* and deformity of the soul."† In the same merely privative sense the expression, "children of wrath," is to be

---

* *Ubi supra*, § 139. † *Ubi supra*, § 460, not. 3

understood as denoting that we are born destitute of the special gifts belonging to the state of children of predilection; just as the phrase, "Jacob have I loved, Esau have I hated," is interpreted to mean, "I have loved Jacob more and Esau less."

Thus Kenrick explains it: "Filii quidem iræ nascimur, iis donis spoliati, quæ filiis dilectionis concessurum se decreverat Pater beneficus; sed non constat ultionem aliquam eos manere qui decesserint solo peccato originis maculati." "We are indeed born children of wrath, despoiled of those gifts which the beneficent Father had decreed to bestow upon the children of predilection; but it is not evident that any vengeance awaits those who depart this life stained with original sin alone."* In the same sense, we are said to be "enemies of God;" that is, excluded from that special friendship of God to which no creature has a natural right. The *culpa* and *reatus*, *fault* and *guilt* of original sin, are, as the sin itself, relative to supernatural perfection and sanctity, denoting that human nature denuded of grace is unworthy in the divine judgment of celestial glory, and therefore doomed to remain excluded from it until restored through Christ. What Perrone says of the word sin is equally applicable to all these cognate words and phrases. "Sedulo est animadvertendum, duplicem subesse peccati nomini notionem seu acceptionem; altera est vulgaris, ut ita dicam; altera vero theologica." "It must be carefully observed that a twofold

---

* § 139.

notion or acceptation lies under the word sin ; one is what may be called *popular;* the other, *theological.**
The misapprehensions of the doctrine of original sin, and the objections to it which are so common, arise chiefly from the confusion of the popular and theological sense of terms, and the confusion of the Catholic sense of terms with the Calvinistic sense, which has become so closely associated with the same terms in the minds of Protestants. Hence the necessity of explaining fully and carefully the theological sense of the term sin, and similar terms used in reference to the lapsed state of the human race, when we are writing in the vernacular on the subject, for the benefit of the general reader. The penalty of neglecting to do so is, that we are inevitably misunderstood, and strengthen, instead of lessening, the prejudices of non-Catholic readers as well as perplex the minds of some Catholics.

If there are some who think that we have attempted to make this doctrine more intelligible than its mysteriousness permits, and that it would be better to acknowledge with St. Augustine that, while no doctrine is more manifestly revealed, none is more hidden from the intelligence, we reply: The doctrine is indeed abstruse, and in the days of St. Augustine had received no adequate explanation, as we have proved in the essay on the doctrines of the saint. But it is no wonder if, after the labors of the scholastics, and the controversies with Calvinists and Jansenists

---

* § 460, not. 3.

on one side, and rationalists on the other, the doctrine should now be so fully developed that its conformity with reason can be clearly shown. This is the judgment of Perrone; who declares boldly that all the difficulties which rationalists can bring against the doctrine of original sin, " ex data explicatione ita **evanescunt, ut nullum amplius locum habeant**:" "vanish and disappear completely before the explication which has been given."*

* *Ubi supra*, § 480.

CHAPTER XI.

THE MYSTERY OF REDEMPTION.

THE next article of the Creed, in order, is that which expresses the Mystery of Redemption: "Crucifixus etiam pro nobis sub Pontio Pilato, passus, et sepultus est." "Who was also crucified for us under Pontius Pilate, who suffered, and was buried." The redemption implies the incarnation, and is based on it. The incarnation having been already treated of, in immediate connection with the trinity, we have only to proceed with the exposition of the doctrine of satisfaction for sin and restoration to grace through the sufferings and death of the Divine Redeemer.

It is no part of the Catholic doctrine that it was necessary for the second person of the Trinity to take upon himself human nature and suffer an infinite penalty, in order that God might be able to pardon sin without violating his justice. All Catholic theologians, from St. Augustine down, teach that God is free to show mercy and to pardon, according to his own good pleasure. The reason and end of the incarnation has been shown already to be something far above this order of ideas. The incarnation does not of itself, however, imply suffering or death. We have to inquire, then, why it was that in point of fact the Incarnate Word was manifested as a suffering Redeemer; and why his death on the cross was constituted the meritorious cause of the remission of sin and restoration of grace.

The church has never made any formal definition of her doctrine on this point, and it is well known how various have been the theories regarding it maintained at different times. We shall endeavor to present a view which appears to us adequate and intelligible; without, however, claiming for it any certainty beyond that of the reasons on which it is based.

The original gift of grace not having been due to Adam, or to any one of his ordinary descendants, in justice, the restoration of that gift, when lost, was not due. Aside from the incarnation, there was no imperative reason why Adam and his race should not have been left in the state to which they were reduced by the original transgression. God, having determined to accomplish the incarnation in the human race, owed it to himself to complete this determination, in spite of all the sins which he foresaw would be committed by men. The foreseen merits of Christ furnished an adequate mode for conferring any degree of grace upon any or all men, he might see to be fitting and necessary for the fulfilment of his eternal purposes. It was not necessary, however, that the Son of God should suffer or die in order to merit grace for mankind. By the divine decree, indeed, the shedding of his blood and his death was made the special meritorious act in view of which remission of sins and grace are conferred. But all the acts of his life had the same intrinsic worth and excellence, which was simply infinite on account of the divine principle of imputability to which they must be referred. There must have been some reasons, therefore, of fitness, on account of which it was determined that Jesus Christ should suffer death for the human race.

We may find one of these reasons in the law of suffering and death which God has imposed, out of a motive of pure love, on the whole human race. This law was, indeed, promulgated under the form of a penalty, but in its substance it was a real blessing. The way to heaven through the path of penance and by the gate of death is a surer and safer way than the one in which Adam was first placed; it is one, also, affording higher and more extensive scope for virtue, heroism, and merit. It was, therefore, fitting that the chief and prince of the human race should go before his brethren in this way of sufferings. "For it became him, for whom are all things, and by whom are all things, who brought many sons to glory, to perfect, by suffering, the author of their salvation."* As a particular consequence of this general law, heroes, patriots, reformers, prophets, and saints have

---

* Heb. ii. 10.

always been specially exposed to suffering and to violent modes of death. They have been obliged to sacrifice themselves to their own fidelity to conscience and to the sacred cause to which they have been devoted. And this sacrifice of life has consecrated their memories in the hearts of their fellow-men more than any other acts of intellectual or moral virtue, however brilliant. It was fitting, therefore, that the Saint of saints, the Saviour of the world, should not exempt himself from the peril of death, to which the very character of his mission exposed him.

Another reason for the suffering of the Divine Mediator is found in the manifestation thereby made of the love of God in Christ to the human race. There is no need of dwelling on this, or of noticing other reasons of a similar kind which have been so frequently and so fully developed by others.

We pass on, therefore, to the consideration of the final and highest reason for the death of Jesus Christ, the expiation of sin.

The true and only possible notion of expiation or satisfaction is that which apprehends it as a compensation for the failure to perform some obligatory act, by performing another act of at least equal value in the place of it. Every noble soul, when conscious of having been delinquent, desires to repair the injury which has been done, as well as to redeem its own honor, by some act which shall, if possible, far exceed the one which it failed to perform. The same principle impels those who have a high sense of honor to make reparation for the delinquencies of others with whom they are closely related in the same family, the same society, or the same nation. Now, the human race has been delinquent in making a proper return to God for the infinite boon of grace. The fall of man and the innumerable sins of the individuals of the human race have deprived Almighty God of a tribute of glory which was due to him, and have brought ignominy upon mankind as a race. Although, therefore, Almighty God might provide for the glorification of the elect who are to share with the Incarnate Word in his divine privileges, by an act of pure mercy; it is far more glorious both to God and man that a superabundant satisfaction should be made for the injury which has been done to the creator by the marring of his creation, and a superabundant expiation accomplished of the disgrace which man has incurred. It was, therefore, an act of divine wisdom and love in God to determine that this satisfaction and expiation should be made by the second person of the Trinity in his human nature. The Incarnate Word, being truly man, identified with the human race, and its chief, necessarily made its honor and its disgrace his own. Although he could redeem his brethren without any cost to himself, his solicitude for their honor and glory would not permit him to do it. He desired that they should enter heaven on the most honorable terms, without any of the humiliation of the delinquency of the race attaching to them, but, on the contrary, with the exulting consciousness that every stain of dishonor had been effaced. Therefore, as their king and chief, he fulfilled the most sublime work of obedience to the divine law which was possible ; he made the most perfect possible oblation to God, as an equivalent for his boon of grace which had been abused by sin. In lieu of that glory which God would have received from the perfect obedience of Adam and all his posterity, and that glory which would have been also reflected upon the human race, he substituted the infinitely greater glory of his own obedience unto death, even the death of the cross. By this obedience Jesus Christ merited for the human race the concession of a new grant of grace, more perfect than the first, by virtue of which not only the original sin which is common to all men was made remissible to each individual, but all actual sins were made also pardonable on certain conditions.

That this statement completely exhausts the true idea of the satisfaction of Christ, we will not pretend to affirm. It appears to us, however, sufficient to give a clear and definite meaning to the language of Scripture and the fathers, and to include all that Catholic faith requires a Christian to believe.

Jesus Christ having merited by his death the right of conferring grace without stint or limit upon mankind, and all the grace given after the fall and before the redemption having been bestowed in the foresight of his death, every spiritual blessing enjoyed by men is referred to the death of Jesus Christ as its cause and source. Strictly speaking, it is only the meritorious cause. By giving himself up to die, he merited the right to communicate the grace contained in the incarnation to men, notwithstanding the failure of the father and head of the race to fulfil the probation on which the transmission of the grace to his descendants depended. He merited also the right to renew this grace in those individuals who should lose it after having once received it, as often as he pleased, without regard to the number or grievousness of their sins, or the frequency of their lapses. It is, however, the Holy Spirit; dwelling in the Incarnate Word in the plenitude of his being, and communicating to his human nature the fulness of grace, not for itself alone, but for all men; which is the ultimate and efficient cause of all spiritual life. It is the grace of the Holy Spirit which actually removes all guilt and stain of sin from the soul, and constitutes it in the state of justice and sanctity. The Holy Spirit is, therefore, the efficient cause of justification. The formal cause is the personal sanctity of each individual. That is, this personal sanctity is that which makes each one worthy of the complacency of God, of fellowship with him, and of everlasting life. The work of the incarnation and redemption must, therefore, produce its results and attain its consummation through the Holy Spirit as the sanctifier of the human race. Consequently, the Creed, after finishing its expression of the Catholic faith so far as the person of Christ is concerned, proceeds to enunciate it as regards the person and operation of the Holy Spirit, who is sent by Christ to complete his work. The articles containing this enunciation complete the Creed, and bring man to his final destination.

CHAPTER XII.

THE CATHOLIC CHURCH, AS THE INSTRUMENT OF THE SANCTIFICATION OF THE HUMAN RACE.

THE next articles of the Creed are: "Et in Spiritum Sanctum, Dominum et Vivificantem, qui ex Patre Filioque procedit, qui cum Patre et Filio simul adoratur et conglorificatur, qui locutus est per prophetas; et in unam sanctam, catholicam, et apostolicam ecclesiam; confiteor unum baptisma in remissionem peccatorum." "And in the Holy Ghost, the Lord and Lifegiver, who proceedeth from the Father and the Son, who with the Father and the Son together is worshipped and glorified, who spake by the prophets; and in one holy, catholic, and apostolic church; I confess one baptism for the remission of sins."

The relation of the Holy Spirit to the Father and the Son in the Trinity has been already considered. The temporal mission of the Holy Spirit as the consummation of the divine work *ad extra* is exercised through the Catholic Church; and, therefore, the article concerning the church follows immediately in the Creed the one concerning the Holy Spirit.*

The organic unity of the Catholic Church follows necessarily from the principles laid down in the foregoing essays. It is an immediate consequence of the unity of the race, and of the incarnation, which are two distinct facts, but which have one principle. The order of regeneration must follow the order of generation. Mankind exist essentially as a race; as a race they received the original gift of supernatural grace; as a race they lost it. All human life and development is generic. The redemption of mankind must, therefore, reëstablish the generic relations which were disturbed by the fall. Jesus Christ, the second Adam, must become the head of a redeemed and regenerated race of men, organized in a supernatural society. Continuity and perpetuity of life are, therefore, the essential notes of the divine society, or human race regenerated, in which true spiritual life is communicated to the individual. The sole possession of these notes demonstrates the divine authority of the Catholic Church.† The continuity of life, embracing integrity of doctrine and law and the faculty of conferring grace, descended from the patriarchal church through the Jewish, with the increment added by the immediate intervention of the divine Lord of the world in person, to the Catholic Church.

---

* *Vide* Archbishop Manning's *Temporal Mission of the Holy Ghost.*
† *Vide* Leo, *Univ. Hist.*, vol. i., Lacordaire's *Conferences*, and the Works of Dr. Brownson, *passim*.

The Catholic Church is, therefore, the human race, in the highest sense. In early times, one nation after another broke away from the unity of the race, carrying a fragment of the integral, ideal humanity with it. Integrity, continuity, and perpetuity of life were, therefore, rendered for them impossible. The same phenomena are exhibited at the present time in all nations and societies outside of the Catholic Church. Partial and temporary developments only can be made of that integral, universal, perpetual life, whose seat is in the bosom of the church; and which is sufficient to vivify the whole human race, if the impediments were removed. The proof *a posteriori*, or by induction, of the Catholic Church, must be sought for in those works which treat professedly of the subject. Our object is merely to show the conformity of the idea of the Catholic Church with the idea of reason, by deduction from primary, ontological principles. The attributes of the church follow so immediately from its primary note, as the human race restored to unity in the fellowship of God in Christ, that they require no special elucidation; especially as this particular branch of theology has been so repeatedly and so amply treated by authors.

In regard to special dogmas of the church, most of those which present any great difficulty to the understanding have already been discussed in the former part of this essay; and the remainder find an easy explication from the same principles.

The doctrine of the sacraments is explicated from the principle that the church is the instrument of sanctification. The sacraments are the particular acts by which the church communicates the spiritual vitality which resides in her to individuals. They have an outward, sensible form, because the nature of man is corporeal, and all human acts are composed of a synthesis of the sensible and the spiritual. They contain an inward, spiritual grace, because the nature of man is spiritual, and receives life only from a spiritual principle. The only one of the sacraments which presents any special difficulty to the understanding is the holy eucharist; on account of the mystery of transubstantiation which is included in its essence. The ground of this difficulty, which lies in crude, philosophical notions, and is, therefore, purely a spectre of the imagination, has been already removed by the doctrine we have laid down respecting the nature of substance and the proper conception of space and extension. The senses transmit to the soul nothing more than the impressions of the phenomena, which the soul, by an intellectual judgment, refers to a real, intelligible substance, or active force, as their productive cause. The substance itself is not sensible, but intelligible; is not seen, as an essence, by the eye, but concluded by a judgment of the mind. By divine revelation it is disclosed to us, that the substance of bread and wine in the eucharist is succeeded by the substance of the body and blood of Jesus Christ; the phenomena or sensible effects of the former substances till continuing to be produced in an extraordinary manner. There is a mystery here, it is true; but it is only the mystery which belongs to the inscrutable nature of the essence of matter as active force, and the mode in which this active force produces various sensible phenomena. The definitions of the church do not furnish a complete explanation of the Catholic dogma, which is left to theologians; and even theologians do not precisely coincide in their conceptions or expressions. All we can do then, after stating the Catholic dogma, is to give the explanation which appears to be the most probable, according to the judgment of the best authors and the most weighty intrinsic reasons. This is enough, however, for our purpose; for all that is required is to furnish a conception which is, on the one hand, theologically tenable, and, on the other, rationally intelligible.

We may separate the synthetic judgment pronounced by the church, in the definition of the dogma, into four analytic judgments. First, the absence of the substance of bread and wine after the consecration. Second, the presence of the substance of the body of Christ. Third, the absence of the natural phenomena of the body of Christ. Fourth, the presence of the natural phenomena of bread and wine. In order to reconstruct these elements of the church's dogmatic judgment into a more perfect synthesis, it is necessary to analyze further these separate propositions. There are three principal, distinct conceptions contained in them: the conception of substance; the conception of presence, or relation in space; and the conception of phenomena, or, to use the precise term employed by the schoolmen, of *acci-*

dents. There is, also, the conception of the mode in which the phenomena of bread and wine subsist out of relation to their proper productive substances, or, the conception of the immediate, efficient cause to which they must be referred. These first three conceptions have been sufficiently analyzed in a former part of this treatise. The absence of the substance of bread and wine after consecration may be explained, in accordance with the conception of substance, by annihilation, removal, or identification with the substance of the body of Christ. The senses cannot take cognizance of its presence before consecration, it being their office merely to report phenomena; they cannot, consequently, take cognizance of its absence. They are not, therefore, deceived in reporting the phenomena as unchanged after the consecration, since they really remain unchanged; nor is the mind qualified to pronounce, on the report of the senses, that the substance is unchanged, by an intellectual judgment; since the judgment which would otherwise be validly made is superseded by a divine judgment, made known through revelation, that in this instance the substance has been changed for another by the creative power of God. The simplest mode of conceiving the effect of consecration on the substances of the bread and wine is to suppose their annihilation. St. Thomas, however, denies that they are annihilated, because the terminus of annihilation is nothing, whereas the terminus of the act of transubstantiation is the body of Christ. In p'ain words, the argument is: if the substances were annihilated, the effect of consecration would be properly expressed by saying that they are reduced to nothing, whereas the language of the church is, that they are converted into the body and blood of Christ. The same argument applies to the notion of their removal elsewhere. Nevertheless, since they are not supposed to be annihilated or removed simply for the sake of getting rid of them, and their destruction or removal is not the end or final term of the act of divine power, but only its proximate term, in order to the substitution of the body of Christ, this argument is not decisive. It is proper to say that the substance of bread is changed into the body of Christ, if the body of Christ is substituted for it; the natural phenomena which formerly indicated the presence of the one substance remaining the same, and indicating the presence of the other substance instead of that of the former substance.

Another explanation is based on the notion of one generic substance individualized in all distinct, material existences. According to this explanation, the bread and wine, being deprived of their individual existence, are not thereby destroyed; but, as it were, withdrawn into the generic substance, which is identical with the substance individualized in the body of Christ; and therefore properly said to be converted into the substance of his body. We are unable to understand how the notion on which this explanation is based, which appears to require us to accept the realism of William de Champeaux and the schoolmen, can be made intelligible; and, therefore, prefer the former, which, we believe, is the one more commonly adopted.

The presence of the body of Christ, without its natural phenomena, and under the phenomena of bread and wine; which presents usually much the greatest difficulty to the understanding; is really capable of a much more easy and certain explanation. It is present not by its extension, but by its pure substance, or *vis activa*, that is, as Perrone says, "*per modum spiritûs*," "after the manner of spirit." Spirit, as all Catholic philosophers teach, is related to objects in space, by the application of its intrinsic force to them. The presence of the body of Christ in the eucharist is, therefore, the application of its *vis activa;* which is, indeed, finite, but, by virtue of its supreme excellence in the created order, through the hypostatic union, commensurate with the whole created universe and all its particular parts. The body of Christ, therefore, while it is circumscribed as to its extension; and, according to the ordinary sense of the word, is present only in one place; is, in a different but real sense, present everywhere where the species of the eucharist are present. These species or phenomena of bread and wine in the eucharist are the signs indicating its presence by its substantial force, or *vis activa*. They may be produced, as every one will admit they can be, by the immediate act of God; or by the *vis activa* of the body of Christ; which, as a perfect body containing eminently all the perfection of inferior material substances, can produce their proper effects. The body and blood of Christ contain substantially and essentially the virtue of bread and wine, and, being in hypostatic union with the divine nature, may be capable of producing the phenomena and effects proceeding naturally from this virtue in many places at once. It appears to us more in accordance with the language of Scripture and the church to make this latter supposition. We sum up, therefore, the explanation of the mystery which appears to us the most probable and rational, in this short formula. By the effect of the divine power, exercised through the act of consecrating the eucharist; the sensible phenomena, indicating before the act the presence of the *vis activa* of bread and wine, cease to indicate it; and indicate, instead of it, the presence of the *vis activa* of the body and blood of Christ. The language of the definition pronounced by the church is thus exactly verified. There is a change of substance, without any change of phenomena. There is a transition of the substance of the bread and wine; which ceases either altogether as a distinct existence, or, at least, as the cause of the phenomena; in order to give way to the substance of the body of Christ; which is properly called a transubstantiation.

The mystery still remains, and must remain, incomprehensible by the human understanding, however clear the explanation of the difficulties which beset it may be made. Neither the senses nor the intellect can perceive the presence of Jesus Christ in the eucharist. It is believed by an act of faith in the word of Jesus Christ. The mode of this substantial presence and of its action on the soul is, moreover, but dimly apprehended; because substance itself, as a *vis activa*, and the mode of its activity, are impenetrable to reason. The rational argument respecting the dogma of faith, therefore, merely proves that it is not contrary to reason; and that it is partially intelligible by analogy with other known truths and facts. We thus understand that the presence of Jesus Christ in the species of the eucharist is *possible*. And, the revelation of its reality once made, we see also its fitness. It is most fitting and congruous that Jesus Christ should unite himself in the most perfect manner which is consistent with the condition of man in this life, with his human brethren; and that this union should be manifested to the senses. This is accomplished in the eucharist in such a way that the intellect, the imagination, or the heart of man cannot conceive or desire anything more perfect and admirable.*

We shall simply note with the greatest brevity the remaining doctrines whose consideration falls under the present head.

The absolute necessity of grace for works worthy of eternal life, and the inability of man to perform them by his natural strength, is explained by the supernatural principle of which we have already given the exposition.

The merit of good works is explained by the doctrine of probation; and the distinction between this

---

* *Vide* F. Dalgairns's work on the *Holy Communion* for a more complete elucidation of the philosophy of substance and accidents.

kind of merit and the merits of Christ, as well as their mutual relation and harmony, is obvious from the exposition which has been made of the latter.

The Catholic doctrine respecting the Blessed Virgin and the saints is explained by the doctrine already laid down of the glorification and deification of human nature through the incarnation.

The whole exterior and visible *cultus* of Catholic worship is explained by the doctrine, of sensible things as signs and representations of the invisible, and of the essentially corporeal constitution of man. These, and all other particulars of Catholic doctrine, are contained in the universal or Catholic idea, which shines by its own light, and proves itself by its sublimity, integrity, symmetry, and correspondence with all the analogies of the natural world.

CHAPTER XIII.

THE FINAL DESTINATION OF ANGELS AND MEN; CONDITION OF THE UNREGENERATE IN THE FUTURE LIFE; ETERNITY OF THE PENALTY OF SIN; THE STATE OF FINAL BEATITUDE.

THE closing articles of the Creed are: "Expecto resurrectionem mortuorum, et vitam venturi sæculi, Amen." "I look for the resurrection of the dead, and the life of the world to come, Amen."

Thus, the creation, which proceeds from God as first cause, is shown to have returned to him as final cause. This is especially accomplished in the beatification of the elect; and consequently it is the glory and blessedness of heaven which is immediately and explicitly affirmed in the Creed. The entire Creed, however, implies, what the Catholic Church in her exposition of the Creed teaches dogmatically, that only a portion of the angelic hierarchy and the human race attain heaven. The doctrine of hell, or the place and state of those who are excluded from heaven, is, therefore, the necessary correlate of the doctrine of heaven. So far as the human race is concerned, we have to consider, first, what is the condition in eternity of those who are subject to the consequences of original sin only.

It follows from the doctrine already laid down, namely, that the state to which man is reduced by original sin is entitively the same with that in which consists the state of pure nature, that the condition of this class of human beings in eternity is the same that it would be if they had never been constituted in the order of the supernatural. They are destitute of supernatural beatitude, but attain to all the felicity of which they are capable in the natural order. They are elevated in the due course of nature to that integrity and perfection of soul and body which, in the case of Adam, was anticipated by a gratuitous gift. Their felicity consists in a perfect exemption from all liability to sin, in the complete evolution of their natural capacities, and in the possession of the proper object of their intelligence and will, that is, in the knowledge and fruition of the works of God, and of God himself by abstractive contemplation. This last expression needs some explanation in order to show its conformity with the doctrine that the original intuition of reason is the intuition of that idea which is afterward demonstrated by reflection to be identical with the being of God. Some, rejecting this doctrine of the idea, object to it that it leads to a confusion of the act of intelligence constitutive of rational nature with the act proper only to beatified nature, that is, the intuitive vision of God. Others, who accept it, endeavor to rebut this objection, and to show the distinction between the knowledge of God derived from rational intuition and that which is communicated by the light of glory. But in doing this they make the first to be only the inchoation of the second, and the second the completion or full evolution of the first. It would follow, then, that a rational creature cannot attain to the proper object of his intelligence and will, consequently cannot attain perfect felicity, without the beatific vision. We cannot admit either that the objection is a valid one or that the explanation which is made in order to do away with it is sufficient. We venture, therefore, to suggest another.

It is real and concrete being, not possible and abstract being, which is the intelligible object of reason. Reason, however, does not, by an intrinsic perceptive power, actively elicit the intuition of its intelligible object. In other words, it is not by its virtue as intelligence that real being, or the intelligible, becomes intelligible to it. The intelligible has the precedence and the superiority in the act of intelligence. The presence of the object makes the subject intelligent in the first act, and this first act is one in which the creative spirit is the agent and the created spirit the terminus of the act. The original, immediate contact of the intellect with real, concrete being, that is, with God, is, therefore, a contact in which the soul is passive, because this contact precedes and is the cause of its activity. It is only by reflection, or bending backward upon itself, that the intellect can have distinct self-consciousness and elicit thought. When it does so, it takes always the affirmation of real, necessary being, by which God created it rational, as the first and absolute element of its thoughts. But this affirmation, as soon as it enters into reflection, and becomes an element of the spontaneous activity of the soul, becomes *abstract*. It is not a pure abstraction, or an act which terminates on the abstract or possible as its ultimate object, but an abstraction formed from the concrete object as apprehended by the passive intelligence, or an abstract conception of the concrete idea. It would require too much time to develop this statement fully. But it is plain at a single glance that it is justified by the facts of consciousness. All our judgments respecting necessary and universal truth are abstract. The judgment respecting necessary cause, that respecting the infinite and the eternal, that respecting ideal space and time, those which respect mathematical relations, and those which form the data of logic, are all of this kind. There is no direct, immediate intuition of God to be found in our consciousness; as we have previously proved in our demonstration of the being of God. The necessity of using the term *intuition* in reference to our apprehension of the idea is, therefore, an unfortunate one, and gives rise to a confusion of the act in which we conclude the existence and attributes of God by a rational, deductive judgment, with the act in which the soul immediately beholds him by an intellectual vision. Intuition and vision are, strictly speaking, identical. Experience teaches us that our first distinct vision is the vision of sensible objects, and that we refer constantly to this as the standard of clear vision, since there is nothing which appears to us equally clear and distinct. By the aid of our perception of the sensible, we attain to the perception of ourselves as existing, thinking spirit, and of other spirits like our own. But we never attain a similar intuition of God by the mere exercise of our intellectual activity. It is of the essence of a created spirit that its active intuition or intellective vision is limited to finite objects as its immediate terminus, commensurate to its finite visual power. It sees God only mediately, as his being and attributes are reflected and imaged in finite things, and therefore its highest contemplation of God is merely abstractive. The natural felicity of created spirits is, therefore, at its maximum, when they attain the most perfect exercise of their faculties in this mode of action which is connatural to them. It is the fruition of God mediately through his creation.

We now proceed to show that the Catholic doctrine permits us to believe that this perfect felicity, which is possible without supernatural grace, is actually conceded to those who die in original sin only. It is reasonable to believe that any felicity which these souls can attain, consistently with their position as liable to the eternal consequences of original sin, will be actually attained by them. For God has created them for good : and to what end has he made them

Problems of the Age. 273

capable of this felicity, unless it be that they may possess and enjoy it? We shall quote from a treatise written in the seventeenth century by F. Maria Gabrielli, in defence of the doctrine of Cardinal Sfondrati, a very thorough summary of the opinions of theologians on this point :*

"Joseph Maria de Requesens† enumerates in his little book on the state of infants many theologians of great name who concede to these infants a certain kind of imperfect natural beatitude. He says that Richard (of St. Victor) teaches that these children will have more goods and greater joy in their possession than sinners have who possess created goods in this life. Lyra says, that according to the opinion of all doctors they will enjoy a happier life than would be naturally possible in this present world. Almost in the same way speak Origen, Marsilius, St. Buonaventure, Cajetan, and others cited by Cornelius à Lapide, who all teach that children dying without baptism lead a happier life than those who are living on the earth. Lessius writes, that although they may be said to be damned because eternally deprived of the celestial glory for which they were created, it is nevertheless credible that their state is far happier and more joyful than that of any mortal man in this life. Salmeron says, these children will rise again through Christ and above this natural order, where they will daily advance in the

---

* *Dispunctio Notarum*, 40, etc. Colon. 1699.
† *De Statu Parvul.* Rom. 1684.

knowledge of the works of God and of separate substances, *will have angelic visits*, and will be like our rustics living in the country, so that, as they are in a medium between glory and punishment, they will also occupy an intermediate place. Suarez says, that children will remain in their natural good and will be content with their lot; and, together with Marsilius as quoted by Azor, he ascribes to them a *knowledge and love of God above all things*, and the other natural virtues. Didacus Ruiz, a theologian of extensive reading, lays down this conclusion: Great mercy will be mingled with the punishment of infants dying in original sin, although not in diminution of the punishment of loss, since that is incapable of diminution; yet in the remission of death which was the punishment directly due to original sin, and would naturally have endured to eternity, so that in spite of this infants will be resuscitated at the day of judgment nevermore to die, endowed with supernatural incorruptibility and impassibility, and they will also supernaturally receive accidental, infused sciences, and will be liberated from all pain, sadness, sickness, temptations, and personal sins, which are naturally wont to arise from original sin. Consequently, they are liberated from the punishment of hell which they might have incurred. Albert, (the Great,) Alexander, (de Hales,) and St. Thomas agree with this doctrine. Suarez shows that these children obtain some benefit, in a certain way, from the merits of Christ; and says that it pertains to the glory of Christ that he should be adored and acknowledged as prince and supreme judge on the day of universal judgment even by infants who died without grace. He also considers it more probable that they will understand that they have done neither good nor evil, and therefore receive neither glory nor pain of sense, and also that they are deprived of glory on account of sin, (that is, original.) He adds the reason of this, to wit, that they may understand the benefit which they received, first in Adam and afterward in Christ, and on this account may worship and adore him. Martinonus adds: When even the demons love God in a certain way even more than themselves as the common good of all, according to St. Thomas, why shall not these children love Christ as their benefactor and the author of their resurrection, and of the benefits which they receive with it through Christ, who is the destroyer of corporeal as well as spiritual death? He cites also what Suarez says, that although one who should speak of the bodies of infants in the same way as of the other damned would say nothing improbable, since St. Thomas speaks of all indifferently, nevertheless since those bodies will have a greater perfection and some gifts or benefits which are not at all due to nature, therefore, in regard to these gifts, Christ may be said to be their model. The same Martinonus subjoins: Although those words of the apostle, 'In Christ all shall be made alive,' Suarez affirms, must be properly and principally understood of the predestined, nevertheless they can probably be applied to a certain extent to these children, inasmuch as they will have in their risen bodies a certain special conformity and relation to Christ, which will be much less and more imperfect in the damned than in the predestined. Nicholas de Lyra affirms that 'infants dying without baptism do not endure any sensible punishment, but have a more delightful life than can be had in this present life, *according to all the doctors** who speak concerning those who die in original sin alone.'"

Those who die in actual sin, and the fallen angels, although in the same state of existence with those who die in original sin only, that is, in the Infernum, or sphere below the supernatural sphere of the elect angels and men, have to undergo a punishment corresponding to their individual demerits. This truth, which is clearly revealed in the Holy Scriptures and defined by the church, is confirmed by the analogies of this present life. The transgression of law is punished in this world in accordance with the sense of justice which is universal among men. There is no reason, therefore, for supposing that the same principle of retribution is not continued in the future life. Moreover, there is positive proof from reason that it must continue. There has never been a more absurd doctrine broached than that of the Universalists. To suppose that all men are saved on account of the merits of Christ, without regard to their moral state or personal merits, is most unreasonable; and subversive of the moral order as well as destructive of the idea of a state of probation. It is equally

---

* This is true of the great majority, but not of all.

absurd to imagine that the mere fact of death can make any change in the state of the soul, or that separation from the body causes the soul to make a mechanical rebound from a state of sin to a state of holiness. The soul can be made happy only from its own intrinsic principles, and not by a mere arbitrary appointment of God, or a bestowal of extrinsic means of enjoyment. Sin brings its own punishment, and the state of sin is in itself a state of misery. Plato and other heathen sages taught the doctrine of future punishment. Mr. Alger, who has written the most elaborate work on the subject of the history of the doctrine of a future life which has appeared in recent times, has fully proved the universality of the doctrine of future punishment. Other rationalistic writers of ability have also of late years seen the impossibility of removing this doctrine from the teaching of Christianity and from universal tradition. We have already fully proved, that God does not deprive any of his rational creatures of the felicity which is proper to their nature by his own act. It follows from this that it is the creature himself who is the author of his own misery. Existence is in itself a good, a boon conceded from love by the creator. So far as this good is turned into an evil, it is by a voluntary perversion of the gift of a benevolent sovereign by the subject himself. The punishment which he must undergo in eternity is, therefore, the necessary consequence of his own acts, together with such positive penalties as are required by the ends of justice and the universal good. This doctrine, which is the doctrine of the Catholic Church, based on the clear evidence of Scripture and ecclesiastical tradition,* is also the doctrine of calm, unbiassed reason, and of the common sense of mankind. The probation of the angels having been finished with their first trial, and the probation of men ending for individuals at death, and for mankind generically at the day of judgment, the epoch of grace is closed for ever with the completion of this present cycle of providence; and consequently the state of all angels and men is fixed for eternity. Hell is, therefore, an eternal state out of which there is no possibility of transition into heaven.

Heaven, or life everlasting, is the eternal state of supreme, supernatural beatitude, to which the elect angels and men are elevated by the grace of God, and in which they participate in the glorified and deific state of the Incarnate Word, through an ineffable fellowship with the three persons of the Blessed Trinity.

Man being integrally composed by the union of soul and body, and his corporeal nature being hypostatically united with the divine nature in the person of the Word, the resurrection of the body must necessarily precede his complete glorification. The only difficulty which the doctrine of the resurrection of the

---

* It is now considered by the best authorities as fully proved that Origen and St. Gregory Nyssen, who have been so often cited by the advocates of the doctrine of universal salvation, did not teach anything contrary to the Catholic doctrine of eternal punishment.

body presents to the understanding relates to the principle of identity between the earthly and the celestial body. This principle of identity, or unity and continuity of life, must be the same with that which constitutes the unity of the body in all the stages of its natural growth; and through all the changes of its material particles, from the instant of its conception to its disintegration by death. It is the soul which is the form of the body, its vivifying principle. The soul and body have an innate correspondence with each other, not only in the generic sense, but in the sense of an individual aptitude of each separate soul for its own body, and each separate body for its own soul. The soul and body act and react upon each other perpetually while the development of both is going on, producing a specific type in each individual which is a modification of the generic type of manhood. The determination of the active force of the soul to the production of this type remains with it after the separation from the body. At the resurrection, it forms anew its own proper body in accordance with this type which is the product of the conjoint action of the soul and body during the earthly life. There is, therefore, the same continuity and identity between the earthly body and the celestial body that there is between the body of the embryo and that of the full-grown man. The celestial body is the same that it would have been if there had been no death intervening between the two corporeal states, but a transformation of the earthly body into the celestial perfection and glorification of its proper type. If this is not all which is included in the definition of the church respecting the identity of the body into the two states, we may suppose, in addition to what has been stated already, that there is a material monad which forms the nucleus of the corporeal organization and is a physical principle of identity. This physical principle must contain virtually the whole body, as the germ does the plant; it must be preserved when the body is disintegrated; and reunited to the soul at the resurrection, in order to become the physical germ from which the celestial body is developed.

The natural beatitude of the glorified angels and saints, which is only a more exalted grade of that felicity which is accorded to the inferior intelligent creation, need not be specially noticed. It is the essential and supreme beatitude consisting in the clear, intuitive vision of God, which is the principal subject of the divine revelation proposed by the Creed as the object of faith.

The possibility of this divine vision will not be called in question by any who are properly speaking theists and rationalists, and with others we have nothing to do at present. Much less will it be questioned by any class of believers in the divine inspiration of the Scriptures. We have not, then, the task of laboring to show the intrinsic reasonableness and credibility of the doctrine, but merely of setting forth that which can be made intelligible respecting the *relation between our present state in which we are unable to see God, and the future state in which we may*

Problems of the Age. 281

be enabled to see him. The examination of this relation includes that of the means and method by which the soul is elevated to an immediate intuition of that which constitutes the divine essence and personality. It requires a statement which shall show what is the *nexus* between the act which constitutes the soul in the power to exercise intelligence, and that which constitutes it in the power to behold God immediately. It may be said, that the essence of the soul is transformed or enlarged in such a way that it becomes able, *per se*, to see God as it now perceives the creation. But this would be equivalent to the creation of a new essence with a new personality; which would destroy the identity of the subject who is supposed to be elevated to this new grade of existence. Moreover, according to the doctrine we have laid down, that supernatural grace elevates the soul *super omnem naturam creatam atque creabilem*, the supposition is impossible. We cannot go over again the principles already discussed, but merely endeavor to state such a theory of the mode of the beatific vision as shall be in harmony with these principles. We therefore dismiss this first supposition without further discussion. Another supposition may be made, that the complete evolution of the idea of God which the soul possesses in the present state in an obvolute manner would bring it to that relation *vis-à-vis* to God as its intelligible object, which corresponds to the relation of the visual faculty to the visible, material object. We cannot accept this supposition any more than the other. It contradicts the principles we have previously laid down, and the generally accepted maxims of Catholic theology respecting the supernatural quality of the power conceded by God to the creature of beholding his intimate essence, just as palpably as the first one. We do not deny that the reason of man is to a great degree in an obvolute condition in this life, and that it is capable of evolution in another and higher life. In this higher life the soul may be capable of perceiving immediately the essence of things, and spiritual substances, after the mode of intelligence which is proper to the angels. But the angels themselves, according to Catholic theology, though created at the summit of the intelligent order, with the complete exercise of intelligence in the highest possible grade, have no natural power to see God immediately; and their natural knowledge of him, though very perfect, is merely abstractive contemplation like that of men. The power of seeing spiritual substances, and the perfect evolution of the idea of God in the soul, therefore, do not give the intuition of the essence of God which constitutes the beatific vision. The beatific vision is supernatural, by means of an immediate light communicated by God to the intelligence, called by theologians *lumen gloriæ*, the light of glory. By means of this light the intelligence perceives God by an active intuition, or a clear, distinct act of reflective consciousness, as immediately present to it in the creative act, the cause of its existence, the source of its active power, the light of its reason, in whom it lives and moves and has its being. God presents himself to the intelligence immediately in his concrete being, as the visible world is presented to the eye by the light of the sun. This is not accomplished by the creation of any new essential faculty in the soul or the addition of anything to its substance. The very same intelligent, thinking principle, or subject, which in this present state of existence affirms to itself the existence of God by an intellectual judgment, beholds him in the beatific state by an intuitive vision. It must be, then, by a concurrence of God with the same faculties of the mind by which we think and reason and perceive, and are self-conscious, in our natural mode of rational activity, that the intelligence is raised to this higher power of supernatural intuition. That act which constitutes it rational in the natural order, must be the basis and substratum of its supernatural intuition of the divine essence. It has already been proved that a created spirit cannot be constituted rational in the first instance by the beatific vision of God; that is, cannot have an essence whose intrinsic, necessary act is a clear intuition of the divine essence, like that act in which God has the eternal, necessary intelligence of himself. The created spirit must first be constituted a rational, intelligent subject, before it can be capable of a supernatural illumination. It must be extrinsecated from God; made a distinct, thinking substance, and constituted in its own finite, rational activity; before there can be any subject, or really existing active force, with which God can concur, with which he can unite himself, and to which he can communicate the power of looking back upon himself by a distinct intuition. The created spirit must be, therefore, in a certain sense, self-subsisting, or containing in itself its own rational principle. It must have its own separate self-consciousness as a thinking substance, containing within itself all the necessary principles of thought. The necessary, the universal, the eternal, or, in a word, the idea, cannot be contained in a created spirit in its concrete being, but only in an abstract form, an image, or a created word. This is identical with the intelligence itself; it is what constitutes its intellective force and principle of activity. In man, as we have already seen, this intellective activity needs the concurrence of exterior, sensible objects, acting on it through the senses and occasioning perceptions and reflections, before it can attain distinct reflective consciousness of itself, and evolve its own ideal formula. This reflective consciousness cannot go back of the soul itself, where it finds the abstractive idea passively received from concrete being. The contact of being, or of God who is alone being, gives the apprehension of being to the soul by creating it. The creative act and the being who produces the creative act lie back of its existence, which is the terminus of the creative act. The soul's separate activity begins at the terminus of God's activity, and is projected forward to its own proper terminus, which is the sensible world. Its natural activity would never bring it face to face with its creator, God, or enable it to contemplate him in any other way than it is now able to do so, by a vividly apprehended demonstration of his being from its own first principles and the exterior works of his hand. In order that the soul, in its reflective acts, may see God continually and clearly, it is necessary that he should unite himself in a new and ineffable manner to its substance and its faculties, and concur with them in such a way that they can look beyond their natural limit of vision into the infinitude of the being of God which surrounds the creation like an ocean on every side. The soul, which is, so to speak, projected from God by creation, must receive a movement of return, which does not arrest itself at the mere fact of self-consciousness, but brings the soul to a consciousness of God as immediately and personally producing its self-consciousness. This act is most perfect in the human soul of Jesus Christ, the Incarnate Word. The personality of the human and divine natures in him being one, there is but one Ego. The human soul, therefore, terminates its act of self-consciousness, not upon itself, as its own *subsistentia*, but upon the divine Ego or person. It is conscious of itself as a distinct substance, but not a substance completed and brought to distinct subsistence in itself. Its consciousness terminates in the divine person, and is referred to it, so that Jesus Christ, in every human act, affirms himself by self-consciousness as both God and man in one person. The union of glorified spirits to God is similar to this hypostatic union, though not so perfect, and not implying personal identity. The nature and mode of this union of the created spirit with God, by which it is glorified, beatified, and even deified—as the doctors of the church fear not to affirm, in accordance with the declaration of the Holy Scripture—is impenetrable to the human understanding. The Indian philosophers, having retained a confused idea of it from the primitive revelation, have expressed this idea in their sublime mysticism with all the superb imagery of their luxuriant imaginations. With them, it is an absorption of all individual souls in the infinite fount of being. Nearly all their language may, however, be adopted, in a good sense, as expressing the Christian dogma, if clear, philosophical conceptions are substituted for their obscure and unscientific notions of the creative act. Without these clear conceptions and definitions, it is impossible to escape running into pantheism. The language of Christian mystic writers, even, is liable to misapprehension as expressing the pantheistic notion of the identity of God and the creature, unless their terms are properly explained. In point of fact, Eckhart did give expression to some propositions which implied pantheism and were condemned by the Holy See. The mystic writers continually affirm that the soul is made *una res cum Deo*, and becomes God by participation. By this, however, they do not mean that the soul loses its distinct substance or becomes identified with the divine nature. They intend to signify an ineffable union between the soul and God, in which, each remaining distinct in its own proper essence, God communicates his own knowledge, sanctity, glory, and beatitude to the soul, and admits it into the fellowship of the Blessed

Trinity. This is the vanishing point of all theology, and of all science, beyond which even the most illuminated eye cannot penetrate. The return of all things which proceed from God as first cause to God as final cause, consummated in this beatific union, solves all the problems of time; there remains only the problem of eternity, which eternity alone can solve.

Studies in St. Augustine.

STUDIES IN ST. AUGUSTINE.

CHAPTER I.

INTRODUCTORY.

THERE are many indications in widely different sections of the theological and philosophical world of a renewed interest in the study of the writings of St. Augustine. Those who are able to appreciate the genius of this great man cannot wonder that this should be so. He has been much underrated and misunderstood in modern times, as a harsh, austere, dry system-maker in theology; his doctrines have been greatly misrepresented by enemies and professed friends alike; and the claims of his works to be ranked among the masterpieces of human thought and language, apart from their dogmatic value, have not been properly recognized. No one of the great doctors of ancient Christendom is better worthy of our study and admiration, whether as a man or a writer. Endowed with a rich and vigorous nature, as luxuriant of vitality as the tropical climate in which he was nurtured, he bloomed like a glowing flower, and was ripened like a luscious fruit, beneath the hot sun of Africa and the burning radiance of the old Greek and Roman intelligence. In the early and half-pagan period of his life, this wild, unrestrained vitality of his intellectual and sensitive nature carried him into the excesses of passion, and of dreamy, extravagant speculation. At the later, or Christian period, when reason, conscience, and divine grace had brought his mighty but chaotic elements into order and harmony, it served to fire his heart with the most sacred and pure enthusiasm, and to impel his soul in its bold, swift, and steady flight toward the highest regions of celestial truth. Such a man could not be a dry, commonplace, mechanical agent for other minds, to elaborate their thoughts into systems made to order, and clothe their ideas with logical and rhetorical forms. When he came into the position of a teacher, a pastor, a ruler and councillor in the church, an expositor and champion of faith, in the most active and the most critical times, he must necessarily throw himself into all the living questions of the day with the whole warmth and energy of his mind and character, and become himself an original, formative, and powerful actor on the mind of the church and of the world ; one of those creative spirits that brood over the chaos of thought, and evolve its hidden cosmic order and harmony. He brought with him, in addition to the gifts of genius, the most perfect heathen culture of the day, and all the wealth of heathen science and art ; to these were superadded the choicest graces of the Holy Spirit, and an intimate knowledge, through personal intercourse or the study of their works, of all the great witnesses and teachers of Christian faith from the still recent times of the apostles to his own day.

His own disposition and the urgency of affairs led him to study Christian doctrine in all its parts and bearings, to penetrate its meaning, to search for the method of vindicating it against all objections, and to pour forth during thirty or forty years a continuous stream of didactic, polemic, or hortatory writings, to explain, defend, or enforce its teachings. These works contain specimens of the highest class of philosophical writing which entitle their author to be called the Christian Plato ; and, in regard to rhetorical elegance, and the charms of a finished style, are often ; as, for instance, in the *Philosophical Dialogues*, written just before his baptism ; worthy to be compared with the similar compositions of Cicero. St. Augustine was not one of those timid advocates of religion who are disposed to ignore, despise, and condemn all science, philosophy, rhetoric, and literature, and who are willing to have a schism between faith and reason. He was not content simply to believe what God has revealed without effort to understand it ; to put away all difficulties and objections by the reflection that God knows of some way to answer them ; to congratulate himself on his own safety, and leave others to accept the faith as authoritatively proposed to them, or be lost, as they pleased. His intelligence could not rest until it had penetrated as deeply as possible into the intrinsic truth and reason of revealed doctrines. He advocates this spirit of research and inquiry, condemns those who disgrace religion by ignorant opposition to science, disavows all servile adhesion to the opinions of Catholic doctors, and counsels tolerance in regard to doctrinal questions which have not been formally decided by the church. The method and general principles adopted by him in the exposition and defence of the faith were sanctioned by the popes and leading bishops and theologians of his own time, with whom he acted in the most intimate concert. Since his own immediate period, the church has always paid him the highest honor and homage she can ever accord to any private doctor. So far, therefore, as ecclesiastical sanction is concerned, there is no collection of merely human works which we can study with a greater feeling of security and confidence than those of St. Augustine. Their influence has been great in all ages, from the time they were produced until the present.

Although what is called the Augustinian School has, in more recent times, been supplanted to a great extent by more modern systems, there seems to be a disposition at the present to return to it once more. We may venture to express the hope that this return may not be a merely retrograde movement; a falling back upon St. Augustine's theology as a finished and unchangeable collection of doctrinal formulas, which are to be maintained in the exclusive spirit of a rigid school; without regard to the results of thought and study in periods of time and conditions of intelligence different from those in which he lived and wrote. To do this would be to depart entirely from his spirit. It was not possible for him to exhaust Catholic theology and philosophy in his single lifetime. It cannot be done by any man or any age. If we would make a right use of his works, we must seek there for living principles and generative ideas, and endeavor to develop these by the aid of all the theological science of subsequent periods, and by original and independent thought and investigation. The study of the writings of St. Augustine and the other great fathers, carried on in this spirit, will, we believe, infuse new life and vigor into Catholic theology and philosophy, without engendering a patristic formalism fatal to all true freedom of mind and all progress. The writings of St. Augustine have a great importance in the eyes of the Protestant as well as the Catholic world. Protestants, as well as Catholics, look on him as one of the great saints and doctors of Christendom, and appreciate his influence on Christian theology at the highest. The Calvinistic and Lutheran orthodox Protestants claim him as their great father, and a teacher of what they call their Evangelical System, a claim which also binds them to accept the Catholic Church of his period as orthodox and evangelical. The Anglican section must necessarily recognize him as one of the chief Catholic doctors, and accept the dogmatic action of the

Catholic Church in his century, against all the heretics and schismatics with whom he warred as her champion. The Pelagian, Unitarian, and Rationalist Protestants unite with the others in their acknowledgment of his greatness and virtue, and exaggerate his influence on the doctrines of the church beyond all bounds. They regard him as the original author and propounder of a class of doctrines in the Calvinistic system which they reject, and which they erroneously suppose were introduced into the theology of the Catholic Church by St. Augustine, and afterward sanctioned by formal definitions. This is an additional reason for studying the works of the great doctor, and endeavoring to bring out his true doctrine. We have this in view, in great measure, as our reason for undertaking the present essay. We wish to show that neither the saint himself, nor the church of his period, held the Calvinistic or Evangelical system, and thus remove the misconceptions of both Calvinists and Pelagians. We desire also to adduce the evidence of his writings to show that he and the church of his period held the system of Catholic doctrine prescribed by the See of Rome at the present day as a term of communion with herself and the churches under her jurisdiction.* That is to say, we cite St. Augustine as a witness whose veracity and Christian piety are acknowledged and venerated on all hands, against Protestantism in

---

* By this is meant the principal parts of the system. It is not the aim of the author to consider each and every doctrine in detail.

general, but particularly that form of it called Evangelical. We do not cite him as an authoritative judge of doctrine whose dictum must be accepted as final. But we cite his evidence to the fact that certain doctrines of faith and principles of organization were universally accepted by orthodox Christendom in his day, as identical with those of the preceding centuries; and we leave the fact thus proved to work its own legitimate results in candid minds. We have understood that not only in the Anglican communion where patristic studies have been more or less in vogue, but also among non-Episcopal Protestants, some thoughtful minds are turning toward the study of St. Augustine, and that these studies are drawing them near to Catholic doctrine. We cherish the hope of being able to assist this class of minds, with whom our own early education enables us to sympathize, in their laudable efforts to arrive at a knowledge of true Christianity in its earliest and purest sources. The happiest results are to be looked for from such studies. The *bonâ fide* and earnest perusal of the works of even one of the great fathers will avail more toward a true knowledge of ancient Christianity than the reading of volumes of arranged, systematized extracts from the entire body of patristic literature. We therefore offer our humble labors to the students of St. Augustine, not as a substitute for, but as an aid in, personal investigation.

In the explanation and vindication of the teaching of St. Augustine, we disclaim any intention of discussing formally the questions on which the several schools of theology are at issue. We do not appear as an advocate of the Augustinian, the Thomist, or the Molinist system as such. Our opinions or leanings may appear incidentally, but our principal object is to elicit the intrinsic and extrinsic evidence of the truth of the great Catholic doctrines defended in all the schools from the pages of a great master in Christian philosophy whom all venerate. We desire to recommend the Catholic faith to the reason and conscience of those who love and seek the truth. We do not underrate the value of scholastic theology, or censure the earnest advocacy of religious and philosophical convictions. We cannot exclude them entirely from any exposition of the faith which gives beyond a mere recital of defined propositions. Our great desire, however, is to make men Catholics, and not Augustinians or Molinists; and therefore we shall endeavor to employ theological and philosophical reasoning in subordination to the one great object of presenting the evidence of the Catholic faith. We may appear in the ensuing pages to show more severity toward Calvinists than toward other classes of non-Catholics. We are therefore anxious to explain that our hostility is directed against Calvinism as a logical system and not against the individuals who hold it. We do not conceive that any system is entitled to mercy or consideration, but only to fairness and justice. The system of Calvinism, taken as isolated from the Catholic doctrines combined with it, and regarded as a philosophy of God, of man, and the relation between them, we regard as the most irrational form of nominal Christianity.* It is based on the doctrine of the existence of positive and eternal evil, and, logically carried out, leads to the doctrine of the Manichæans, that there is a self-existent and absolute principle of evil, that is, an eternal and necessary dualism in the order of being. Not being logically carried out to the conception of two eternal beings, it makes a duality in the one eternal essence of God, which is equally absurd, and more repugnant to the moral sense. For the Manichæan conception of God, though imperfect in regard to his absolute sovereignty, preserves the idea of his absolute and unmixed goodness. The Calvinistic conception, on the contrary, though preserving the idea of sovereignty, corrupts the idea of goodness. It ascribes to God two archetypes of creation, one good, the other evil; and, as the ideas of the divine intelligence are identical with the divine essence, it represents the divine essence itself as both good and evil. It ascribes to the Creative Mind two purposes, one to communicate the good of being, the other the evil of being. All the good of excellence and felicity, on the one hand, and all the evil of depravity and misery, on the other, are the necessary sequel of these two creative purposes. Therefore, fatalism and physical necessity are the law of the universe. Those who are within the sphere of the creative act which creates evil are doomed to sin and to suffer eternally by a physical

---

* It is, nevertheless, the most logically consistent with itself of all Protestant systems.

necessity. All human beings but the small number of the elect are born under this dark and irresistible doom. This doctrine has done, and is doing, more to generate antipathy to Christianity than any other cause. It has excited a revolt against Protestant orthodoxy, which includes in its hostile feelings the Catholic faith also. On that account, the good of religion and of the human race requires that it should be vigorously combated, and, if possible, destroyed, on Christian and Catholic principles. It is necessary that Christian orthodoxy should clear its skirts of complicity with this doctrine. For the mistaken opinion that the former had incorporated the latter with itself, and given it all the sanction of tradition and authority, works greatly to the prejudice of orthodoxy. This is even the more necessary, because this mistaken opinion is founded on some apparent and plausible reasons. All error is a travesty of some portion of the truth. Calvinism is a travesty of one side of the Christian doctrine. It is therefore easy to confound statements of the Catholic doctrine with the corresponding Calvinistic exaggerations. This is especially the case with the statements which were made before heresy had travestied that particular portion of the orthodox system, and which were more unguarded in their verbal expression. Moreover, heresies which consist, not in a positive denial of the fundamental dogmas of the faith, but in an alteration of the dogmas by a false philosophical explanation, are commonly generated from crude and imperfect conceptions floating in the current theology of preceding ages. These form the raw material of heresy, which is not detected and condemned until it has been elaborated in some ill-regulated brain and shaped into formal heresy. The controversy with any particular heresy brings out the opposite Catholic doctrine into a clearer and more definite verbal expression. It eliminates from the portion of theology occupied with the explication of that doctrine, crude and imperfect conceptions and inaccurate expressions. Calvinism and afterward Jansenism were formed out of such imperfect conceptions of the doctrines of the Fall, Predestination, and the Necessity of Divine Grace in order to all salutary acts leading to celestial blessedness, together with the denial of free-will in any proper sense of the word, either entirely or at least as regards the lapsed state of man. It is, therefore, important to show that the ancient doctors of the church did not formally hold or teach these misconceptions, but that, so far as they exist materially in their statements, they merely lurk there as unformed and accidental defects of thought and expression; that their doctrine, as a living and concrete whole, apprehended in its true principles and spirit, is the same with that which the later church has more clearly and formally defined. We have occasion also to combat, in conjunction with the Calvinistic system, that which is commonly called "Evangelical." The two are partly identical. The latter is completely included in the former. Yet, as the Evangelical system is, to a certain extent, dissociated from technical Calvinism, and is denominated more from its practical than its metaphysical doctrines, it must be spoken of as distinct. A special word of explanation regarding our opposition to this system is therefore necessary. It must not be thought that we are contending against the ideas legitimately expressed by the word "evangelical," that is, belonging to the Gospel of our Lord Jesus Christ. We use the word for want of a better, to designate a system which appropriates to itself, unjustly, a designation belonging rightfully to the doctrine of the Catholic Church. The dominant idea of this system, as taught by its original authors, is, that justification is an imputation of the extrinsic righteousness of Christ appropriated by a purely mental act called faith, and distinct from inward sanctity, or outward means as instruments of sanctification. As modified by some of its later advocates, it includes sanctification under the idea of faith, but maintains that it is produced by purely spiritual operations, without visible forms or instruments. This system is sometimes denominated the Lutheran, because this particular doctrine of justification stands out so boldly in the preaching and writings of Luther, while the metaphysical doctrines springing from the predestinarian theory of Calvin are called after him as their principal champion. It is this Luthero-Calvinistic system which we are intending specially to combat with weapons taken from the armory of St. Augustine. While we combat the system, however, as such, as subversive of the dictates of reason and the dogmas of revelation, we admit that the body of

Studies in St. Augustine. 15

religious and moral doctrines held even by strict Calvinists contains a great mass of Catholic truth, and we respect the goodness and virtue which it has produced. We acknowledge also that the system called "Evangelical" has undergone great modifications as held by the majority of its adherents. We adopt fully the words of Döllinger: "Nevertheless, Protestants and Catholics have theologically come nearer to each other; for that main doctrine, those 'articles with which the church was to stand or fall,' and for the sake of which the Reformers declared separation from the Catholic Church to be necessary, are now confuted and given up by Protestant theology, or are retained only nominally, whilst other notions are connected with the words."*

We have, then, no quarrel with any, and no words of bitterness for any one, whether he be a Christian believer under any name, or an unbeliever, if he only loves that portion of truth and goodness which he can see, and desires to see all its other portions, in order to love them in their completeness. Being Catholic, and thus possessing the perfect circle of truth, our sympathies touch all minds, and we recognize in all the truths which they severally possess, but only in an inchoate and imperfect form, because they have no universal formula which reconciles them all. We respect, then, the truth contained in error, but have no mercy for error itself, as error.

* *The Church and the Churches.*

So far as theological systems are concerned, we neither give nor ask for quarter.

We will attack falsehood with all the energy in our power, and claim no deference for the doctrine we profess, on any other ground than as being the truth. Toward the persons of those whose belief clashes with our own, we hope to preserve all Christian courtesy and kindness.

The more strictly the rules of this Christian courtesy are observed in all discussions of religious questions, the better we think it will be for the cause of truth; and we may add, that the manner of St. Augustine furnishes in this respect an excellent model for our imitation.

The whole controversy in which we are about to engage relates to the nature of the lapse of the human race from its original destiny, and the mode of its restoration through Christ the Redeemer.

We shall commence, therefore, in the next chapter, with the subject of the Fall of man and the questions related to it.

CHAPTER II.

THE PROBLEM OF MORAL EVIL AND ITS CAUSE.

THE existence of moral evil in the universe, its origin and reason, and its ultimate consequences, form the most difficult of all the problems which have ever perplexed the human mind. All religions and all philosophies contain some kind of attempt at a solution. We cannot wonder that the solution given by those which have corrupted the primitive revelation should be unsatisfactory. The absence of a clear revelation from God accounts for the fact. But how shall we account for the fact that those who profess to have such a revelation are equally perplexed and distressed by the same dark problem? We account for it in this way. God made known in the patriarchal and Judaic revelation certain great facts and truths concerning the original state, the fall, and the redemption of the human race, which were afterward more clearly and widely promulgated by Christ and the apostles. This revelation was sufficient to satisfy the demands of the soul for all practical and necessary purposes. The common people before the time of Christ were in a state of mental and spiritual childhood, in which they were required to know only the simplest and plainest articles of religious faith. They knew that the grace and favor of God were attainable by keeping his commandments, and were more occupied with securing the blessings of a virtuous life on earth and enjoying here the true good of existence, than with questioning about their origin and ultimate destiny. They had an indistinct faith in a Redeemer, who would deliver his people from all evils in this world and the future, and conduct them to final happiness; and this was enough to take all fear and gloom from their minds. The *élite* of the people had a clearer and more extensive knowledge of the sacred truths handed down by Scripture and Tradition. But their minds were not metaphysical; and they either did not reflect on the difficult problems of human destiny, or were easily satisfied with some plausible solution. The Christian revelation has made a great change in this respect. The human intelligence has had a new world thrown open to it, and has been powerfully stimulated to enter and examine it. The great data for a complete explanation of the plan of God in the universe have been set out in a strong and conspicuous light. But with the light there is also an increase of darkness, a revelation of the obscurity and difficulty which accompany truth as a shadow. God has revealed articles of faith, but not a theology. We believe that the reason of this is, that he has imposed on the Christian intelligence the task of making a theology for itself. The greatest minds in the church have been at work on this task in all ages, from the time of St. Paul down to our own day. As in all other theologies, so in the Christian, human intelligence has busied itself to grasp, explain, and reconcile with other great truths the data furnished by revelation in relation to sin and its penalty, and thus to solve the problem of the cause and end of evil. It has found here its most difficult task. The data furnished it to work upon, while they complete our information regarding the genesis of sin in the human race, and the method of regeneration to holiness and bliss, appear at first sight to be irreconcilable with the justice and goodness of God. These data are, the fall of the human race through the sin of Adam, the birth of all men in original sin, the gratuitous salvation of a portion of mankind through a Redeemer, and the final perdition of the remainder. These doctrines appear to contradict the necessary and universal judgments of our rational and moral nature, that the creative act is essential love, that each individual rational being who is subjected to moral probation must have a fair and impartial trial, that sin is a voluntary transgression of known law by a free and conscious agent, and that penalty is proportioned to the personal demerit of the sinner, of which it is the legitimate fruit. The doctrine of the fall of all men in the first Adam, and the restoration of a part of men in the second Adam, appears to introduce the idea that sin and holiness, misery and blessedness, are operations of a law of physical necessity proceeding from the irresponsible will of the Creator, and that we are therefore created under a doom or destiny of good or evil, over which we have no control. Are not, then, Christian believers equally distressed and perplexed by the problem of evil, with others? What advantage does revelation give them? And how is it that God has left them in such distress? To this we reply: First, that between ideal and eternal truths there can be no contradiction. The contradiction is only apparent, and lies in our imperfect conceptions. Second, that by the light of faith there is given to the soul a true and complete idea of all these truths, although it may not be perfectly evolved into reflective consciousness. Thirdly, that the great mass of the faithful have never distinctly reflected on the difficulty we are considering, or been distressed by it. And fourthly, that the *élite* of the faithful have been able to find in theology a solution of their difficulties, which, if not perfect, has always been adequate and progressive, and, like the arc of a circle which is partly invisible, suggestive of the complete rotundity of truth.

These last two observations need to be explained more fully.

The mass of the Catholic people, where the faith prevails universally, find themselves and the whole population around them in the church from infancy. They regard themselves as regenerated and made the children of God by baptism. They do not in their habitual reflections go behind that fact. The fall of Adam and original sin are done away with, so far as concerns themselves and the world around them. They live in the world of grace and redemption. Heaven is open to them, and the means of reaching it are at hand. The unregenerate world is too distant and foreign from their own world to awaken any vivid sympathy in their bosoms. As Christians, they have the principle of universal charity. But the active, practical sentiment of sympathy with the whole human race in all times and places is something which is beyond the actual capacity of their minds, being the result only of the highest state of mental education. They feel no desire for, and have no need of, any theology except what is given them in catechisms, sermons, and such pious books as they are able to read. The worry and fret of the mind over religious questions, the dark and melancholy state of a soul brooding over doubts and perplexing itself with fearful problems, are not found among them. Their religion is peaceful, joyous, and full of hope. Mr. Alger, in his recent work on the *History of the Doctrine of a Future Life*,* is mistaken in the opinion he has adopted from Neander, that terror predominated in the Catholic mind during the middle ages. Hope is always the predominant sentiment in the bosom of the Catholic people. Bright and cheerful images habitually fill their minds. It is only a guilty conscience that awakens terror in their bosoms, and this terror usually leads them to make their peace with God. The body of the Catholic people now, closely

* Part iv. chap. 2.

connected as they are by an unbroken tradition with the middle ages, have substantially the same ethical and religious temper with their forefathers. The only source of trouble, anxiety, or fear, in regard to religious matters in their minds, arises from their own personal sins. There is no anxiety about election and reprobation, grace and free-will, no gloomy feeling of a doom hanging over them from birth, or a law of fatal necessity impelling them to sin and misery. They are convinced that they can keep the law of God if they will, that pardon is always open to the repentant, and that heaven is within their reach. If the idea of hell in their minds is vivid and terrific, it is usually in the background, and the fear of incurring its doom personally is a subdued apprehension controlled by the more powerful sentiment of hope, except at times when a guilty conscience brings its terrors near. For the Catholic people generally there is therefore no need of theological explanations of perplexing questions which have never arisen in their minds.

The deep perplexity and gloom of soul existing in such a multitude of minds in our own day, is the result of the morbid, analytical, metaphysical habit of mind, superinduced by Protestantism, working on the perverted and distorted ideas of Calvinistic theology. It appears to have reached its most aggravated stage in the land of the Puritans. That gifted daughter of New England, Mrs. Stowe, has given a most perfect delineation of it in *The Minister's Wooing*. Her sister, Catharine Beecher, has described it with no less tragic power, not under the form of fiction, but with the matter-of-fact accuracy of logic and historical narrative. We have had experience of it ourselves, having been brought up from childhood in the doctrine of the Puritans, and having learned Calvinistic theology thoroughly, both theoretically and practically. We made the most earnest endeavors to find a way of reconciling it with reason and the moral sense, without any success; and it was with a feeling of unspeakable relief that we discovered that there was no reason for believing it to be a part of the Christian revelation. It is our ardent desire to bring the same relief to souls that are weighed down by this incubus. There are many who stand in need of the clearest light that theology can shed on these dark questions, for the health and welfare of their souls; to make faith possible to them, and to give them the peace necessary for the practice of Christian virtue. The light of theology, as we have said above, has always been possessed by the *élite* of the faithful. The number of this class of believers of more developed intelligence, who are capable of receiving, and who really need, theological knowledge, in addition to the rudimental instruction suited to the mass, is increasing. A great number of the Catholic laity are converts, who need to have the difficulties raised by their early education removed. Another large number share in the intellectual movement of the age, and are brought in contact with the uncatholic world of thought and speculation. It is our duty to guide, direct, and instruct all these classes of persons within the fold of the church, in a manner suited to the wants of their minds. It is also our duty to endeavor to make the Catholic doctrine intelligible to those who are without. We believe that the restless anxiety of their minds, perpetually brooding over the problem of human destiny, is left there by the creator, and permitted to torment them, in order that they may search after the solution of their doubts until they find it in the Catholic faith. If we have a solution for these doubts, sufficient to give the most perfect intellectual and spiritual tranquillity to all the right-minded and sincere, we ought to be most anxious to put it forward in the clearest manner possible. We are endeavoring to do this to the best of our power, in the present essay, by presenting the doctrine of St. Augustine concerning some of the most difficult doctrines of Christianity, in contrast with the distortions of Calvinism. The whole system of Calvinism may be said to be included and summed up in the doctrine of Total Depravity. Human nature is essentially and totally evil, capable of producing only evil, and deserving only evil. As we are born in this state, we must refer our sin and misery to a destiny beyond our own control, established eternally by our creator, who made us for evil. If we are rescued from this state, it is by a similar act of Omnipotence, irrespective of personal acts or desert, and by virtue of a destiny equally beyond our control. This is the fearful system contained in and springing from the doctrine of Total Depravity. We shall begin an attack upon it, therefore, with this doctrine in our next chapter.

CHAPTER III.

THE CAUSE AND NATURE OF SIN, AND THE REASON OF ITS PERMISSION.

THE Calvinistic doctrine that sin is a total depravation of nature, which makes it and all its acts substantially evil, is nowhere taught by St. Augustine. On the contrary, he uniformly affirms that nature remains always substantially good, not only in the state of original, but even also of actual sin. It is his invariable doctrine that there is no such thing as a positively evil nature or substance, and that there can be no such thing, because the existence of such a substance is metaphysically impossible. The principles of his philosophy destroy the very notion of essential and total depravity. This notion is Manichæan, and necessarily presupposes the notion of an eternal, intrinsically evil being, by participation in which contingent or derived existences are made evil. For a created existence whose being is in the Supreme Good cannot be intrinsically evil, since it has nothing in its nature except what is derived from the Creator.

The notion of an infinite, self-existent principle of evil is, however, absurd, since it is self-evident that absolute being is identical with absolute good. The philosophy of St. Augustine and of the Catholic Church, being based on the doctrines of the unity of God and the creation of all things out of nothing by his Word, cannot admit the existence of any evil substance in creation. The Word, in whom the archetype of all possible things has an eternal being, is identical in nature with the Father. Creation is nothing but the reduction into act, in time and space, of the possibilities which exist in an eminent sense in the idea of God from eternity and in infinity; the extrinsication of something real which imitates the being of God, so far as it is imitable under finite conditions. Creation is, therefore, a finite, imperfect image of the Word, as the Word is the infinite, perfect image of the Father: *Figura substantiæ ejus.** Nothing can be extrinsicated in the creation which is not in the archetype, therefore nothing which is not good in so far as it is anything positive. The notion of evil, sin, depravation, corruption, etc., is merely privative. It is the notion of a limitation or diminution of good. The intrinsic liability to evil or sin which is inherent in all created nature, arises from its limitation as something finite, and not having being in and of itself. Drawn from nothingness, it tends of itself to revert back to nothingness. A total lapse into nothingness would be annihilation. A par-

---

* Heb. i. 3.

tial return to it is a loss of some of the modes of actual or potential being which it once possessed. Total depravation of substance implies annihilation. An organized form may be corrupted by the dissolution of its component parts. But the soul, being simple, has no components which are separable. It must, therefore, remain essentially incorrupt as long as it exists at all.

We now proceed to show that this is the doctrine of St. Augustine, by the citation of passages from his works.

"Nature, being that very substance which is capable both of good and evil, is capable of good by participation in that good by which it was made; it is capable of evil, however, not by participation in evil, but by a privation of good; that is, not by the commixture of a nature which is an evil thing in itself, for *no nature is evil inasmuch as it is nature*, but inasmuch as it recedes from that nature which is the sovereign and immutable good, for the reason that it was not made from that nature, but from nothing."*

"Every nature, inasmuch as it is nature, is good; for, if it is incorruptible, it is better than that which is corruptible; but if it is corruptible, it is also without doubt good, since by corruption it becomes less good. Now, every nature is either capable or incapable of being corrupted. Therefore every nature is good; and by nature I mean the same with that

---

* *Con. Julian.* i. 37.

which is commonly called substance. Therefore, every substance is either God or from God."*

In these passages we have the whole of the philosophy of St. Augustine on this particular subject, in a nutshell. He had been in his youth a Manichæan, and, having sounded all the absurdities of the dualistic system to the bottom, he seized hold of the contrary principle of the unity of being in God with such a firmness of grasp, that he never let go his hold for a single instant, even in his controversy with the Pelagians. Every substance, he says, is either God or from God; that is, there is no substance existing outside of God, except those substances which God has created out of nothing. In God, being and good are identical, self-existing, eternal, unchangeable, and infinite. In creation, the entity of all existing things consists in a participation in the infinite being which is the infinite good, according to a finite mode. Therefore, the entity of all things is good, and they cannot cease to be good without ceasing to have entity and becoming nonentities. So, then, the only corruption possible in created things is a resolution of composite forms into their simple elements, in the case of material existences; and in the case of spiritual substances, the resolution of the relations or modes in which they subsist in the order of the universe. This corruption cannot, therefore, touch the essence of any substance, nor can it destroy all its modes of activity or relations to other substances,

---

* *De Lib. Arb.* iii. 35.

since nothing created can exist except in some kind of act, and therefore in some relation to the universe of which it is a component part. This is what St. Augustine affirms in the following passage:

"Therefore, these two created things, body and life, (that is, matter and spirit,) since they are of the class of things which exist by their form, (that is, by the actuation of their nude potentiality in some generic and specific grade of individual existence, complete in itself and distinct from every other,) according to the doctrine we have laid down above, and when they lose their form entirely fall back into nothingness— sufficiently show that they have their substance from that form which is ever the same, (that is, from God, who is being and act in the simplest and most absolute sense.) Wherefore, all kinds of things which are good, however great or however small they may be, can have no being except from God. For what is greater among creatures than intelligent life? (living, intelligent spirit,) or what can be less than body? Now, these, however deficient they may become, and however much they may tend in the direction of non-existence, nevertheless retain some form in order to exist at all. But whatever there is of form remaining in any deficient thing, is from that form which knows no deficiency."*

From this it follows necessarily that those rational creatures who sin become only relatively and not

---

* *De Lib. Arb.* ii. 46.

absolutely evil, and that sin or evil is also a relative and not an essential quality of their acts.

"The work of God remains good in all works, however evil, of the wicked. . . . And the very unclean spirit himself is good, inasmuch as he is a spirit, but evil inasmuch as he is unclean."*

"The things which are made need this good, namely, the chief good, that is, the highest essence. They become less than they were when, by the sin of the soul, their motion toward him is lessened ; but they are not, therefore, entirely separated from him, otherwise they would become nothing at all."†

"They inquire of us, Whence is evil? We answer, From the good, but not from the sovereign and unchangeable good. Therefore, evils have arisen from inferior goods and such as are mutable. And although we perceive that these evils are not natures, but vices of natures, yet we also understand that they could not exist except from and in certain natures ; and that there is no evil except a defection from good."‡

"There is a nature in which there is no evil, and in which, indeed, there can be no evil ; but there cannot be a nature in which there is no good. Hence, not even the nature of the devil himself is evil."§

Having now sufficiently proved that the doctrine of St. Augustine is entirely opposed to the doctrine of essential and total depravity, we proceed to show that it is also opposed to the doctrine that God posi-

---

* *De Peccat. Orig.* ii. 44. † *De Ver. Rel.* xiv.
‡ *Con. Jul.* i. 37. § *De Civ. Dei.* xix. 13.

tively decreed sin and evil as necessary means to the greatest common good.

The whole of St. Augustine's doctrine on the divine permission of sin is included in four propositions:

First. God foresaw, but did not predetermine, the fall of some angels and of man.

Second. The fallen angels and man fell by their own free-will.

Third. God left rational creatures free to sin, because the possession of this freedom made the rational creation more excellent.

Fourth. God created those rational beings who he foresaw would sin irrecoverably, because their existence is, in itself, and in its relation to the final cause, a positive good.

These four propositions, which are radically contrary to the whole Calvinistic theory, are invariably maintained by St. Augustine throughout his writings, as many Catholic writers have most thoroughly and minutely proved. Every treatise and every passage has been carefully scanned and discussed, on account of the Jansenistic controversy, by theologians of various scholastic opinions. We propose merely to cite a sufficient number of passages to illustrate and confirm each of the four propositions laid down above; and to exhibit the doctrine of St. Augustine on such other topics as are naturally connected with them.

In support of the first proposition, we will first cite an explanation of the relation between the prescience of God and the sins of the creature, showing that the former does not predetermine the latter. There are two interlocutors in the extract we are about to give, Evodius and Augustine:

"E. Since these things are so, I am unspeakably anxious to know how it can be that, on the one hand, God should be prescient of all future events, and, on the other, that we should not sin by any necessity. For whoever says that anything can happen otherwise than as God has foreseen it beforehand, attempts to destroy the prescience of God by a most insane impiety. Wherefore, if God foresaw that the first man would sin, which every one must necessarily grant to me who holds with me that God is prescient of all future events; if, therefore, it is so, I do not say that he ought not to have created him, for he made him good; nor can the sin of one whom he made good in any way injure God; yea, as in making him he showed his goodness, in punishing him he showed his justice, and in liberating him he showed his mercy. Therefore I do not say he ought not to have created him; but I do say that, since he foreknew that he would sin, that must necessarily happen which God foresaw was to be. How, therefore, is the will free, when such an inevitable necessity is apparent?

"A. It is plain that what troubles you and excites your wonder is this: how these things should not be contrary and repugnant to one another, that God should be prescient of all future events, and that we should sin, not by necessity, but voluntarily. For, you say, if God knew beforehand that a man will sin, it is necessary that he should sin; but, if it be necessary, there is therefore not the choice of the will in sinning, but rather an inevitable and fixed necessity. By which reasoning you fear lest it should result that either God should be impiously denied to be prescient of all future events, or, if we cannot deny that, we should confess that sin is necessary and not voluntary: does anything else trouble you?

" E. Nothing else at present.

" A. Therefore, you think that all things of which God is prescient happen by necessity and not by will?

" E. That is my opinion.

" A. Bestir yourself, now, and look into yourself a little, and tell me, if you can, what kind of will you will have to-morrow, whether of sinning or of doing right?

" E. I do not know.

" A. How, then; do you think that God also is ignorant of this?

" E. I do not think so, by any means.

" A. If, therefore, he knows your will of to-morrow, and foresees the future wills of all men who are, and who are to be, much more he foresees what he will do with the just and the impious.

" E. Certainly. If I say that God is prescient of my works, much more confidently I should say he foreknows his own works, and most certainly foresees what he himself is about to do.

" A. Ought you not, then, to beware lest one should say to you that he also will do those things which he is going to do, by necessity and not by will, if all those things of which God is prescient are done by necessity and not by will?

"E. When I said that all things are done necessarily which God has foreknown as future, I intended only those which are done in his creation, but not those which are in himself; for these are not done, but they are eternal.

"A. Therefore God works nothing in his creation.

"E. He has already once determined how the order of the universe which he has constructed should be carried on; and he does not administer anything by a new will.

"A. Does he never make any one blessed?

"E. Truly he does.

"A. He does it, then, at the time when the person is made so?

"E. It is so.

"A. If therefore, for example, you will be blessed after a year, after a year he will make you blessed?

"E. Yes.

"A. Therefore, he foreknows to-day what he will do after a year.

"E. He has always foreknown it; I acknowledge he also foreknows it now, if it is to be so.

"A. Tell me, I pray you, are you not his creature, or is your beatitude not accomplished in yourself?

"E. Yes, I am his creature, and it will be in myself that I shall be blessed.

"A. Therefore, not by will, but by necessity your beatitude will be accomplished in you by the act of God?

"E. His will is my necessity.

"A. Therefore, you will be unwillingly blessed?

"E. If it were in my power to be blessed, I would be blessed immediately, for I will to be so, even now, and I am not, because not I, but he makes me blessed.

"A. Excellently does the truth cry out concerning you. For you could not possibly think that any other thing is in our power, except that which we do when we will. Wherefore nothing is so much in our power as the will itself is. For that, without any interval whatever, as soon as we will, is at hand. And therefore, we can rightly say that we do not grow old by our own will, but by necessity; or, we do not die by our own will, but by necessity; or anything of the same kind: but that we do not will by our own will, what madman would dare to say? Wherefore, although God may foreknow our future wills, that does not cause that we should will anything not by our own will. For what you have said concerning your own beatitude, that you are not made blessed without yourself, you said in such a way as if I denied it; but I say that, when you will be blessed, you will not be blessed unwillingly, but voluntarily. When, therefore, God is prescient of your future beatitude, and nothing can occur otherwise than as he has foreknown, else it would be no prescience, we are not on that account obliged to think, what is most absurd and far from the truth, that you are not to be voluntarily blessed. But as the prescience of God, which is this very day certain of your future beatitude, does not take away your will of beatitude when you begin to be blessed; so, also, your culpable will, if any such is to be in you, will not therefore become no will, because God has foreknown that it is to be so. Consider now, I beseech you, with what great blindness it is said : If God foreknows my future will, since nothing can happen otherwise than as he has foreknown, it is necessary that I should will what he has foreknown ; but, if it is necessary, it must be acknowledged that I will it not voluntarily, but by necessity. O singular folly ! How, therefore, can nothing else be done than what God has foreknown, if that shall not be will, which he has foreknown shall be will ? I omit the equally monstrous assertion which I have a little before said was made by the same man, It is necessary that I should so will ; thus striving to take away will by supposed necessity. For, if it is necessary that he should will, whence will he will, when there will be no will ? But if he does not speak in this way, but shall say that he does not have his will itself in his own power, because it is necessary that he should will, he is met by that which you said yourself, when I inquired whether you would become blessed unwillingly ; for you answered that you would be blessed now, if it were in your power ; for you said that you willed to be so, but were not yet able. Whereupon I subjoined that the truth cried out concerning you ; for we cannot deny that we have power, unless when that which we will is not present to us ; but while we will, if the will itself is wanting to us, we do not will. But if it cannot be that, when we will, we should not will, the will is present to those who will ; and nothing else is in our power, except that which is present to us when we will. Therefore, our will would not be will, unless it were in our power. Moreover, because it is in our power, it is free to us. For that is not free to us which we do not have in our power, and it is impossible that what we have in our power should not be free to us. So it comes to pass, that we do not deny that God is prescient of all future events, and nevertheless we will what we will. For since he is prescient of our will, that of which he is prescient will be. Therefore the will will be, because he is prescient of the will. Nor can it be will unless it shall be in our power. Therefore he is prescient of our power also. Power is not, therefore, taken from me by his prescience, but will be present with me more certainly on this very account, because he whose prescience is not deceived has foreknown that it will be present with me.

"E. Behold, now, I do not deny that those things which God has foreknown happen necessarily in such a way, and that he foresees our sins in such a way, that the will in us nevertheless remains free, and placed in our power.

"A. What disturbs you, then? Have you perhaps forgotten what was done in our first disputation; and will you deny that, without compulsion from any one, superior, inferior, or equal, but by our will itself, we sin?

"E. I dare not deny any of these things at all; but, nevertheless, I confess that I do not see how these two things are not opposed to each other—the prescience of

God concerning our sins, and our free-will in sinning. For we must necessarily confess that God is both just and prescient. But I would wish to know how he can justly punish sins which must necessarily be done; or how it is not necessary that those things should be done which he has foreknown are to be; or how that is not to be imputed to the creator which it is necessary should be done in his creature.

"A. For what reason does our free-will appear to you contrary to the prescience of God: because it is prescience, or because it is the prescience of God?

"E. Rather because it is of God.

"A. What, then! if you should foreknow that some one would sin, would it not be necessary that he should sin?

"E. Indeed, it would be necessary that he should sin; for I could not otherwise have prescience, unless I foreknew things that are certain.

"A. It is not, therefore, because it is the prescience of God that what he has foreknown must necessarily happen, but only because it is prescience; which is no prescience unless it foreknows things certain?

"E. I agree; but why do you make these assertions?

"A. Because, if I am not deceived, you do not compel the person to sin, who you foreknow will sin; nor does your prescience itself compel him to sin, although, without doubt, he is about to sin; for otherwise you could not foreknow that that will be. Therefore, as these two things are not opposed to each other, that you by your prescience should know what another is about to do by his own will, so God, compelling no one to sin, nevertheless foresees those who will sin by their own will. Why, then, shall he not avenge as just those things which he did not compel to be done as prescient? For as you by your memory do not compel those things to be done which have passed, so God, by his prescience, does not compel those things to be done which are future. And as you remember some things which you have done, but have not done all the things which you remember, so God foreknows all things of which he is the author, and yet is not himself the author of all these things which he foreknows. But of these things of which he is not the evil author, he is the just avenger. Understand, then, from this, with what justice God may punish sins, because he did not do those things which he foreknew would be done; for, if, for this reason, he ought not to repay punishment to sinners because he foresees that they will sin; neither ought he to pay rewards to those who act rightly, since he equally foresees that they will act rightly. And, moreover, we must confess that it belongs to his prescience, that nothing of all those things which are to be should be hidden from him, and also to his justice, that sin, because it is committed by the will, should therefore not be done with impunity from his judgment, because his prescience does not compel it to be done."*

This long extract shows very clearly and sufficient-

---

* *De Lib. Arb.* iii. 4-11.

ly what was the doctrine of St. Augustine concerning the relation between the prescience of God and the sins which are committed by his creatures, namely, that God foreknows, but does not predetermine, them; which establishes the truth of our first proposition : *God foresaw, but did not predetermine, the fall of some angels and of man.*

The second proposition—namely, that the fallen angels and man fell by their own free-will—follows from the first, and equally with it is proved to be St. Augustine's doctrine by the foregoing extract. We will support it, however, by a few more citations :

" A. Every rational nature being created with a free dominion of the will, if it remain in the enjoyment of the supreme and immutable good, is without doubt praiseworthy; and every one which tends to remain in it is also praiseworthy; but every one which does not remain in it, and does not wish to strive to remain, in so far as it is not there, and in so far as it does not strive to be there, is blameworthy. . . . On account of that which he has not received, no one is guilty; but on account of that which he ought to do and does not, he is justly guilty. He ought to do it, however, if he has received a free-will and an entirely sufficient power. . . . For, if each one is under a debt for that which he has received, and man is made so that he sins necessarily, he is under a debt of committing sin. When he sins, therefore, he does that which is due from him. If it is a crime to say this, then no one is compelled by his nature to sin. Nor does any other nature compel him.

For one does not sin when he suffers that which he does not will. For, if he suffers justly, he does, not sin in that which he suffers unwillingly, but he sinned in that which he did willingly, and which caused him to undergo justly this involuntary suffering. But if he suffer unjustly, how does he sin? For it is not sin to suffer something unjustly, but to do something unjustly. But if one is compelled to sin, neither by his own nature, nor by another nature, it remains that he must sin by his own will. . . .

"E. But I would wish to know, if possible, why that nature does not sin which God foreknew would not sin, and why that one sins which was foreseen by him as going to sin. . . . But I do not wish that the will should be given me as an answer; for I seek the cause of the will itself. . . .

"A. Since the will is the cause of sin, but you seek the cause of the will itself, if I could find this for you, would you not ask for the cause of that very cause which had been found? And what will be the method of inquiry, and what will be the end of delaying and discussing, whereas, we ought not to seek for anything beyond that which is itself the root? . . . But what, in fine, can be the cause of the will, before the will? For either it is the will itself, and we do not depart from that same root of the will, or it is not the will and has no sin. . . . Remember the many things which we have previously said concerning sin and free-will. But if it is laborious to commit it all to memory, keep this, which is very short. Whatever the cause of the will is, if it cannot be resisted, it is yielded to without sin ; but, if it can be, let it not be yielded to and sin will not be committed. But does it deceive one who is incautious? Let him take care not to be deceived. Is its fallaciousness so great that it cannot be avoided at all? If it is so, there are no sins ; for who sins in that which cannot in any way be avoided? But sin is committed, therefore it can be avoided?"*

" If the efficient cause of this evil will is sought for, it is found to be nothing. For what is that which makes the will evil, when it performs an evil work? Accordingly, an evil will is the efficient cause of an evil work, but there is no efficient cause of an evil will. . . . Let no one, therefore, seek for the efficient cause of an evil will : for it is not efficient, but deficient ; because that will itself is not an effective but a defective act."†

" Finally, some angels, the chief of whom is the one who is called the devil, by free-will became apostates from the Lord God. Nevertheless, although abandoning his goodness by which they were blessed, they could not escape his judgment, by which they became most miserable. But the rest, by the same free-will, stood firm in the truth, and merited to have a most certain knowledge that they should never fall. . . . So also he made man with free-will, and, although ignorant concerning his future fall, nevertheless therefore blessed, because he felt that it was in his power not to die and not to become mi-

---

* *Ubi supra*, 37, 45, 46, 47, 48, 49, 50.   † *De Civ Dei*. xii. 6–7.

serable. In which upright and faultless condition, if he had willed to remain by his own free power of determination, immediately, without any experience of death and unhappiness, he would, by the merit of that stability, have received the fulness of beatitude by which the holy angels are blessed, that is, that he could not any more fall, and knew this most certainly. . . . But because, by his own free choice, he deserted God, he experienced the just judgment of God, so that he was condemned with his entire race, which was as yet totally contained in him, and sinned in him."*

Page after page might be filled with similar extracts, containing and fully developing the same doctrine; that God created the angels and Adam in the order of supernatural beatitude, and constituted them in a state of grace, with full and complete power to persevere in it or to abandon it, according to the free determination of their own wills; that Lucifer and his host, and Adam, fell by the abuse of their own freedom; and that no other cause of their fall is to be sought for lying back of their free-will. The second proposition is then established, namely, that according to St. Augustine's doctrine, *the fallen angels and man fell by their own free-will.*

The third proposition is, that God left rational creatures free to sin, because the possession of this freedom made the rational creature more excellent.

The ground on which he asserts this is, that without

---

* *De Correptione et Gratiâ*, xxvii. xxviii.

free-will there could be no merit. We will not delay long in proving this proposition, but merely cite one or two passages, which, though brief, are explicit and perfectly conclusive :

"As even a shying horse is better than a stone, which does not shy because it lacks sense and motion in itself, so a creature which sins by free-will is more excellent than one which does not sin because it does not possess free-will."*

"E. Explain to me, now, if possible, why God gave to man the free determination of his will, which, if he had not received, he could not have sinned. . . . Man himself, inasmuch as he is man, is something good ; because he can live rightly when he will.

"A. Evidently, if these things are so, the question which you have proposed is solved. For, if man is something good and cannot do rightly unless when he wills, he ought to have free-will, without which he cannot do rightly. For it is not to be believed that God gave it for this reason, because by it sin also is committed. It is therefore a sufficient cause why it ought to be given, because without it man cannot live rightly. . . . There would be no sin and no right action if it were not done by the will. And so both punishment and reward would be unjust if man did not have free-will. But there ought to be justice both in punishment and in reward ;

---

* *De Lib. Arb.* iii. 15.

since this is one of the goods which are from God. Therefore God ought to give free-will to man."*

This is as much as to say, that a universe in which a moral order, or period of probation, was established, in which rational creatures should work out their own eternal destiny by their personal merit or demerit, is more excellent than one which contains no such order. The existence of this moral order implies liberty to sin, as a concomitant of liberty to do right. *Therefore, God left rational creatures free to sin, because the possession of this freedom made the rational creation more excellent.*

The fourth proposition is, that God created those rational beings, who, he foresaw, would sin irrecoverably, because their existence in itself, and in its relation to the final cause, is a positive good.

Under this head we shall content ourselves with one long citation from the *Treatise on Free-Will,* without giving any comments or explanations of our own:

"His most liberal goodness would most justly merit our praise, even though he had created us in some inferior grade of the creation. For although our soul may be defiled with sins, it is nevertheless better and more sublime than it would be were it changed into that light which is visible to the eye. Thus, from the excellence of this light itself, you can discern how much more even those souls which are given up to the bodily senses praise God. Where-

* *De Lib. Arb.* ii. 1, 2, 3.

fore, let not the fact that sinful souls are vituperated move you to say in your heart that it would be better they should not exist. For they are vituperated in comparison with themselves, when we consider what they would have been if they had not sinned. Nevertheless, their creator, God, is to be praised in the highest degree that our human faculties will permit, not only because he disposes of them justly when they have sinned, but also because he has made them of such a kind that, even when defiled by sin, they are in no respect surpassed by the dignity of corporeal light, on account of which he is nevertheless justly praised. Therefore, I also admonish you to beware lest you should say, perchance, not indeed that it would be better that they should not exist, but that they ought to have been made otherwise. For, whatever may present itself to you as having a greater degree of good in it according to right reason, you may know that God, as the creator of all good things, has made it. But it is not according to right reason; on the contrary, it is an envious weakness, that, when you consider something better to have been made, you should wish that nothing should have been made inferior to that; as if, for instance, in the contemplation of the heavens, you should desire that the earth had not been made; which would be altogether wrong. For you might justly find fault if you saw that the earth had been created to the exclusion of the heavens, since you might say that heaven, such as you are able to think it, ought to have been made. But when you see that this also has been created to whose kind you would wish to bring the earth, which would then no longer be called earth, but heaven ; I believe that since you are not defrauded of the better thing, you should not grudge that the inferior thing has also been made, and called earth. Then, again, the earth itself contains, in its particular portions, such a great variety, that nothing pertaining to the species of the earth occurs to the thinking mind, which God, the creator of all good things, has not made in some part of its entire mass. For, from the most fertile and delightful earth to the most desolate and barren, it proceeds by degrees through intermediate conditions in such a way that you cannot venture to find fault with any of them, except by comparison with those that are better ; and so you ascend, by all the degrees of praise, in such a way that what you find to be the highest kind of earth, you would nevertheless not wish to be the only kind. But, now, how great is the distance between the entire earth and heaven ? For the natures of vapor and wind are interposed between them. And from these four elements other species and forms which cannot be numbered by us, but are numbered by God, are varied. Therefore, there may be something in the nature of things which you do not think of by your reason. It is not possible, however, that anything which you think of by true reason should not exist. For you cannot think of anything better in the creature which has escaped the creator, the artificer of creation. For the human soul—naturally connected with those dim reasons on which it depends when it says this would be better than that, when it says the truth and sees what it says—sees it in those reasons with which it is connected. Therefore, let it believe that God has made that which by true reason it knows ought to have been made by him, even if it does not see this in the things which are made. Because, if it could not see the heavens with its eyes, and nevertheless by true reason saw that something similar should have been made, it ought to believe that it has been made, though it could not see it with the eyes. For it could not in thought see that it ought to have been made, except in those reasons according to which all things have been made. But what is not in these reasons, no one can see by a true thought, because it is not a true thing. Most men err in this, that, when they see the better things with their mind, they do not look for them with their eyes in their proper places. As if one, who by reason comprehended perfect rotundity, should be angry because he did not find it in a nut, and had never seen any other round body except fruits of this kind. Thus it is that some persons, when they see with the truest reason that a creature is better which, though possessed of free-will, nevertheless, being always fixed in God, has never sinned, and consider the sins of men, grieve, not because they do not cease to sin, but because they were made; saying, He ought to have made us so that we should always will to enjoy his immutable truth, but never to sin. Let them not clamor, let them not be angry; for he did not compel these beings to sin, since when he made them he gave them power to do as they would; and there are angels who are such that they never have sinned and never will sin. Therefore, if that creature delights you which, with a most persevering will, never sins, without doubt it is reasonable that you prefer it to the one which sins, and think that every one else must prefer it, and, moreover, God the creator has preferred it in his ordering. Believe that there is such a creature in the superior seats and in the sublimity of the heavens; for, if the Maker has shown his goodness in creating the one whose future sins he foresaw, he would by no means withhold that goodness which would make the creature which he foresaw would not sin. For that sublime creature possesses its perpetual beatitude in the continual enjoyment of its creator, having merited it by a perpetual will of persevering justice. Besides, even that sinful creature has its own order, having lost beatitude by its sins, but not having forfeited the power of recovering beatitude. Moreover, it is itself superior to that nature which a perpetual will of sinning possesses, between which and the first one that remains in a righteous will, this one holds an intermediate state, deriving its exaltation from the humility of penitence. Nor did he withhold the largesse of his goodness even from that creature which he foresaw would not only sin, but remain in the will of sinning, so as not to create it. For, as even a shying horse is better than a stone, which does not shy because it lacks all motion and sense of its own so that creature is more excellent which sins by free-will than the one which does not sin because it has no free-will. And, as I should praise wine good in its own kind, and vituperate a man inebriated by the same wine, and yet should prefer the same man vituperated and while still intoxicated to the wine on which he was made drunk, though I had praised the wine; so, the corporeal creature is justly to be praised in its own grade, while they are to be vituperated who are turned away by its immoderate use from the perception of truth; although, on the other hand, the same persons already perverted, and, as it were, reeling with excess, are preferred, not on account of the merit of their vices, but on account of the dignity of their nature, to the same creature which in its own order is praiseworthy. Because, therefore, every soul is better than every body, and every sinful soul, however low it may have fallen, is by no change made body or entirely ceases to be soul, and therefore in no wise loses its superiority to body, but among bodies light holds the first place; it follows that the last soul is to be preferred to the first body, and though it may happen that to the body of a certain soul some other body may be preferred, to the soul itself it cannot be preferred. Why, then, should not God be praised, and praised by an ineffable ascription, who, when he made those who would remain in the laws of justice, made also other souls whom he foresaw would sin or even persevere in sins, since even these are better than those who cannot sin, because they have no rational and free determination of the will? Yet, these again are better than the most resplendent lustre of any corporeal forms, which some persons, although most erroneously, worship as the substance of the Most High God himself. Now, if in the order of corporeal creatures, from the choirs of the stars themselves even to the number of our hairs, the beauty of good things is so arranged in successive degrees that it would be most silly to say, Why is this? For what is that? since all things have been created in this one order; how much more foolishly is the same thing said of any soul, which, no matter to what diminution and defect of its own glory it may come, without any doubt will always surpass all bodies in dignity. Therefore, God made all natures, not only those that would remain in justice and virtue, but also those that would sin; not in order that they might sin, but that they might adorn the universe, whether they should will to sin or not to sin. For, if among existing things souls were wanting who should occupy the summit of order in the universal creation, so that, in case they should will to sin, the universe would be weakened and disordered, there would be a great lack in the creation; for that would be wanting whose absence would disturb the stability and connection of all things. Such are the excellent and holy and sublime creatures who are the celestial and supercelestial powers, who are in the place where God alone rules, and to whom the whole world is subject. Without the just and perfect functions of these spirits, the universe could not exist. Likewise, if those were wanting, who, if they sinned or did not sin, there would be no diminution of the order of the universe, there would still be a great lack. These are rational souls, unequal indeed to those superior beings in office, but equal in nature; having also under them many other inferior and yet praiseworthy grades of existence constituted by the Supreme God."*

The philosophy of St. Augustine is totally contrary to the idea of a sphere of absolute and infinite evil, which is Manichæan, and conducts logically to the idea that evil, as well as good, is a substantive existence, having its root and principle in an eternal, self-existent, and necessary evil being; which is dualism; and therefore totally destructive of the unity of God, and of the very idea of God, which is unintelligible except as absolute unity of essence. When the mind has come thus far, the gulf of atheism or pantheism yawns before it; the inevitable terminus of every path except that of Catholic faith; the seething abyss into which all the currents of heresy and infidelity must finally tumble headlong, no matter how apparently wide apart from each other their devious and seemingly placid course may be. Here at last the Calvinist, the Pelagian, the Unitarian, the Kantian, the Positivist, must meet; to find that they have all been conspiring together to destroy all possibility of a rational Theodicea, and to reduce the universe to a chaos, in which and over which there is no God.

Even Miss Catharine Beecher, the most uncompro-

* *De Lib. Arb.* iii. 12–32.

mising antagonist of Calvinism that has appeared of late years in New England, has ended by destroying the idea of God. Her intention was to vindicate the goodness and freedom of human nature, and the benevolence of the creator, and in her zeal she accused not only St. Augustine, but the Catholic Church, of Calvinism. She accused the Catholic Church of being gloomy and cruel; of making God the author of evil; and ascribing to nature an intrinsic principle of sin and wretchedness. Flying from this dark and abhorrent system, she sought, by the unaided strength of her own mind, to raise herself to a region of more serene and enlightened philosophy; but has fallen instead into the more obscure night of the doctrine, that evil is a necessity in the very nature of being, and domineers over God himself.

"It has been shown that the creator himself is limited by the eternal nature of things to a system which, though the best possible, makes him, in one sense, the author of some evil, both natural and moral. He is the author only as the creator of all things, and thus the author of all the consequent results of creation, even of those that are morally evil. In this sense alone is he the author of either natural or moral evil. The infinite and eternal mind of God is limited, not by want of wisdom and knowledge, but by THE ETERNAL NATURE OF THINGS OF WHICH HIS OWN EXISTENCE AND NATURAL ATTRIBUTES ARE A PART. . . .

"What, then, is the cause or origin of evil as taught by reason and experience? *It is the eternal nature of things existing independently of the will of the creator or of any other being.* . . . What is the cause or reason that any given event, however evil, is not prevented by God? It is because any change that would prevent it would alter the best possible system, and thus make more evil than the one thus prevented. . . .

"God himself is called holy, on the supposition that there are rules of right and wrong in the nature of things, independent of his will, and that his will is conformed to these rules, while men are called holy in reference chiefly to the will or service of their creator. In the creator, holiness signifies perfect voluntary conformity to that which *is for the best*, according to the eternal nature of things. . . .

"Still more are we to regard the feelings and wishes of our Creator and Supreme Lord. HE HAS INFINITE SUSCEPTIBILITIES OF ENJOYMENT AND SUFFERING, and thus whatever retards or promotes his wishes and plans must be of as much more value as his powers of enjoyment or suffering are greater than ours. . . .

"The following, then, are the deductions of reason and experience as to the future condition of our race after death:

"The soul, at the dissolution of the body, remains unchanged in its tastes, habits, and character. The *tendencies* indicated in this life are continued indefinitely, and eventually will result in the separation of the good and the bad, into two separate communities; the one being obedient to all the laws of God will be

Studies in St. Augustine. 55

for ever and perfectly happy, and the others are to reap the natural results of disobedience, and whatever added penalties the best good of the universe may demand.

"The final consummation in which this separation will be achieved may be at the distance of ages, and, in the meantime, all those minds that have passed or will pass from this life are in the same process of culture, discipline, and upward or downward progress, which exists in this life. Whether these advantages and temptations will be greater or less in the disembodied state, we have no data for inference or conjecture.

"The conduct and character formed in this life will have an abiding influence on the character and happiness of every mind through eternal ages."*

Here we have an eternal nature of things independent of God, and therefore abstract, but not real, necessary being, containing in itself the necessity of evil. This destroys the only intelligible idea of God, and leaves a divinity limited in nature, not holy by essence but by voluntary choice, and therefore essentially mutable, capable of suffering, and only superior to man in degree; in a word, mere existence, and not absolute being. Miss Beecher supposes that he is the creator of all other existences, but without reason; and a more consistent philosopher would tell

---

* *Appeal to the People*, pp. 143, 144, 150, 153, 180. The Italics are the author's, the small capitals are our own, in the above extract.

her that the abstract idea of God, which is individualized in him, is also individualized in us, and for the same cause ; which is pantheism. There is an indefinite evolution of good and evil through long ages, which Miss Beecher supposes must finally bring the virtuous to a state of perfection, but without reason. For the essential mutability of the will, and the necessity of evil which lies in the nature of things, precludes the possibility of an unchangeably perfect state of being. There is an everlasting flux and reflux in the universe. The sphere of God and of the supernatural world is destroyed, and nothing is left but the hell of Catholic theology as the heaven of God and the saints ; while the hell of the wicked is something far worse than hell has ever been imagined to be by those poets or preachers in the Catholic Church who have depicted its horrors the most vividly.

We know very well that Miss Beecher had no intention of teaching such a doctrine as this, and would recoil from it with horror. We respect highly her intellectual gifts and moral excellence ; but we cannot refrain from pointing out the errors into which the best and most enlightened must fall, when they set up their own judgment against the Catholic Church.

The gifted lady from whose work we have quoted has, we think, signally failed, in common with all other Protestant writers, to give any satisfactory solution of the profound problem of the origin of evil. We trust that we have shown, as far as we have gone, that the one given by St. Augustine and Cathlic theology is more rational and consoling. But our task is not yet finished, and we hasten to resume it.

We have already proved beyond a question that the absurd and odious doctrine of an evil nature, determined by intrinsic necessity to sin, and doomed to endless excruciating suffering for its necessary and inevitable acts, is not the doctrine of St. Augustine and of the Catholic Church. We have shown by ample citations from the writings of the great Catholic doctor that all merit and demerit, all liability to punishment and title to reward on the ground of justice, originate in the voluntary and free acts of intelligent beings. The doctrine of freedom and liberty of choice, or the self-determining power of the will, which lies at the basis of the whole moral order, has thus been vindicated and shown to be a first principle of Catholic theology. A vast mass of difficulties relating to the nature of sin and its penalty has thus been swept away at one blow. The reason and moral sense are relieved from the insupportable weight laid upon them by the notion of an ineluctable law in the universe emanating from the will of its supreme ruler, by which a large portion of the intellectual creation is utterly excluded from the sphere of good and transferred to a sphere of absolute, indefinite, and eternally progressive evil. Instead of this, they behold a law of liberty and moral probation, by which the creator proposes the sovereign and infinite good to be gained as a premium of merit, giving at the same time full and complete ability to attain it, and leaving the creature to work out for himself, dur-

ing a short period of trial, his own eternal beatitude
if he chooses to do so ; or if he does not choose to do
it, to fall from it and forfeit it for ever. It is true that
the great problem, How is the permission of sin and
the annexation of an eternal penalty to it consistent
with infinite goodness and wisdom? is not hereby
fully solved. But it is simplified. The ground is
cleared for theology to discuss the question, Why
should God leave the creature the power of forfeiting
his eternal beatitude? Why does not God give the
beatific vision at once, as a pure gift of grace, to all
intelligent creatures? Why does he expose any to
a trial and probation which endangers their losing it?
In the first place, he need not give it to any. It is a
reward beyond the bounds of nature, which is not
due to any creature. To love God with the beatific
love, by necessity of nature, and to enjoy the beatific
vision of God by nature, belongs only to the Blessed
Trinity, and not even to the humanity of our Blessed
Lord, except by virtue of the personal union with the
Word. To say, then, that supernatural beatitude is a
pure and free gift of God to the creature, is to cut
off the question why he does not give it uncondition-
ally to all. He actually does give it without previous
probation to thousands of millions of infants who die
after baptism before they attain any use of free-
will.* He gives it to many more after a very short
and easy trial, and to a number, how large or how

---

* The number of baptized infants who have already died before
coming to the use of reason is about 6,000,000,000.

small we know not, after they have misused the greater portion of their time of merit, on the simple condition of a change of will. God chooses to exhibit his pure goodness and mercy in this way in some cases. But in all his creative acts he is perfectly free. It is as foolish to ask why he does not act thus in all cases, as it would be to ask why he does not create more worlds, more angels, and more men.

We may, perhaps, find a reason which will convince us that this plan of God is not only reconcilable with his goodness, but that it exhibits it in a far higher degree than any other could do. God has chosen to raise the creature to the summit of being, and thus to carry the creative act to its apex. He has elevated human nature to the hypostatic union with the Second Person of the Blessed Trinity. As a consequence of this, created nature is made in the highest possible sense concreative cause with God, concurring in the highest effects of omnipotence. He has willed that the hypostatic union should be communicated to a vast multitude of individuals, personally distinct from his Son, but made in his image. Each one of these ought, therefore, to be a concreative cause with God. The highest effect of God's creative act is the elevation of the creature to the beatific union. The creature ought, then, in order to become concreative with God in the most perfect manner, to concur in this effect, which he does by meriting his own beatification.

In Christ, personal beatification could not fall under merit, for it was the principle of merit itself. By the personal union of the human with the divine nature, it was necessarily beatified. For the same reason, it was impeccable. In Christ merit had a more restricted, though a more dignified sphere. He could merit only by choosing among all possible good works certain ones which were very illustrious and perfectly voluntary, and merit only for others, but not for himself. The Blessed Virgin was also impeccable; though she merited for herself, and not for others, by merit of condignity; because her office required that she should receive a grace incompatible with sin. Probably others, for a like reason, have received a grace incompatible with *mortal* sin. We cannot say, then, that liability to sin is a necessary concomitant of liberty of will.

It is true that St. Augustine, in some of the passages we have quoted, speaks as if it were. He had not, however, so fully mastered the philosophy of free-will as later theologians have done. He does not accurately distinguish voluntary action from freedom of choice, or note the distinction between liberty from necessity and liberty from violence. All action of the will is voluntary or spontaneous, as such; even when the will is necessarily by nature determined in one direction. Thus God's love of himself, by which the Son is generated, and the Holy Spirit proceeds, that is to say, the whole inner life of God, is voluntary and yet necessary. The human will of Christ, and of every beatified angel and man, is necessarily determined to the beatific love of God, and yet this love is voluntary. Free-will, or free choice, is another thing. It is not merely freedom from coercion or external violence, but also from inward necessity. In God this liberty is only exercised in his works *ad extra*. In those creatures whose wills are determined toward the supreme good, it is exercised in electing, among all good actions in general, which particular acts they will perform. It is only exercised in choosing between the sovereign good and created good, by creatures who are still *in viâ*, whose wills are in an equilibrium or indifference toward all kinds of good, but not determined by necessity to any choice excepting the choice of good *in genere*, to which all are determined physically and necessarily by nature. This equilibrium can only exist in a creature which has a dim and imperfect perception of the supreme good, and is therefore able to turn itself toward it as its final end, or away from it to created good. Error in the will can only come from error in the understanding, or a false practical judgment, by which the finite and imperfect good is apprehended as an apparent supreme good, and the real good is put aside. This possibility of error is a defect, and hence the power of sinning is called by theologians *nævus libertatis*.* An intelligence which apprehends God as he is, is incapable of this error, and therefore impeccable. The moral probation of angels and men consists in being left

---

* "A blemish of liberty." Figuratively used in the later Latin, but literally signifying a mole or spot on the skin.

for a time in this imperfect and defective state, with a precept from God to choose the sovereign good, to which is annexed the promise of receiving as a reward the perfect knowledge of God, which will make them incapable of sinning and impart to them eternal beatitude. The only question is, whether God can leave a creature destined to supernatural beatitude as its final end in this state of defect and liability to error, and for what cause he does so. He can do it justly, because the possession of the sovereign good is not due to nature. The reason why he does so is because it is more glorious for God and the universe that the creature should act as concreative cause with God, in raising itself to beatitude. We cannot say that holiness and aptitude for glory demand *per se* that the creature should have the power of sinning ; for our Lord and the Blessed Virgin were impeccable. We cannot say that God cannot give glory without merit ; for Christ did not merit for himself the right to glory, and baptized infants do not receive it for any personal merit of their own. We cannot say that merit absolutely requires it ; for Christ and the Blessed Virgin merited without the power of sinning. But we can and do say, that the most full and complete exhibition of the principle of concreative causality and merit in the creature requires that some should be left to work themselves up by the use of their own liberty, from the state of defect to the state of perfection. The great chief of creation being God as well as man, ought to have, and must have, the right to beatitude as inherent in his Person. His Blessed Mother ought to have the right as inseparably joined to the grace which destined her to her high office; not as due to her nature, but as due to her own and her Son's dignity. The human will of Christ, and the will of Mary, could not therefore act as concreative cause with God, by raising themselves from a defective and peccable condition to the summit of being, since they were created on the summit. They glorified God in a higher order by concurring with those acts by which he communicates grace and glory to creatures. But God would also glorify himself and the universe, by exhibiting the principle of concreative causality and merit in a multitude of creatures of a great diversity of rank and grade concurring by their own free act to their own elevation. It is not necessary that all should do so, or that those who do should do it to an equal extent. Therefore God admits into heaven, as ornaments of the lower circles of the celestial sphere, a multitude of beings without personal merit, or with very little, who exhibit chiefly his gratuitous goodness and mercy. But the highest places are the reward of high merit, signal services, arduous labors, great sacrifices, difficult exploits, good works of a magnificent order; they have been gained at the risk of losing heaven; and with the actual loss of it, to a large proportion of those who originally were placed in the lists of trial and combat.

This is our solution of the problem: How is it consistent with the goodness of God to expose his creatures to the risk of forfeiting their eternal destiny, with the foreknowledge of its actual forfeiture by many? God left them to work out their destiny by their own free concurrence, as more glorious to themselves and to him, and the risk of sinning was incidental to this freedom. God chose to carry the creative act, not only to completion, but to the very apex of possibility, and to do it in the very highest and noblest way. There is nothing which brings a creature so near to God as the power of being concreative cause with him. God could not carry the act of creative love farther than he has done in the actual plan of the universe, including the Incarnation. Those who are excluded by their personal sins from sharing in this elevation of created nature in Christ, and have thus missed their glorification, were included in it by the purpose of God, and have excluded themselves by their own voluntary act. They are simply left in the place they have chosen, and receive the destiny they have created for themselves.

This solution is not our own private and personal discovery. We are speaking the thoughts of the greatest Catholic theologians and philosophers in all times, and giving the results of whole ages of study on these subjects. Although we have not borrowed the language of St. Augustine, and have enucleated his doctrine of liberty more perfectly than he himself was able to do, by the help of the later theology; yet, every one who has read attentively the extracts we have heretofore cited must see that we have been only working out his great principles. His doctrine of free-will and liberty is the key to the vindication of the moral order, and of the eternal retribution meted out to merit and demerit in the future life.

CHAPTER IV.

ST. AUGUSTINE'S DOCTRINE OF ORIGINAL SIN.

THE object of this chapter is to point out the great difficulty which the doctrine of original sin presents as taught by St. Augustine, and to suggest a solution, derived as far as possible from the principles laid down by the great doctor himself.

It is evident at first sight that the difficulty consists in the introduction of an element of sin and consequent misery into the universe, proceeding from the will of the creator, which the creature has not incurred by the exercise of his own liberty of will, and which therefore is to him inevitable. The exposition of the philosophy of St. Augustine made in the foregoing chapter has already developed principles absolutely contradictory to this notion. It has been proved that St. Augustine ascribes the origin of sin to the free-will of the creature. He does not account for the fall of Lucifer and Adam by referring to the decree of predestination or the merits of a grace *in se* infallibly efficacious. His doctrine of predestination and efficacious grace is not a pure metaphysical doctrine belonging to his theory of the universe and of the necessary influx of the divine will on the acts of the creature. It is a doctrine relating merely to the particular case of mankind after the fall. It will appear more clearly if we take the case of Adam singly and apart from his character as head of the human race. His creation, destination, probation, and fall are explained by St. Augustine in accordance with the general principles of his philosophy of the universe. He was created for eternal beatitude, endowed with liberty of will and sanctifying grace, placed on probation, that he might merit beatitude by his own acts, sinned by the abuse of his own liberty, and incurred the sentence of death in consequence of sin.

Having now voluntarily and justly forfeited his beatitude, God may leave him where he is, or he may save him by an act of grace. If he leaves him where he is, we have an illustration of the negative part of the decree of predestination, in which some are passed by in the grant of gratuitous grace. If he determines to save him, he gives him, according to St. Augustine, a grace which not only enables him to make a right choice by his free-will, but secures infallibly his choosing aright and persevering to the end. This illustrates predestination to eternal life and to grace efficacious *in se* as the necessary means to execute the decree. The absoluteness of the decree of predestination and the infallible efficacy of the grace are represented as a manifestation of the mercy of God for the sake of Christ, who has merited for the sinner more grace than was accorded in the state of justice by the mere goodness of the creator. If we take Eve into consideration, the illustration can be made more perfect. Suppose that God discloses to Adam and Eve his purpose to save one of them without specifying which one. He predestines Adam and passes by Eve. He grants to both sanctifying grace through some outward sign. Adam is kept from sinning by an efficacious grace, while Eve is left to sin by her own free-will, and dies without forgiveness. The question arises, How is this just? The reply is, Because God was bound to save neither one from the state in which they had placed themselves by their free and deliberate choice. The salvation of Adam is an act of pure grace, the damnation of Eve an act of simple justice. She had her probation once and failed in it. She must attribute her ruin to herself alone.

If we include, now, the whole human race in the same category with Adam, we shall have St. Augustine's way of arguing completely presented. He makes the case of every individual of the human race precisely as the case of Adam, precisely as if he himself were Adam. Let us take the most extreme case, which will bring out the explanation of St. Augustine into the clearest light and to the most searching test, and at the same time bring the difficulty contained in this explanation into an equally clear light. An infant dies without baptism. St. Augustine says: This infant is a sinner, and is, therefore, doomed to suffer the pains of hell for all eternity. You inquire, How could it be just for God to bring this infant into the world in the state of sin and then punish it for a sin which it could not avoid? St. Augustine replies: This infant sinned when Adam ate the forbidden fruit. God made mankind upright and free, with full liberty to choose between life and death. Mankind sinned in Adam by the abuse of free-will, and original sin with its penalty is the just punishment of this sin. You reply that this identification of the infant with Adam is precisely the difficulty. It is, we admit, just the Gordian knot. The whole difficulty regarding predestination and kindred doctrines in St. Augustine's theology is involved in this. Remove this identification of the individuals of the human race with Adam, and the general principles of St. Augustine's philosophy of the universe become at once as applicable to every unit of the human race in its fallen condition, as to Adam before he fell. St. Augustine does not discuss the question of predestination in any universal and purely metaphysical relation, and therefore we do not feel bound to do it. We leave it aside, therefore, except as it is involved in the exposition of original sin by St. Augustine. And as we have shown that the whole difficulty is concentred in the instance of a child dying in the state of original sin alone, the actual condition of its soul in relation to God and its future destiny; we will confine ourselves strictly to this point.

It is necessary, in the outset, to justify the statements already made concerning the doctrine of St. Augustine by citing his own words. In the first place, then, he lays down the doctrine of original sin as a dogma of Catholic faith, in general terms, in these words:

"I say this, that original sin, and its remission in the case of infants in the laver of redemption, is so manifest according to the sacred Scriptures, confirmed by such a great antiquity and authority of Catholic faith, and so perfectly made known by the clear manifestation of the church, that whatever opinion may be set forth by way of question or assertion by any person concerning the origin of the soul, if it be contrary to this doctrine, cannot be true."*

"Wherefore every one condemns and avoids both alike; who, according to the rule of Catholic faith, glorifies the creator for his good creation of the flesh and of the soul in men as they are born; (which the Manichæan will not do;) in such a sense that he nevertheless confesses that a Saviour is necessary for infants on account of the vice which has passed over to them through the sin of the first man; (which Pelagius will not do.")†

In the first of these passages we have a simple statement of the dogma of original sin, as held from the first by the Universal Church, which the deniers of this dogma will find it very difficult to impugn or evade. In the second, St. Augustine brings out his

* *Con. 2 Epist. Pelag.* iii. 26.   † *Ibid.* iv. 3.

own theological view of the doctrine as we have already explained it. While he shuns carefully the notion of a substantial and total corruption of nature, he nevertheless defines original sin to be a vice of nature, or congenital defect in the natural powers of man, transmitted from Adam ; and implies that this defect could not exist in him from the creative act of God. He then refers in this passage, as also in the first one, to the original act by which Adam was created, as including the creation of all men. He justifies the operation of God in creating man by reference to the original state of Adam, and by referring the present defect of nature to a sin committed. This is more clearly brought out in the following passage :

"The nature of man, truly, was primarily created blameless and without any vice ; but that nature of man with which every one is born of Adam, now needs a physician, because it is not sound. All the good things, indeed, which it has from its formation in life, in the senses, in the mind, it has from its creator and artificer, the Most High God. But the vice which darkens and weakens these natural goods, so that it has need of illumination and healing, was not contracted from the blameless artificer, but from original sin, *which was committed by free-will.*"*

This passage establishes the truth of what we have said above, that St. Augustine identifies all individual men with Adam in regard to the exercise of

---

* *De Nat. et Grat.* iii.

free-will in that primary state of probation in which human nature fell from original justice. He accounts for God's treating an infant who has committed no actual sin, as a sinner, by saying that he was created perfect, and fell by his own free-will. This is equivalent to the identification of the infant with Adam not merely in nature but in personality. The general scope of St. Augustine's writings bears out this interpretation, as we understand them. It explains and accounts for, in like manner, his well-known doctrine in regard to the eternal suffering of infants dying in original sin, from which he has received the name *durus pater infantium*. He maintained this opinion because he thought it a necessary consequence from the doctrine of original sin. In his mind there appeared to be the same dialectic connection between original sin and eternal suffering as between the sin of the individual committed with knowledge and deliberation and the same penalty. This could not be unless the infant who had committed no individual act constituting him a sinner, and whose original sin was the effect of the first sin of Adam, was in some way identified with Adam in his own person in the commission of that sin. If Adam and the infant merit the same punishment and for the same reason, on account of the same act; both must be regarded as having a share in the act. According to the philosophy which St. Augustine everywhere teaches, such an act is necessarily an act of free-will. But there can be no participation of the infant in an act of the free-will of Adam unless his will is identified with Adam's will. St. Augustine does not teach that the infant is punished for a sin forensically imputed to him, or that he suffers an eternal pain which is a mere disaster consequent on the fall of Adam, but that he suffers because he is really guilty of a transgression of the divine law. The following passages express clearly what St. Augustine teaches on this point.

Speaking of the exorcisms used in administering baptism, he says : " He is breathed upon indeed, but it is the devil *who holds the child as guilty by the contagion of sin*, that when he has been cast out, the child may be transferred to Christ. But if the child is not snatched from the power of darkness and remains in it, why should you wonder that he should be *with the devil in eternal fire*, who is not permitted to enter into the kingdom of God ?"*

The foregoing is a sample of some of his strongest passages, and we subjoin another, which shows how he was accustomed to modify and qualify his doctrine, in order to make it as lenient as he could, consistently with his theology :

" I do not say that infants dying without the baptism of Christ are chastised with such a great punishment that it would have been expedient for them rather not to have been born, since the Lord said this not of all sinners, but of the most criminal and impious. For, if, as he said of Sodom, without intending to be understood of it alone, one will be punished

---

* *Opus Imp. con. Julian.* iii. 199.

more tolerably than another in the day of judgment; who can doubt that unbaptized infants who have only original sin, and are not burdened with any of their own, will be in the lightest damnation of all? Although I cannot define what, of what nature, or of what intensity it will be, nevertheless I do not dare to say that it would be expedient for them rather to be nothing than to be in it."*

Once more he says: "When we approach the question of the punishment of infants, believe me, I am pressed by perplexities, nor can I at all find out what answer is to be given to it."†

We think the great difficulty is brought out now with sufficient distinctness, and we have aimed to place it in as clear a light, and to draw around it as dark and distinct an outline, as possible, for the sake of making the solution more intelligible. We shall endeavor to solve it, first, by showing how far St. Augustine himself furnishes the means of diminishing the difficulty, and then, by supplying what is defective in his theology from later theologians who have enucleated the subject more perfectly.

We begin by remarking that St. Augustine himself perceived and acknowledged the difficulty of making the doctrine of original sin completely intelligible. He never professes to be able to make a perfectly satisfactory statement of it, or to solve its difficulties. Although it occupied his mind intensely

---

* *Con. Julian. Pelag.* v. 44.
† *Con. Julian.* lib. v. c. 8 et *Epist.* 28 *ad Hier.*

to the last, he never came to any definite conclusions. We are not, therefore, to take that part of his theology relating to the doctrine which we have now under consideration, as a definite and finished philosophical system which he professes to prove scientifically. It is rather by way of hypothesis and conjecture that it is proposed. The identification of all human beings with Adam which we have pointed out as the real knot of the difficulty, is not a formal, metaphysical doctrine with him, but rather a confused and indistinct notion involved in his statements, and resulting from the lack of clear and precise conceptions. He perceived himself that the most puzzling part of the question lay precisely in this point. If the souls of all individual men are completely distinct existences, created singly and separately, how can they come into the world in a state of sin and under a sentence of eternal punishment, without making God the author of sin? How can sin be infused into an innocent soul, in consequence of the act of another and by means of corporeal generation? This question seemed to him so difficult of answering, that although his metaphysics inclined him strongly to believe in the distinct creation of individual souls, and he repeatedly said he should admit it as a truth if it could be reconciled with the dogma of original sin, he was never able to accept it decisively. It appeared to him that the dogma of original sin implied in some way the creation of all souls in the soul of Adam and their derivation from him. His mind was too acute, however, not to see the extreme difficulty contained in this theory, and the apparent impossibility of making it intelligible. He refused, therefore, to propound this theory in any definite and scientific form, and to the very last regarded a scientific solution of the problem involved in the question of the origin of the soul as a *desideratum* in theology. .

In his *Treatise on the Soul*, which is a sort of critique on a recent work of Vincent Victor, addressed to the monk Renatus, he says : " He attempts to solve that most difficult question concerning original sin, how it pertains to the body and soul, if the soul is not derived from the parents, but is inspired new, by God ; striving, therefore, to unravel this so vexatious and profound question : ' Justly,' he says, ' it regains, by the flesh, that ancient habit which it had appeared to have lost by the flesh a short time before, that it may begin to be regenerated by that by which it had deserved to be defiled.' You see at once that the man has ventured on a task above his strength, and thereby fallen down such a tremendous precipice as to say that the soul has merited to be defiled by the flesh ; when he cannot in any way tell whence it contracted this merit before assuming the flesh. For if from the flesh it begins to have the merit of sin, let him tell if he can whence before its sin it deserved to be defiled with the flesh. For it must have had this merit for which it was sent into sinful flesh to be defiled by it, either from itself, or, which is much more abhorrent, from God. From the flesh certainly it could not have the merit, before it had flesh, on account of which it was sent into the flesh to incur defilement. If, therefore, it had this merit from itself, how could it have it, when before having flesh it had done no evil? But if it is said to have had this merit from God, who can hear it, who can bear it, who can permit it to be said with impunity? For we are not in this place inquiring what it merited, that after taking flesh it should be judged worthy of condemnation; but what is merited before the flesh, that it should be so condemned as to be sent into the flesh to be defiled. Let him explain this if he can."*

"Why is (the soul) condemned to incur this sin, we ask, *if it is not derived from that one* which sinned in the first father of the human race? . . . How much better for him to preserve *my hesitation* concerning the origin of the soul, and not to venture to affirm that which he neither comprehends by human reason, nor defends by divine authority, lest he should be compelled to proclaim his foolishness because he is ashamed to confess his ignorance."†

"Wherefore I say also concerning my soul, that I know not how it came into my body, for I have not given it to myself; he who gave it knows whether he drew it from my father or created it new as he did for the first man. I also shall know if he teaches me, whensoever it shall please him. But now I am ignorant, and I am not ashamed, as that man is, to confess that I do not know that which I do not know."‡

---

* *De Animâ et Ejus Orig.* i. 6.   † *Ibid.* 16.   ‡ *Ibid.* 25.

In the course of this same treatise he calls this question, "*molestissima, periculossissima, scopulosissima*," "most vexatious, most dangerous, and full of breakers."

Writing to Oceanus concerning the same question, and referring to something which St. Jerome had written on it, he says : " If you have read anything from that source by which that question can be solved, or have heard anything from him orally, or the Lord has enabled you to learn it by your own thoughts, I beseech you to impart it to me, that I may give you abundant thanks."*

Again, writing to Optatus, he says :

" If you shall find what I have admonished you to seek, which, I confess, I have not yet found, defend it to the extent of your ability, and assert that the newness of the souls of infants is of that kind that they are not derived by any propagation ; and communicate to us with fraternal charity what you have discovered.

" But if you shall not find why or how the souls of infants become sinful, not having in themselves any malice by which they are compelled to receive from Adam the cause of their damnation, but that they are enclosed, new-made, and guiltless in sinful flesh ; still, do not let your assent be rashly drawn aside to another opinion, so as to believe that they are derived by propagation from that one soul ; *lest perhaps another may be able to discover that which you are not able to discover, or you may at some future time discover that which you cannot at present.*"†

* *Ep*. cl. xxx. † *Ep*. cxc.

One of the most curious and interesting passages on this subject in all St. Augustine's writings is found in his magnificent *Treatise on Free-Will*, written before Pelagius broached his heresy, and therefore better fitted to exhibit the spontaneous working of St. Augustine's own mind than his controversial works. In it he speculates in a very singular way on the manner in which a newly created soul becomes a partaker in Adam's sin, showing clearly how far the saint himself and the other theologians of his period were from any satisfactory solution of the question.

"If, then, one soul was made, from which are derived the souls of all men who are born, who can say that he did not sin when that first one sinned? But, if they are made singly in each one of those who are born, it is not a perversion; on the contrary, it appears most convenient and according to good order, that the evil merit of the preceding should be the nature of the one which follows. . . . But, if souls already existing in some secret place of God are sent to inspire and rule the bodies of each single individual who is born, they are deputed to this office, that by well regulating the body which is born of the penalty of sin, that is, the mortality of the first man, that is to say, by castigating it through the virtues and subjecting it to a well-ordered and legitimate servitude, they may obtain, in a fitting time and order, a place of celestial incorruption. . . . But, if souls constituted elsewhere are not sent by the Lord God, but come of their own accord to inhabit bodies; it is easy to see this, that whatever ignorance and difficulty may have followed their own choice, the creator is on no account to be blamed for this. . . . But of these four opinions concerning our souls, whether they come by propagation, or are made new in each of those who are born, or already existing elsewhere, are either divinely sent or spontaneously come into the bodies of those who are born, neither one ought to be rashly affirmed. *For either that question has not yet been evolved and made clear by Catholic interpreters of the divine books, as its obscurity and perplexity demand, or the treatises which are of this nature have not yet fallen into our hands."*

It is very plain that, so long as the dogma of original sin was left untouched, St. Augustine would not only tolerate but welcome any explanation of it which would render it more intelligible. He writes to Julian:

"Accuse my hesitation concerning the origin of souls, because I dare not teach or affirm what I am ignorant of; bring out yourself whatever you please from the profound obscurity of this matter; so long as that doctrine remains fixed and unshaken that the fault of that one is the death of all, and in him all had perished when the new Adam came to take and to save that which was lost."

The dogma is here stated, namely, that by the transgression of Adam his descendants are born in sin, which is the death of the soul, and only restored in Christ. This dogma has always been held by the Universal Church, and is maintained equally by every

* *De Lib. Arb.* iii. 5, 6, 59.

school of Catholic theology. It is thus defined by the Council of Trent: "If any one asserts . . . that Adam, when he was defiled by the sin of disobedience, transmitted only death and the pains of the body to the whole human race, *but not also sin which is the death of the soul;* let him be anathema." The nature of that sin or death of the soul is the matter to be explained and made intelligible, and if that is made intelligible the dogma itself is made so also.

All that has been said in explanation of St. Augustine's doctrine concerning the nature of evil comes in place here, to throw light on this question. Sin is not positive and substantial, but merely privative. It has not entity, but is a mere lack of entity. The sin of human nature which is derived from Adam does not make it evil in that which it retains, or make it cease to be good so far as it is nature, but deprives it of some excellence which it ought to have had. The death of the soul has also been already explained in his own words, as "another life, which, in comparison with the former life, is death." In this sin, or death of the soul, is included, as has been proved already, the incapacity of attaining to the proper and original destiny of the human race. The difficulties connected with the Calvinistic doctrine of total depravity having been all swept away, there remains only one to be met, the very one that occupied the mind of St. Augustine so intently. How can it be just to deprive a soul of the capacity to attain its true and proper destiny on account of the sin of its progenitor? There are some passages in one of his earliest works, the oft-cited *Treatise on Free-Will*, and also in his latest, the *Retractations*, which seem to anticipate the reasonings of later schools on this subject.

"Beatitude was not taken away from the first man by his condemnation in such a way as to deprive him also of fecundity. For even from his offspring, although carnal and mortal, something could be made which was in its own kind the glory and ornament of the earth. . . . For if one has commenced its existence in that state which the other reached after a culpable life, not only before sin, but even before having any life of its own, it possesses no small good for which to give thanks to its creator; because its very origin and beginning are better than any corporeal thing in its perfection."*

Here is the idea which will be later developed: that human nature, though fallen from the order of regeneration, remains capable of good in the order of genesis, or the cosmical order. And again:

"Even though ignorance and difficulty had been the natural, primordial condition of man; not even then would God be blamable, but praiseworthy."†

Here we have the idea that God might have created man at first such as he is now born. It is not inconsistent with the goodness and holiness of God to create such beings as infants now are, being born in original sin. For there is nothing evil in the nature of either soul or body. God might have made

---

* *De Lib. Arb.* iii. 56.   † *Retract.* i. 9.

Adam at first under the same conditions, and caused him to propagate by the original law of his being a posterity likewise subject to them. There still remains, however, the difficulty, how the existence of these conditions can be called truly and properly sin, or the death of the soul. And, although St. Augustine furnishes us with many principles from which we can solve the other difficulties of this question, and open the way to solve even this one, still we do not think that he was ever able to complete the task, or that it can be completed without rejecting a portion of his theory. The question perpetually recurs, How can an infant that perishes in the embryonic state, or before arriving at the use of reason, and which is therefore in a physical impossibility of performing any rational act, be condemned as a sinner and assigned to eternal punishment, on account of a defect transmitted from its first progenitor? And the answer is always the same, and always unintelligible and unsatisfactory, that this defect is voluntary, because it proceeds from the voluntary fault of Adam. It is thus stated by St. Augustine in his last work, the *Retractations*, in which he reviews and corrects all the works written during his long life:

"That which in infants is called original sin, while as yet they do not use the power of the will to choose, is not absurdly also called voluntary, because, having been contracted from that first evil will of man, it has become in a certain way hereditary. Therefore what I said is not false, *that sin is in such a sense a voluntary evil, that it is in no way sin unless it is voluntary.*"

Here is the obstacle to a solution of the difficulty involved in the doctrine of original sin, which St. Augustine never surmounted. If that obstacle is entirely insurmountable by reason, the difficulty must remain for ever unsolved. Were we attempting to solve it by any new theory of our own, we might lay ourselves open to the rebuke administered by St. Augustine to Vincent Victor, for undertaking a task above our strength. But we are not making any such attempt. We undertake merely to apply the results of the labors of the great Catholic theologians for fourteen centuries, who have discussed this subject to the very bottom, under the watchful eye of the same church whose decisions St. Augustine respected as final and decisive.

The fault of St. Augustine's statements, which renders them in part unintelligible, is to be found, as we view the matter, in the personal identification of Adam with the individuals of the human race, and the consequent confusion of original sin or the sin of human nature, with actual sin or the personal sin of the individual. Almost all the efforts of theologians who have discussed the doctrine of original sin since the time of St. Augustine, and more particularly since the time of St. Thomas, have been devoted to the enucleation of this part of the question. The rest of it was evolved in such a thorough and masterly manner by the great doctor himself, as to leave little else for his successors to do, than to select and arrange in an analytical and systematic order, the treasures of the rich philosophical strata of his genius. The discrimination of the relations between individuals and the race, relatively to the origin and destiny of man; and of the respective qualities and effects of the sin which attaches to human nature, and that which is the result of personal acts; was the task bequeathed by St. Augustine to future ages, and which has tasked the theological mind ever since. A great part of philosophy, also, is occupied with this same question in a wide application, namely, the relation between the genus or species and individuals. Scholastic opinions are variously modified with the variations of philosophical systems in different periods, countries, and individuals. Nevertheless, as all orthodox schools have the true and complete idea of which they are striving to gain a perfect reflective cognition and to make a perfectly intelligible statement, there is a substantial agreement among them. There is also, in spite of more or less diversity and defectiveness in the reflective conceptions of doctrine and in the use of language, a constant and perceptible advance in true theological science. This is true in regard to the particular question under discussion. And we shall endeavor to bring some of the light of science to bear on it, avoiding as much as possible to enter into the limits of particular schools, or to discuss technical questions.

All the individuals of the human race are identical with Adam in their nature; but this identity of nature does not include identity of will, which would imply personal identity. It is entirely irrelevant to the question of our personal responsibility for Adam's sin, whether our souls are created singly, or by common derivation through our parents from him. We are not responsible for any modification of our nature, as such, and irrespective of the free and intelligent judgments and volitions which we make in our individual and personal capacity. It is metaphysically impossible, therefore, that we should be responsible for Adam's sin, or for the injury it did to our nature.

We are not required to have contrition for it, and cannot have it if we would. It is in vain, then, to explain the existence of original sin in an infant by saying that he caused it by his voluntary act. It must be something entirely different from actual or personal sin, which is a voluntary transgression of the divine law. The individual human being when he incurs original sin is passive, when he commits actual sin is active. That is, in the second instance, he places himself in a certain state called sin; and is placed in that same state, in the first instance, by another. These two states differ, inasmuch as one is voluntary and the other involuntary in its cause; and are alike, in that both are strictly and properly denominated *sin*. It is essential, therefore, to understand the proper sense of the word *peccatum* or *sin*. In the widest sense *peccatum* signifies a defect of the perfection proper to any object. It is a maxim of philosophy, "*Bonum ex integrâ causâ, malum ex quovis defectû:*" "Good is from a cause that operates perfectly, evil from any defect." The perfection of an object consists in its complete possession of all the modes of existence necessary to enable it to attain its ultimate term. Its sin is its swerving from, or coming short of, this ultimate term. In its strictest sense it is confined to spiritual substances which are made to attain their ultimate term by a spontaneous movement. In this case sin is the failure of a spiritual being to make the spontaneous movement necessary to bring it to its ultimate term. Actively considered, this sin is a false cognition and a false volition, causing the intelligent creature to swerve from its due course and miss its mark. Passively considered, it is the inability to attain its ultimate term caused by this voluntary swerving away from it. In other words, sin, in the active sense, or actual sin, is something desired, spoken, or done contrary to the eternal law; or a voluntary transgression of a divine precept. Sin, in the passive sense, or habitual sin, is the state or condition caused by this voluntary transgression. For instance, a man in the state of grace commits a murder. This is an actual sin, that is, a voluntary transgression of the divine law. The act of sin is transient. It may not cause a habit of sin, in the sense of a predisposition to commit other murders. The individual may never commit, or wish to commit, another murder; yet he remains in the state of sin habitually unless restored to grace by supernatural means. This habitual sin is nothing else than a state of inaptitude for attaining eternal life, which is the ultimate term of man.

The actual sin which originally caused the human race to deflect from its proper ultimate term was the voluntary transgression of Adam, which was a personal and transient act, completed before his posterity had any distinct and individual existence. The sin in which we are born, which is the sin of the race, or of human nature, is not sin in the active sense, or actual sin, since it precedes all possibility of intelligent and free action on our part. It is, then, sin in the passive sense, or habitual sin, that is, a state of inaptitude for attaining eternal life, our proper ultimate term. It does not answer fully and completely to the definition of sin, unless the sin of Adam is included in it as its cause. The complete human race includes Adam as its head and root, and the position of human nature in the rational universe in relation to the ultimate end of creation must be considered in connection with the condition and destiny of the primordial man. If each human being were a distinct species by himself, as the angels are, separately and distinctly created, with a distinct and independent destiny of his own, and not united with a race in a common destiny and a common nature transmitted from a source common to all its individual members, original sin, or sin of the race, would be an impossibility. Whatever condition one was created in would be his normal condition, and, if that condition were precisely identical with the one in which we are now born, his natural incapacity to perform acts in a supernatural order could not be called a sin of his nature, or his liability to concupiscence, death, and perpetual exclusion from the sphere of regeneration, be called a punishment. The case is otherwise, however. The human race was created in Adam as its principle. His nature was the nature of all his posterity, his destiny was their destiny, and his grace, completing and elevating his nature in the supernatural order, was their grace; subject to the arbitration of his will as their head and sovereign, to be preserved or lost as a common inheritance by his determination. It is therefore strictly true that the whole human race sinned in Adam, and thereby incurred death and condemnation. That is to say, the sin of Adam caused the whole human race to swerve from its appointed destiny, and to be deprived of the gifts of grace and eternal life which were conditionally conferred upon it. Human nature was changed into something worse; that is, it was changed from a nature completed and elevated to the order of the supernatural by sanctifying grace, to a nature incomplete in its own order and destitute of sanctifying grace. In this condition it is transmitted by Adam to his posterity. The obligation of inheriting this condition of our nature is properly called a punishment, since it is the consequence of a violation of law on the part of the head of the human race. The condition itself is properly called the death of the soul, because it is a state of life relatively inferior to the former state of inchoate supernatural beatitude, including corporeal integrity and immortality. It is properly called original sin, because the individual child of Adam commences his separate personal existence in a state of degeneracy from his primitive archetype, and of incapacity to attain the ultimate term originally assigned to the human race.

There is no imputation of Adam's sin, no transmission of actual sin or personal guilt. These things are metaphysically inconceivable. No sane man ever did or could believe them. There is no change of human nature into anything intrinsically evil, or addition to it of any positively evil quality. If it is said to be fallen, changed, degenerate, stained, depraved, etc., these terms are not used absolutely but relatively to its former condition. If it is said to be under the anger of God, the object of his hatred, and subject to the devil, either in Scripture or ecclesiastical writings, it is meant that it is not the recipient of that supreme act of creative love which elevates a soul to grace and glory, and is confined to that cosmic sphere over which Satan has a certain jurisdiction. The little unbaptized infant is not a vile and hateful thing in the sight of God. It is merely disqualified for the beatitude of heaven. It is innocent, good, beautiful, admirable, a master-piece of creative wisdom, and loved by God. We will not discuss the question how far the dignity of human nature is lessened in the natural order by the effects of the fall. It is not necessary to do this. We see a vast difference between different races and different individuals in physical and mental perfection. It is enough that the essential type of humanity remains in all, even when most imperfectly developed. Human nature remains radically the same that it was in Adam when he was created. Whether he was elevated to the supernatural order simultaneously with his creation or subsequently to it, he was naturally as incapable of attaining the glorified state as the unbaptized infant is, and needed the grace of regeneration as much as it does. Sanctity is not a natural quality of any created being, but is always a superadded gift. Glory is not due to any created nature, as such, or otherwise its beatitude would be identical with its essence, and inseparable from it. The common language of theologians is, that sanctifying grace, which is initial beatitude, and has its completion in the state of glorification, elevates the creature "*super omnem naturam creatam atque creabilem:*" "above every nature which has been or could be created." There was, then, no injustice in the compact which God made with Adam by the terms of which the gratuitous gifts of grace and glory were to be transmitted by him to his posterity, if he proved faithful in the trial of his obedience, and to be withdrawn if he proved unfaithful. There would have been no injustice in the immediate infliction of the penalty of death, thus depriving his future posterity of existence in the natural order. Much less would it have been unjust to leave to the human race its existence in the order of genesis, without any hope of return to the order of regeneration. The grace of regeneration is a pure and simple boon from God to those who receive it, to which they have no claim. Those who miss of it, without any fault of their own, are not injured, for they are not deprived of a natural right, but of a gift of grace.

CHAPTER V.

FREEDOM OF WILL AFTER THE FALL, NECESSITY OF GRACE, PREDESTINATION.

THE first point to be considered is the freedom of the will after the fall.

The freedom of the will before the fall has been already established, and with it the principle that a rational creature cannot sin except by virtue of freedom. It has also been proved that original sin is not personal and actual sin. It follows from this, that a human being cannot commit actual sin, even in his fallen condition, without liberty. St. Augustine states this doctrine in the following passage :

" But who of us says that by the sin of the first man free-will perished from the human race ? Freedom perished, indeed, through sin, but it was that freedom which was possessed in paradise, of having a complete righteousness together with immortality ; on account of which human nature needs divine grace, as the Lord says : ' If the Son have made you free, then are ye free indeed,' that is, free to live well and justly. For free-will so far has not perished in the sinner, that by it they sin."*

What, then, was the Pelagian heresy on the subject of free-will?

It was, that man was created with a natural ability to do works meritorious of eternal life, and still retains that ability. The Catholic doctrine is that man was originally constituted with a supernatural ability to merit eternal life, which he lost by the fall. He is incapable of performing any good work in the supernatural order, until he is restored by the grace of the Redeemer. But he is capable of performing works morally good in the natural order, by his free-will, and of freely coöperating with grace, when it is given him.

The Council of Trent has defined that free-will was not destroyed by the fall:

"Si quis liberum hominis arbitrium post Adæ peccatum amissum et exstinctum esse dixerit; aut rem

---

* *Con. 2 Ep. Pelag.* i. 5. The author does not intend to assert that St. Augustine developed in a clear and satisfactory manner the liberty of the will in fallen man. It has been already stated that there is a certain confusion in his language respecting this point, and this confusion has been traced to his theological conception of original sin. What the author wishes to establish is, that St. Augustine clearly asserts that free-will is not extinct in fallen man, although he does not distinctly state all the conditions which are really necessary to the existence and exercise of this freedom. This has been done by subsequent theologians and later ecclesiastical decisions. This more explicit doctrine is, however, implicitly contained in St. Augustine's doctrinal statement that man still possesses free-will after the fall, and is in harmony with his more fully developed doctrine of free-will in man before the fall.

esse de solo titulo imo titulum sine re, figmentum denique a Satana invectum in ecclesiâ; anathema sit."

" If any one shall say that the free-will of man was lost and extinguished after the sin of Adam ; or that it is a thing existing only in name, yea, rather a name without any real thing, in fine, a figment brought into the church by Satan, let him be anathema."*

Also that free-will coöperates with the grace of God in justification :

" Si quis dixerit, liberum hominis arbitrium a Deo motum et excitatum, nihil cooperari assentiendo Deo excitanti atque vocanti quo ad obtinendam justificationis gratiam se disponat ac præparet ; neque posse dissentire, si velit, sed velut inanime quoddam nihil omnino agere, mereque passive se habere ; anathema sit."

" If any one shall say that the free-will of man, moved and excited by God, coöperates in nothing, by assenting to God, exciting and calling, by which it disposes and prepares itself for obtaining the grace of justification ; neither is able to dissent if it will, but, like something inanimate, does nothing at all, and remains merely passive ; let him be anathema."†

It follows from this that concupiscence, which is not a free act, but an involuntary passion, is not in itself sin. St. Augustine affirms this in the following passage:

" But concerning concupiscence of the flesh, I be-

---

* Sess. vi. can. 5, *De Justif.*   † Sess. vi. can. 4, *De Justif.*

lieve that those persons are either themselves deceived, or else they deceive; for it is necessary that even the baptized man, although he progresses with the utmost diligence and is led by the Spirit of God, should contend against it with a pious mind. Yet, although it is called sin, it is not called so because it is sin, but because it was made by sin; as in Scripture that is called the hand of a man which was made by his hand. But those things are sins which, according to the concupiscence of the flesh or ignorance, are done, said, or thought in an illicit manner."*

It would be a waste of time to prove that this doctrine, that the involuntary movements of concupiscence are not sin, until consented to by a deliberate act of the will, is taught in every text-book of moral theology, and every book of practical instruction, used in the Catholic Church.

It follows, also, that the works of those who have not the grace of regeneration, or faith, are not all, necessarily, mortal sins, but may be morally good, as the Council of Trent declares:

"Si quis dixerit, opera omnia quæ ante justificationem fiunt, quacumque ratione facta sint, vere esse peccata, vel odium Dei mereri, aut quanto vehementius quis nititur se disponere ad gratiam, tanto cum gravius peccare; anathema sit."

"If any one shall say that all works done before justification, in whatever way they are done, are

* *Con. 2 Ep. Pelag.* 27.

truly sin, or merit the hatred of God ; or that the more vehemently one strives to dispose himself to grace, so much the more grievously does he sin ; let him be anathema."*

Again : The odious doctrine of Calvin and Luther, that no man can keep the law of God, but that all, even the justified, necessarily commit mortal sins, is condemned by St. Augustine and the Catholic Church.

" God does not, therefore, command impossibilities, but in commanding he admonishes to do what you can, and to ask for what you cannot do.

" For perhaps they would complain justly, if no one of all men should become the conqueror of error and lust; but since he is everywhere present, who, through the creation which serves him as its Lord, in many ways, calls the man who is opposed to him, teaches the one who believes in him, consoles the one who hopes in him, exhorts the one who loves him, aids the one who strives, hears the one who prays ; it is not imputed to you for guilt that you are unwillingly ignorant, but that you neglect to seek that of which you are ignorant ; nor that you do not gather up your wounded members, but that you despise him, who is willing to heal them."†

This last passage explains beautifully the difficulty which lies in the Catholic doctrine.

The church undoubtedly teaches that man is unable to keep the supernatural law of God by his

---

* *De Justif.* can. 18.   † *De Nat. et Grat.* lib. xxxiii. c. xxi.

natural strength, and unable to keep the natural law even, with absolute perfection, for any great length of time, by unaided natural strength. Then God does give to man a law above his strength. But the reason is, because he is created for a supernatural destiny, and even the natural law is ordained in view of it. For attaining this supernatural destiny, appropriate graces are provided, and these graces reach even those who are in the condition of inchoate life. Thus the equilibrium is restored. There is an equality between the natural law and man, aided by the medicinal grace of the creator. And there is an equality between the supernatural law and man, elevated by regeneration and aided by actual graces.

In the chapter on baptism and penance, it will be proved that St. Augustine teaches that a Christian can keep the law so as to commit no grievous sin. This is an article of faith in the Catholic Church, as is proved by the following definition of the Council of Trent:

" Si quis dixerit, Dei præcepta homini etiam justificato, et sub gratiâ constituto, esse ad observandum impossibilia, anathema sit."

" If any man shall say that the commandments of God cannot be kept even by a man who is justified and constituted in grace, let him be anathema."*

The just man remains in the state of justification as long as he keeps this law, and loses justification the moment he falls into mortal sin. Consequently,

* *De Justif.* can. 18.

he is justified, that is, he preserves the state of a just man, by his good works, and by these good works merits eternal life. His continued acceptance before God, and his eternal beatitude, are the consequences of his keeping the commandments, and depend on it.

" Grace preceded your merit; grace is not from merit; but merit from grace. . . . Thou dost precede all merits, that thy gifts may produce my merits."*

" Sowing good works, reaping an eternal reward. The seeds, therefore, are our own, whatever good we have done ; and our sheaves are what we shall receive in the end."†

"But evidently when it has been given (grace) our merits also begin to be good, yet by means of it. But when the Pelagians say that the grace by which the sins of a man are forgiven is the only one which is not according to our merits ; but that what is given in the end, to wit, eternal life, is granted to our precedent merits ; we must answer them, if they would so understand our merits that they would also acknowledge that they are the gifts of God, their opinion would not be deserving of reprobation."‡

That is, the heresy of Pelagius consisted in ascribing to the principles of our nature the power of producing acts meritorious of eternal life. The doctrine of St. Augustine and of the Catholic Church is, that

---

* *Serm.* clxix., Philip iii.   † *Serm.* xxxi. in Ps. cxxv.
‡ *De Gratiâ et Lib. Arb.* xiii. xv.

nature, elevated by regeneration, and aided by actual grace, can produce such works. To quote once more the words of the great doctor :

"Therefore, most beloved, if our good life is nothing else than a grace of God, without doubt also eternal life, which is rendered-to a good life, is a grace of God."*

The greatest difficulty respecting the liberty of the will under the action of sanctifying and actual grace, arises from St. Augustine's doctrine of election, and grace efficacious *in se*. It is well known that he taught the doctrine, that God has chosen from among those who are justified by baptism in the church, a certain number, who are predestined to perseverance and eternal life, and who therefore receive a grace, infallibly efficacious in its own nature, by which their perseverance is secured, the rest being left destitute of this grace.

We leave Calvinists to make as much as they can out of this admission. Their heresy does not consist in simply maintaining the doctrine of predestination, and it is not on that doctrine that the church's condemnation of their system falls. They can maintain it without censure, in common with the Augustinian and Thomist schools, provided they will accept all the definitions of the church on other points.

We leave the liberal Christians also to make as many objections to the doctrine of St. Augustine on

---

* *De Gratiâ et Lib. Arb.* xx.

Studies in St. Augustine. 99

this head as they please, and to refute it, if they are able. For, as the church has not condemned it, so also she has not defined and imposed it. It was not taught by the early Greek fathers, and is disputed in modern times by a large school of theologians. Notwithstanding the most strenuous and persistent efforts of its advocates to obtain the sanction of the Holy See for their own doctrine of predestination and grace, and the condemnation of the opposite, the Holy See, after a long and mature examination of the question, has abstained from deciding it. It is left for the discussion of metaphysicians and theologians, and every one is at liberty to decide the question in his own mind, if he is capable of doing so ; to adopt the opinion of those writers for whose authority he has the greatest respect, or to dismiss the subject from his thoughts. It is very desirable, we allow, to discuss these questions thoroughly, and there are minds which will not be satisfied until they have found a solution which appears to them rational and consistent with the grand fundamental principles of philosophy and theology. We cannot, however, enter into this discussion, nor does our purpose require it. We are endeavoring to prove that, according to the Catholic system, the will retains its liberty under the action of grace. The eternal predetermination by God of all his acts, the necessity and efficacy of grace, and the liberty of the will, are all essential parts of the Christian idea, as expressed in the divine revelation. The difficulty consists in reconciling completely the different parts of the idea, and attaining a distinct reflective cognition of the relation between the act of the creator as first cause and of the creature as second cause. The mode of making the reconciliation differs in different schools. It cannot be made in such a perfect manner as to remove all obscurity from our conceptions. The difficulty itself is nothing else than the fundamental and ever-recurring perplexity that pervades all philosophy, how to explain the relation between the infinite creator and the finite creation. The difficulty lies in the mysteriousness of the creative act itself, which the human intellect, in its present state, cannot fully comprehend. Infidelity and heresy, which are constituted by the total or partial corruption of the Christian idea, deny some part of that which is clear in this mystery, on account of that which is obscure. They deny either something which is necessary to the conception of God as first and final cause, or something which is necessary to the conception of the rational creature as intelligent and free second and concreative cause. This last corruption of the perfect idea of Christianity is the essence of Calvinism and its cognate heresy Jansenism. They have taken the Augustinian doctrine of predestination and grace efficacious *in se* as their standing-point, and have drawn metaphysical deductions from them, which destroy the doctrine of liberty, and subvert the whole moral order. The Pelagians have done just the opposite. They have taken their standing-point on a philosophical doctrine respecting the liberty of the will, and have drawn deductions which destroy the supremacy of God as first cause, and subvert the whole order of grace. The Catholic theologian does not do this. His favorite point of view may be nearer to one side of the Catholic idea than to the other, and his philosophy takes its complexion from that fact. But he admits the opposite side of the idea also, and endeavors to conciliate his philosophy with it. This is just the difference between the Calvinist and the Catholic predestinarian. The first proposes his doctrine of predestination as an article of faith, and deduces from it consequences which are destructive of human liberty. The second does not and cannot propose his doctrine of predestination as an article of faith, he admits human liberty, and strives to reconcile his philosophy with it. The church gives expression to the idea, which she has always possessed and taught in its completeness, from time to time, in clearer and more definite terms, as the exigency of the case demands. The metaphysical explanation of the idea she usually leaves to the labor of human reason, without giving a positive sanction to or censuring any particular theory of explanation, unless there is danger of destroying or corrupting the idea. Thus the idea is preserved in its completeness; and the metaphysical reconciliation of its opposite points can be prosecuted with freedom, can be modified as new light is obtained, and is susceptible of progress. According to this Catholic method, St. Augustine and St. Thomas, while propounding their metaphysical theories of predestination and grace, distinctly assert that the action of the will under the impulse of grace remains free; the church defines the necessity of grace, and the liberty of the will, without giving any metaphysical reconciliation of the two; and we are left free to study the latter question scientifically.

We will endeavor to show this, now, by citing from St. Augustine some passages which prove that he held his doctrine of grace in connection with that of the liberty of the will, and by quoting the definitions by which the church has protected the latter doctrine from any false deductions which might be drawn from the former.

"If I should propose to you the question in what way God the Father draws to the Son men *whom he has left in free-will*, perchance you would solve it with difficulty. For how does he draw them, if he leaves them so that each one may choose what he will? And, nevertheless, each one is here taught, though few are able to penetrate this with the understanding."*

Nothing can be clearer or more pertinent than this passage. It clearly states both the necessity of grace, and the freedom of the will under the operation of grace. It recognizes the difficulty of reconciling the two, a difficulty which does not exist in the theory of Calvinists and Jansenists. For there is no difficulty whatever in understanding how the will may be free from mere external violence, and act spon-

---

* *Con. Petilianum*, ii. 84.

taneously and without reluctance in loving God or any created good, and yet be impelled by an inward necessity. It also recognizes the possibility of solving the difficulty, in such a way that the consistency of the two doctrines is intelligible to the understanding. All that has been heretofore quoted respecting the freedom of the will, from the book *De Libero Arbitrio*, is also pertinent in this place. It is not necessary to repeat these quotations. But, as some endeavor to shut out all reference to the earlier works of St. Augustine, on the ground that he changed his doctrine after the Pelagian controversy arose, it may be well to refute this allegation.

The last work of the saint was the *Retractations*, containing a general review of his writings, with explanations and corrections on those points which in his view needed them. In this book, he cites the strongest passages which are found in the book *De Libero Arbitrio*, disavowing the Pelagian sense which had been attributed to them, but retracting nothing. We may take them, therefore, as expressing his safest and most mature opinions, by virtue of this final ratification and sanction.

He says: "From these words of mine, and others of the same kind, because the grace of God was not mentioned, as we were not treating of it at that time, the Pelagians conclude, or can conclude, that we held their opinion. But vainly do they think so. It is the will, indeed, by which one both sins and lives rightly; which is the doctrine contained in this language of ours. But unless the will itself is liberated from the servitude by which it is made the servant of sin, and aided so that it may overcome the vices; mortal men cannot live rightly and piously."*

This is simply the Catholic doctrine as held universally: that the grace of God gives the faculty of performing supernatural works as distinct from works of natural virtue, and concurs by an actual operation with the free-will in eliciting those works.

These passages show sufficiently that St. Augustine regarded the will as retaining its freedom under the operation of grace.

The Council of Trent has defined this doctrine as of faith:

"Declarat præterea (sancta Synodus) ipsius justificationis exordium in adultis a Dei per Christum Jesum præveniente gratia sumendum esse, hoc est, ab ejus vocatione, qua, nullis eorum existentibus meritis, vocantur; ut, qui per peccata a Deo aversi erant, per ejus excitantem atque adjuvantem gratiam ad convertendum se ad suam ipsorum justificationem, eidem gratiæ libere assentiendo et cooperando disponantur: ita ut tangente Deo cor hominis per Spiritus Sancti illuminationem, neque homo ipse nihil omnino agat inspirationem illam recipiens; quippe qui illam abjicere potest, neque tamen sine gratia Dei movere se ad justitiam coram illo libera sua voluntate possit. Unde in Sacris Litteris, cum dicitur: convertimini ad me, et ego convertar ad vos, libertatis nostræ admonemur. Cum respondemus: Converte nos, Do-

---

* *Retract.* i. c. ix. § 4.

mine, ad te, et convertemur; Dei nos gratia præviniri confitemur."

"The holy Synod, moreover, declares that the beginning of justification itself in adults is to be ascribed to the prevenient grace of God, through Christ Jesus, that is, from his vocation, by which no merits of their own existing, they are called; so that they who by sins were averted from God, are disposed by his exciting and aiding grace to convert themselves to their own justification by freely assenting to and cooperating with the same grace, so that, God touching the heart of man by the illumination of the Holy Spirit, neither does man himself do nothing at all, receiving that inspiration; since he is able to reject it, nor on the other hand can he, without the grace of God, move himself to justice before him, by his own free-will. Whence, in the sacred writings, when it is said, Be converted to me and I will be converted to you, we are admonished of our liberty. When we answer, Convert us, O Lord, to thee, and we shall be converted; we confess that we are previously moved by the grace of God."*

The grace of God, according to the Council of Trent, can be rejected or accepted by the free-will of man. When one is called to justification, therefore, if he coöperates with the grace of God, and continues to do so unto the end, it is with full power to the contrary. There is no necessitating grace given to the elect, which takes away this power. If he re-

* *De Justif.* c. v.

jects the grace, or ceases after a time to coöperate with it, and continues impenitent to the end, it is also with full power to the contrary. The Council of Trent constantly asserts that a man who is justified can keep all the commandments of God. If he does this, he perseveres and is saved. If he breaks the commandments of God, it is by the abuse of his free-will that he does it, and not because he is deserted by the grace of God. This is clearly declared by the Council, in these words : " Deus namque suâ gratiâ semel justificatos non deserit, nisi ab eis prius deseratur." " For God by his grace does not desert those who are once justified, unless he is first deserted by them."* These are definitions binding on all Catholics, and declare the faith once delivered to the saints, which has been held in all ages. The speculations of the schools on the nature of predestination and efficacious grace are not thus binding, and have no authority beyond the authority of reason, which is precisely limited by the conclusiveness of the arguments by which they are supported.

We conceive now that we have done enough for our present purpose by establishing the fact that the liberty of the will is a dogma of Catholic faith, taught by St. Augustine and defined by the church, equally with the necessity of grace, and by vindicating the freedom of speculation on the mode of reconciling the two with each other. And this concludes this portion of our task.

* *De Justif.* c. xi.

Studies in St. Augustine.

We have proposed to show that St. Augustine's system of theology is not the Calvinistic system. That it is identical in its grand, fundamental principles with Catholic theology, as held and taught in the church of the present day. Moreover, that it contains the principles of a philosophy, by which we can remove some of the principal objections made against the Catholic faith, from grounds of human reason. And now we leave what we have written on this part of our subject to the consideration of all candid and truth-loving minds.

CHAPTER VI.

FAITH AND THE CATHOLIC CHURCH.

HAVING already discussed the relation of the doctrine of St. Augustine respecting the fall and its effects to the system of Calvinism, we proceed now to consider his teaching respecting the restoration of man, in reference to the same system, and that which is called Evangelical. We do not intend to include in this discussion the nature of the redemption by which man is restored, but simply the means by which it is applied, and the conditions of participating in it. The discussion of the subject of free-will has already anticipated this in part, but we will now take it up more formally.

One of the most fundamental points of difference between the *soi-disant* Evangelical system and Catholic theology is the nature of faith. Its absolute necessity is recognized by both. Both acknowledge the truth so frequently asserted by St. Paul, that we are justified by faith, and that "without faith it is impossible to please God." The Catholic Church de-

Studies in St. Augustine. 109

clares, in the Council of Trent, that faith is "the root of all justification." The Evangelical system asserts that faith alone justifies. But the latter understands by faith an illumination of the individual soul immediately produced by the Holy Spirit, by which it believes and appropriates the revelation made personally to itself in the Holy Scripture, of Christ as the Saviour. The former understands by faith, the firm belief of the truth which God has revealed and which the Catholic Church proposes. The one says, You must have a fiducial trust in Christ as your Saviour by his righteousness, which is imputed to you, and if you have this, the work of your salvation is completed. The other says, You must hold the Catholic faith as the first and indispensable condition of salvation, as the *sine quâ non* of justification, but faith alone will not save you, unless you have sanctifying grace, and by the aid of that grace and actual graces you keep the commandments of God. The one system does away entirely with the Catholic Church; the other presupposes its necessity. The one isolates the individual, making him his own centre of spiritual life; the other grants him no separate and individual life, except on the condition of receiving it from the common life of regenerate humanity which is incorporated in the church. However much certain classes of Protestants may modify the notion of faith, and connect with it the idea of holiness or virtue, they still keep to this principle of isolation and false independence of the individual. Even when they approach to the Catholic idea, and represent faith as a belief of certain objective truths embodied in what they call the Catholic faith, or the doctrine of the Catholic Church, they cannot escape from the original false principle of individualism with which they started at first. For their Catholic faith, or doctrine of the Catholic Church, is only a form of their own particular minds, or of a sect or party to which they belong, selecting from and interpreting the past records of Christianity according to a private standard of their own. They have no really existing living Catholic Church, whose supreme and final judgment gives the law to their belief. And hence they can never reach the complete Catholic idea of faith, as a belief in revealed truths, proposed to them by the Catholic Church, and received by a participation in her infallible judgment with unerring certainty on account of the infinite veracity of God. The practical difference between Catholics and all others, in relation to the nature and necessity of faith, is clearly defined and well understood by all. With us, the necessity of faith means the necessity of inwardly adhering to a distinctly defined and well-known body, specifically entitled, in the language of mankind, the Catholic Church. Objectively speaking, the Catholic faith is that complete body of doctrine which this communion requires us to believe and profess as the condition of belonging to her fold. The opposite of faith is heresy or infidelity, that is, adherence to some doctrine contrary to her own, either partially or in its totality. To have faith is tantamount to being, in the interior belief of the mind, a

Catholic. To lose faith is to cease to be a Catholic. Hence there is a precise and definite way of speaking among Catholics, in preaching, controversy, the teaching of children and of the faithful generally—and the instruction of converts—which is peculiar to ourselves, and is not nor can be adopted by any other religious body. It marks the perpetual presence of the idea of a living, visible, infallible church, always proposing with unerring authority the doctrine of Christ, and demanding for it the complete and unwavering assent of the mind, as the first and indispensable condition of receiving divine grace and the capacity of performing works which are meritorious in the order of salvation and eternal life. The presence or absence of this peculiar style of speech is a sure test of the presence or absence of the Catholic idea. One cannot speak or write, at large, and with freedom or sincerity, without betraying the theology which lies behind his forms of expression. The Catholic, Anglican, or Evangelical conception of Christianity breaks out as necessarily and unavoidably as the idiom and accent of different languages show themselves in the speech and writing of men of distinct nationalities.

There can be no question as to the style in which St. Augustine speaks on these topics. You recognize the Catholic doctor at every turn. No Anglican or Evangelical can adopt this language or interpret it in his own favor. A Catholic can recognize it, however, as the language to which he has always been accustomed. He argues, preaches, or writes familiarly in letters, just like a Catholic bishop or theologian of modern times. He speaks of the Catholic Church, the Catholic faith, councils, the Holy See, definitions of doctrine, the sin of heresy and schism, the necessity of being in the one true church, and a host of cognate ideas, as precisely and as much like a matter of course as Bossuet, Milner, Cardinal Wiseman, or Bishop England. He not only assumes, in the same way that Catholic bishops and priests now do, that he is always appealing in such matters to principles universally recognized by the faithful of his own communion, but even by those of separated bodies whom he is opposing. He reasons against the heretics of his own day, more as we should now reason with a Jansenist or a Greek, than according to the style of controversy with Protestants. That is to say, he reasons as with men who did not reject the Catholic principle itself, but who acted in inconsistency with it. We remember, on one occasion, many years ago, hearing a very distinguished and learned man, a leader of the new school of High Churchmen in the Protestant Episcopal Communion, express his regret that a young clergyman of Oxford was employed in the study and translation of the works of St. Jerome, for fear that the study of Jerome would make him a Papist. This little outbreak of the honest opinion of a man who was both deeply versed in patristic learning, and also a bitter antagonist of Rome, naturally made a somewhat singular and lasting impression on his auditor, whose mind was just opening to Catholic influences. The just inference from the remark must be that a candid and ingenuous mind would see the doctrine of the Roman Church in the works of St. Jerome and draw the conclusion that it was the doctrine of the Catholic Church in the fifth century. We cannot help thinking that the effect of studying the works of St. Jerome's contemporary and intimate friend, St. Augustine, ought to be the same. We will now produce some specimens which we believe will fully substantiate all we have asserted. The radical idea of faith is explained in the following words :

"Our faith, that is, the Catholic faith, separates the just from the unjust, not by the law of works, but by the very law of faith; because the just man 'lives by faith.' On account of this separation it happens that a man leading a life free from homicide, theft, false witness, and covetousness of his neighbor's goods, rendering due honor to his parents, chaste even to continence from marriage, most generous in almsgiving, most patient of injuries, who not only does not rob others, but does not even claim goods stolen from himself, or perhaps sells all his possessions to give them to the poor, keeping nothing for himself; if with these, in a certain sense praiseworthy, moral virtues, he does not hold a right and Catholic faith toward God, he will depart from this life to incur damnation. Another man, however, having indeed good works from a right faith which works by love, not, however, possessing an equal moral virtue, but in fact appearing to be inferior in morality to the other, on account of the right faith which he has toward God, departs from this world to be made free, and be admitted to the company of those who reign with Christ."*

This passage in the mouth of a modern Catholic preacher would raise an outcry; coming from the source it does, we may safely leave it to the good sense and candor of our readers to make the proper qualification of its meaning. It ought certainly to answer fully and by itself alone the purpose for which we cite it, namely, to show that justifying faith, in St. Augustine's mind, meant a right belief or a conformity to a certain defined standard of orthodox doctrine.

The next passage we shall cite answers a double purpose. First, it proves that St. Augustine did not hold the doctrine of justification by faith alone, against those who would make him out a Calvinist.

Secondly, it proves against those who would accuse him and the Catholic Church of teaching that a man is saved simply because he is a Catholic, without true sanctity and virtue, that we hold no such doctrine.

"But this I say to your charity, that although all bad Catholics hold in words that Christ is come in the flesh, in deeds they deny him. Do not therefore regard yourselves as being secure on account of your faith. Add to a correct faith a correct life."†

It appears that a modern Catholic preacher could not use language more precise and to the point, to express the doctrine which is held and taught in the

---

* *Con.* 2 *Ep. Pel.* iii. 14.   † *Serm.* 183, 1 Jno. iv.

Catholic Church in our own day, than this. First, you must be a Catholic; then you must be a good man. If you reject the Catholic faith, by your own fault, you cannot be saved. If you hold the Catholic faith and are a bad man, you will be lost. To hold the Catholic faith, to be a Catholic, designated in St. Augustine's day, as now, the profession of a distinct and well-defined doctrine, and such phrases were well understood by all persons of whatever church, sect, or religion they might be, without any need of explanation. We will illustrate what we have been saying by a few more citations:

"This is perfectly certain among all faithful Catholics, so that no one dissents from it except one who does not wish to be a Catholic."*

"I speak to those nurtured in the Catholic faith, or who have been gained over to Catholic peace."†

"Behold, by the aid of his mercy, we have the Spirit of Christ; from the very love of righteousness, from an integral faith, from a Catholic faith, we know that the Spirit of God is with us."‡

"There are some things in regard to which the most learned and excellent defenders of the Catholic rule at times differ with each other, without infringing on the substance of faith, and one speaks better and more truly than another concerning the same matter. But this of which we are now treating belongs to the very foundations of faith."§

---

* *Serm.* 161, in Philipp. iii.   † *Serm.* 174, in 1 Tim. i.
‡ *Serm.* 155, *in Verb. Apost.*   § *Con. Julian.* i. xxii.

We will now cite a class of passages of the same general tenor with the foregoing, in which the character and notes of the Catholic Church ; whose teaching furnishes the standard of Catholic faith, and by membership in which a man is constituted a Catholic ; are more clearly exhibited :

"Therefore believing the divine Trinity and the triple Unity, beware, my beloved, lest any one seduce you from the faith and unity of the Catholic Church. *'For whoever shall preach the gospel to you otherwise than as you have received it, let him be anathema.'* You see without doubt, my dearest brethren, even in the very words of the holy Creed, how at the conclusion of all those articles which pertain to the sacrament of faith a certain supplement is added in these words, '*Per sanctam ecclesiam.*' Fly therefore as much as possible these diverse and various deceivers, whose sects and names it were too long to mention, so great is their multitude. For we have many things to say to you, but you cannot bear them now. One thing I recommend to your prayers, that you turn your mind and eyes entirely away from a man who is not a Catholic, so that you may be able to attain to the remission of sins, the resurrection of the body, and the life everlasting, through the one true and 'Holy Catholic Church.'"*

"'*But you shall receive the power of the Holy Ghost coming upon you, and you shall be witnesses to me.*' Where ? '*In Jerusalem.*' It followed from what

---

* *Serm.* 215, *in Symb.*

went before that we should hear this said, for in these words the church is proclaimed, the church is commended, unity is announced, division is accused. It was said to the apostles, 'You shall be witnesses to me.' Where? In Jerusalem, where I was slain, '*and in all Judea, and Samaria, and even to the ends of the earth.*' Behold what that is which you hear, and hold it fast. Be the spouse, and await in security the Bridegroom. The spouse is the church. Where was it proclaimed that she was to be? For many will say, Behold, she is here. I should hear if another did not also say, Behold, she is here. What do you say? Behold, she is here. I was just going, but another recalls me with a similar exclamation, Behold, she is here. You, on one side, say, Behold, she is here; another, on the other side, says, Behold, she is here. Let us ask the Lord, let us appeal to the Lord. Let the parts be silent, let us hear the whole. One says from one corner, Behold, she is here; another says from another corner, No; but, behold, she is here. Do thou, O Lord! speak, and declare which thou hast redeemed, show which thou hast loved. We are invited to thy nuptials; show us thy spouse, lest we disturb thy vows by our litigation. He speaks plainly, he shows us plainly; he does not abandon those who are seeking. He does not love the contention. He says it to his disciples, and he says it to them even when they had not asked him, because he opposes those who contend. It may be that the reason why he was not interrogated on this subject by the apostles was, because the flock of

Christ was not yet divided by robbers. We, who have experienced the miseries of division, seek earnestly the bond of unity. The apostles inquire after the time of the judgment, and the Lord answers them about the place of the church. He does not answer their inquiries, but he foresees our afflictions. 'You shall be,' he says, 'witnesses in Jerusalem.' This is but little. Thou hast not paid so great a price to purchase that place alone. 'In Jerusalem.' Say yet more, 'And even to the ends of the earth.' You have come to the boundaries of earth, why do you not make an end of contention? Let not any say to me any more, Behold, she is here—No; behold, she is here. Let human presumption be silent, let the divine preaching be heard, let the true promise be held fast."*

"After the commendation of the Trinity, follows the Holy Church. God is manifested, and his temple —'For the temple of God is holy,' says the apostle, 'which temple ye are.' This is the holy church, the one church, the true church, the Catholic Church, fighting against all heresies; she can engage in warfare, but she cannot be overcome in it. All heresies have gone out from her, like useless branches cut off from a vine; but she remains in her root, in her vine, in her charity. The gates of hell shall not overcome her."†

"The Christian religion must be held by us, and the communion of that church which is Catholic, and

---

* *Serm.* 265, *in Ascens. Dom.* † *Serm.* 1, *De Symb.*

is called Catholic, not only by its own members, but also by all its enemies. For, whether they will or no, the very heretics themselves and the offspring of schisms, when they talk not with their own friends, but with people outside, call the Catholic Church nothing else but Catholic. For they cannot be understood unless they designate her by that name by which she is denominated by the whole world."*

"Perhaps you may perceive, as I know you are a man of no little discernment, how lamentable it is that we, who are brethren according to the flesh, do not live in one fellowship in the body of Christ, especially since it is easy for you to consider and see the city set upon a hill, of which the Lord says, in the gospel, that it cannot be hid. For this is the Catholic Church, whence in Greek it is called καθολικη, which is diffused through the whole orb of the earth. It is not possible for any one to be ignorant of her; therefore, according to the word of our Lord Jesus Christ, she cannot be hid."†

"It happens sometimes that in the human body some member is cut off from the body, as a hand, a finger, or a foot: does the soul follow the amputated part? While it was in the body it was living, when it is cut off it loses life. So the Christian man is a Catholic while he lives in the body; being cut off, he becomes a heretic, and the spirit does not follow the amputated member. If therefore you wish to live by

---

* *De Ver. Rel.* v. 2.   † *Ep.* 52 *ad Severin.*

the Holy Ghost, preserve charity, love the truth, desire unity, that so you may attain to eternity."*

The authority of the church to define doctrine, clearly implied in all the foregoing passages, is more distinctly stated in the following:

"But because the blessed Ambrose, as a Catholic bishop, said those things according to the Catholic faith, it follows that Pelagius, who had deviated from this way of faith, with Cœlestius his disciple, was deservedly condemned *by the authority of the Catholic Church*."†

"The authority of Catholic councils, and of the Apostolic See, most justly condemned the new Pelagian heretics."‡

The famous declaration, " I would not believe the Gospel, unless the authority of the Catholic Church moved me to do so,"§ sums up the whole doctrine of St. Augustine. Prof. Reuss, of the Protestant faculty at Strasburg University, in his recent work on the *Canon*, thus comments on this passage :

" Ses principes aboutissent à ce mot fameux, diamétralement opposé à la base de toute théologie protestante, ' Je ne croirais pas l'Evangile si l'Eglise Catholique ne m'en garantissait l'authenticité.'" (P. 169.)

" Il est fort curieux de voir la peine que se donnent tous les théologiens protestants, Calvin en tête, pour interpréter de manière à la rendre inoffensive cette déclaration d'un auteur dans la dépendance du quel

---

* *Serm.* 265, *De Ascens. Dom.* † *De Peccat. Orig.* ii. 68.
‡ *De Animâ*, ii. 17. § *Con. Epist. Manich.* i. 6.

ils se trouvaient beaucoup plus qu'ils ne l'osaient avouer." (P. 247.)

"St. Augustine's principles come to their result in the famous saying, diametrically opposed to the fundamental principle of all Protestant theology, 'I would not believe the Gospel, if the Catholic Church did not guarantee to me its authenticity.'"

"It is very curious to see what trouble all Protestant theologians, Calvin at their head, give themselves to interpret, in an inoffensive manner, this declaration of an author on whom they are much more dependent than they dare to acknowledge."

Once more: St. Augustine, reasoning on the moral power and dignity of the Catholic Church, as manifested in its effects, draws this conclusion:

"When, therefore, we see such a remarkable assistance of God, and such great fruits and advantages resulting, shall we hesitate to hide ourselves in the bosom of that church which has obtained the summit of authority, even by the confession of the human race, by the succession of bishops from the Apostolic See, while heretics bark around her in vain, and are condemned, partly by the judgment of the people themselves, partly also by the majesty of miracles? To be unwilling to give the first place to this church is a mark either of the highest impiety or of a headlong arrogance. For, if there is no certain way to wisdom and salvation for souls, unless when faith predisposes them for the exercise of reason, what else is it but ingratitude for the divine help and assistance to wish to resist an authority established with such great labor? And if every species of discipline, however common or easy, requires a teacher or master in order to be acquired, what is a more complete evidence of daring pride than to refuse to learn the books of the divine mysteries from their interpreters, and to be determined to condemn them while they are unknown? Wherefore, if either reason or our entreaty has any influence over you, and if, as I believe, you have a true regard for your own welfare, I desire that you take my advice, and commit yourself to the care of good teachers of Catholic Christianity, with a pious faith, a lively hope, and a simple charity."*

The same thoughts are still more forcibly and distinctly expressed in the following passages, which are in the immediate context of the celebrated dictum, *Non crederem Evangelio*, etc., just now cited:

"For in the Catholic Church, that I may omit that most pure wisdom to the knowledge of which only a few spiritual persons attain in this life, and which they know without any doubt, although in an extremely small degree, on account of their human condition; for the rest of the multitude, not quickness of intelligence, but simplicity of faith renders perfectly safe; that I may therefore omit this wisdom, which you do not believe to exist in the Catholic Church; there are many other things which most justly detain me in her bosom. The consent of peoples and nations detains me; the authority which was initiated by

* *De Utilitate Credendi*, i. 35, 36.

miracles, nurtured by hope, augmented by charity, confirmed by antiquity, detains me ; the succession of priests even to the present episcopate, from the very see of the apostle Peter, to whom the Lord committed his sheep to be fed, after his resurrection, detains me; finally, the very name of Catholic detains me, which that church has alone, and not without cause, obtained among so many heretics, in such a way that, while all heretics wish to be called Catholics, nevertheless not one of the heretics will dare to point out his own basilica or house to a stranger inquiring for a place of Catholic worship. Therefore, these most dear bonds of the Christian name, which are both so numerous and so powerful, justly retain the believing man in the Catholic Church, even if, on account of the dulness of our intelligence or the demerit of our life, the truth does not yet manifest itself with perfect clearness. But with you, where there is not one of these things to invite and retain me, the bare promise of truth resounds ; which, indeed, if it is so manifestly shown that it cannot be called in question, is to be preferred to all those things by which I am held in the Catholic Church; but if it is only promised and not exhibited, no one shall move me from that faith which binds my mind by so many and such strong bonds to the Christian religion.

" Therefore, let us see what Manichæus teaches me, and especially let us consider that book which you call the Epistle of the Foundation, where almost the whole of what you believe is contained. For, when that was read to us in the time of our misery, we were called by you enlightened.

"'Manichæus, the apostle of Jesus Christ, by the providence of God the Father.' These are salutary words from the perennial and living fountain. Now attend, if you please, with good patience, to what I shall ask. I do not believe that he was the apostle of Christ. Do not get angry, I beg of you, and begin to utter maledictions; for you know that I have determined to believe nothing rashly that you assert. Therefore I ask, Who is this Manichæus? You will answer, The apostle of Christ. I do not believe you; and now you will not have anything that you can say or do; for you promised me the science of truth, and now you compel me to believe something which I do not know. Perhaps you will read the gospel to me, and from thence you will try to assert the person of Manichæus. If, therefore, you should find some one who does not yet believe the gospel, what would you do when he says to you, I do not believe? Now, I would not believe the gospel unless the authority of the Catholic Church moved me. Wherefore, why should I not submit to those who say to me, Do not believe the Manichæans, when I have submitted to the same, saying, Believe the gospel? Choose which you will. If you say, Do not believe the Catholics, you cannot rightly compel me to the faith of Manichæus by the gospel, because I have believed this very gospel on the preaching of the Catholics. But if you say, You have rightly believed the Catholics praising the gospel, but you have not rightly believed them vituperating Manichæus, do you think I am so extremely foolish that, without any reason being given, I will believe what you wish, and not believe what you do not wish me to? I shall act much more justly and cautiously if, when I have once believed the Catholics, I do not pass over to you; unless, instead of commanding me to believe, you make me to know something more manifestly and clearly. Therefore, if you are going to give me reasoning, lay aside the gospel. But if you hold on to the gospel, I will hold on to those by whose command I have believed the gospel, and at their command I will not believe you at all. If by chance, however, you can find something very plain concerning the apostolate of Manichæus, you will weaken for me the authority of the Catholics, who command me not to believe you; and this being weakened, I shall no longer be able to believe the gospel, because I have believed it through them; so that nothing whatever that you can adduce from it will have any force with me. Wherefore, if there is nothing manifest concerning the apostolate of Manichæus found in the gospel, I will rather believe the Catholics than you. But, if you can read anything there which is plainly for Manichæus, I will neither believe them nor you; not them, because they have lied to me about you; not you, because you offer to me that Scripture in which I had believed through those who have lied to me. But far be it from me not to believe the gospel. For, believing in it, I do not find how I can also believe in you. For the names of the apostles which are there read do not contain among them the name of Manichæus. And who succeeded in the place of the betrayer of Christ, we read in the Acts of the Apostles, which book it is necessary for me to believe, if I believe the gospel, because Catholic authority equally commends to me either Scripture."*

Let the names of Luther and Calvin be substituted for that of Manichæus in the foregoing passage, and it becomes at once an argument against Protestantism. Few, if any, who peruse it carefully, will deny that the statement of Prof. Reuss, cited above, is fully sustained by it.

"Since these things are so, you perceive at once that episcopal councils, and the Apostolic See, and the whole Roman Church, and the Roman Empire, which, by the favor of God, is Christian, were most justly moved against the authors of such an abominable error."†

"What does the ungrateful man say to those things, whom the Apostolic See, with the most benign lenity, had spared as one who professed himself to be already amended?"‡

Speaking of a bishop who was condemned by a Donatist council, he says :

"He had no need to care for the multitude of the enemies who conspired against him, when he saw that he was joined by letters and by communion both to the Roman Church, *in which the principality of the*

---

* *Con. Epist. Manich.* i. 5, 6.   † *De Pecc. Orig.* ii. 18.
‡ *Con.* 2 *Epist. Pelag.* ii. 7.

Studies in St. Augustine. 127

Apostolic See has always flourished, and to other countries from which the Gospel came to Africa itself."*

"In regard to this matter, two councils have been sent to the Apostolic See, and rescripts have come from there. The cause is finished: would that the error might at last be finished."†

If our design admitted of giving a complete history of St. Augustine's controversies with the Donatists, with an analysis of his arguments against them, supported by copious extracts, the doctrine of the strict corporate unity of the Catholic Church centred in the See of Rome, would appear in the most conclusive manner. This argument has, however, been often drawn out in the controversy with that party in the Anglican Church who set up a claim of abstract Catholicity and unity, against the concrete, living unity of the Roman Church. We prefer, therefore, to leave the passages we have cited to produce their own impression on the minds of candid and truth-loving readers, without going into a more minute and complete discussion of this matter, which is foreign from our main purpose.

* *Ep.* 43, *Glorio et cet.*   † *Serm.* 131, *De Verbo Dei.*

CHAPTER VII.

BAPTISMAL REGENERATION.

THE doctrine of baptism is one in regard to which a fundamental and irreconcilable difference exists between Catholics and Protestants of the Lutheran and Calvinistic stamp. Not only this, but as we shall see elsewhere, the entire system of theology is affected by it. Happily, St. Augustine has not left us in any doubt as to his own doctrine on this subject, having treated of it very frequently, and very plainly and copiously ; which he was naturally led to do by his incessant controversy with the Pelagians respecting original sin. Let us then, without further preamble, inquire what St. Augustine's doctrine is, as set forth in his own words. In doing this, the only difficulty is to know what to select and what to pass by in such a wealth of materials. The ensuing citations are the first that presented themselves, in an examination of only a small portion of the works of the great doctor.

In one of his sermons, he speaks quite incidentally and as a well-understood fact, of the complete remission of sins in baptism :

"For whatever past sins, that concupiscence of the flesh wrought in us, whether by actions, by words, or by thoughts; all has been effaced by holy baptism, one indulgence has obliterated all debts."*

In another sermon he proves against the Pelagians that infants need salvation by the fact that they are baptized and made partakers of the grace of Christ, which on the other supposition they would not need :

"He who says that the age of infancy has nothing in it for Jesus to save, denies that Christ is Jesus in respect to all faithful infants. I repeat it, he who says that the age of infancy has nothing in it for Jesus to save, says nothing less than this, that Christ the Lord is not Jesus in respect to faithful infants, that is, infants baptized in Christ. For what is Jesus? Jesus signifies Saviour. Jesus is our Saviour. He is not Jesus to those whom he does not save, because they have nothing in them which requires him to save them. Now, if your heart can tolerate the thought that Christ is not Jesus to any who have been baptized, I do not know whether your faith can be acknowledged as according to the sound rule."†

In the same sermon, he thus forcibly expresses the doctrine that an infant, born in original sin, is trans-

---

* *Serm.* 155, *De Verb. Apost.*   † *Serm.* 174, in 1 Tim. i.

ferred from Adam to Christ, and regenerated, by the sacrament of baptism :

"That poisoner wounded the entire mass of the human race in the first man; and no one can pass from the first to the second man, except by the sacrament of baptism. In infants who are born, but not yet baptized, Adam may be recognized; and Christ may be recognized in infants who are born and baptized, and therefore born again. . . . You, that you might not die eternally, have been born, and have been regenerated; he (your unbaptized infant) has already been born, but has not yet been regenerated. If you live because you have been regenerated, permit that he also may be regenerated and live. Suffer him, I say, to be regenerated, suffer him to be regenerated. Why do you contradict? Why do you try to break down the ancient rule of faith by new disputations?"

In the following passage he describes the eagerness with which Catholic mothers, then as now, hastened the baptism of infants, on account of their belief that they were cleansed from original sin by the sacrament:

"Behold, I see the Mother Church, bearing testimony by her very breasts. Mothers run with their little children and present them to the Saviour to be saved, not to Pelagius to be damned. Any woman who has become a mother, moved by piety, will run with her infant child, exclaiming, Let him be baptized, that he may be saved."*

* *Serm.* 184, in 1 Joann. iv.

Addressing the catechumens who were to be baptized, he says:

"Behold, you are about to approach the holy font, where you will be washed in baptism; you will be renewed by the saving laver of regeneration; and ascending from that laver you will be without any sin. All those past sins which were poisoning you will be there destroyed. Your sins will be like the Egyptians who pursued the Israelites, but who pursued them only to the Red Sea. . . . Therefore, baptism, that is, the water in which you will be dipped, and, as it were, pass over the Red Sea, is signed with the sign of Christ. Your enemies are your sins. They follow you, but only to the sea. When you shall have entered in and escaped, they will be destroyed, as the Egyptians were covered by the waters while the Israelites marched over on dry ground. And what says the Scripture? *Not one of them remained.* You have committed many sins, you have committed few sins; you have committed great sins, you have committed little sins; the least of them all has not remained."*

On another similar occasion he thus addresses the neophytes:

"Not to delay, since we have many things to do, a brief but solemn charge must be given to those who have been regenerated in baptism and to-day are to be mingled with the people. . . . You are called infants, because you are regenerate, and have entered

* *Serm.* 213. *in Symb.*

on a new life, and have been born again to life eternal, if you do not suffocate that which has been born again to you, by evil living."*

The following passages are taken from two sermons preached against the Pelagians:

"I inquire now in regard to an infant, who is brought to the church to be baptized and made a Christian, in order, as I suppose, that he may be made one of the people of Jesus, of what Jesus? 'Of him *who saves his people from their sins.*' If he has nothing in him that makes him need to be saved, let him be taken hence. . . . Do we institute another baptism for infants, in which there is no remission of sins? Evidently, if that little one could speak for himself, he would refute the words of the adversary, and cry out: Give me the life of Christ; I am dead in Adam, give me the life of Christ; '*In whose sight not even the infant is pure, whose life on the earth is but of one day.*' . . . We evidently ought not to dispute in so great a danger of these infants, lest by disputing we should seem to defer their salvation. Let him be brought forward, let him be washed, let him be liberated, let him be made alive."†

"On the Feast of St. John, our discourse led us to speak, among other things, of the baptism of infants; and because it was already long, and we were obliged therefore to think about bringing it to a close, we did not say as much respecting this important subject as our anxiety would demand of us at such a perilous

---

* *Serm.* 270, *in Oct. Pasch.*   † *Serm.* 293, *in Natal. S. Joann. B.*

time. Our anxiety arises not from the doctrine long ago founded on the highest authority in the Catholic Church, but from the disputations of certain persons, which threaten to gain ground and to overturn the minds of a large number. Therefore to-day, with the Lord's assistance, we have determined to speak to this point. . . .

"They concede that infants ought to be baptized. The question therefore between us and them is not, whether infants should be baptized, but concerning the reason why infants are to be baptized. . . . We say that they cannot otherwise have salvation and life eternal unless they are baptized in Christ; but they say, it is not for salvation or eternal life, but for the kingdom of heaven. . . . Bring forward, therefore, your authority, and we will stand by it together against our common adversary. For, that an unbaptized infant cannot enter into the kingdom of heaven, both you say and I, let us therefore both resist our common adversary, who says that an unbaptized infant can enter into the kingdom of heaven, and let us hold up the shield of faith against his most insidious weapons. . . . We will both say to this man, Are you a Christian? I am, he replies. Hear the gospel, you who would send unbaptized infants into the kingdom of heaven; hear the gospel: '*Unless a man be born of water and of the Holy Ghost, he cannot enter into the kingdom of heaven.*' . . . Tell me, I beseech you, does Christ profit anything or not to unbaptized infants? He is compelled to say that he does profit them, for he is pressed by the weight of Mother Church. . . . If these persons said that Christ does not profit anything to baptized infants, this would be saying nothing else than that the baptism of infants is superfluous. Since, however, they do not dare to say that their baptism is superfluous, they acknowledge that Christ does profit baptized infants. . . . But God forbid that I should say that infants are not believers. I have already in a former part argued that he who has sinned in another believes also in another. It is said by some one he believes, and it avails, and he is reckoned among the baptized faithful. So much the authority of Mother Church effects, so far the established canon of truth prevails; whoever tries his strength against this, or butts himself against this impregnable wall, will be himself broken. Therefore, Christ profits something to baptized infants; and as I speak, so also the whole church says with me: He profits the believing; he profits the faithful. Choose now whichever side you will. . . . But some one says, Saints ought to be born of saints; as says the apostle, '*Otherwise would your children be unclean, but now are they holy.*' How do you take that? In what way do you understand that a child born of faithful parents is in such a sense holy that he ought not to be baptized? Tell us, if you please, how you can explain that kind of sanctity? For there are many kinds of sanctity, and many kinds of sanctification. Not everything that is sanctified is sent to the kingdom of God. The apostle says of our food: '*It is sanctified by the word of God and prayer.*' Although our food is sanctified, do we not know where it goes? Learn, therefore, that there is a certain kind, so to speak, a sort of shadow of sanctification, which does not suffice to salvation. There is a difference, and what that difference is is known to God. Nevertheless they run with the child of faithful persons to baptism; for the parents do not entertain the erroneous opinion that he has been born faithful. That he has been born they can say; but not that he has been born again. That you may understand now in what sense the children of the faithful are sanctified, without inquiring into the mode of this sanctification at too great length, take the case of an infidel husband who has a believing wife. The apostle says: '*The unbelieving husband is sanctified by the wife, the unbelieving wife by the brother.*' Now, although there may be in that case a certain kind of sanctification by which the unbelieving husband is sanctified through his believing wife, ought he, therefore, to take security to himself that he shall enter into the kingdom of heaven, though not baptized, not regenerated, not redeemed by the blood of Christ? Therefore, just as the unbelieving husband is sanctified by his wife, and nevertheless perishes unless he is baptized, so the children of the faithful, even if they are in a certain sense sanctified, nevertheless perish, if they are not baptized.

"I beg your indulgence, now, for a short time longer. I am merely going to read a little. It is St. Cyprian, an ancient bishop of this see, that I hold in my hand. Listen a little to what he thought and the church has ever shown that she thinks concerning the baptism of infants. It is of little moment what these persons say, disputing of I know not what impious novelties, and trying to accuse us, as if we said something novel. For this purpose, therefore, I read St. Cyprian, that you may see how the canonical and Catholic sense of those words which I have just been treating of is to be understood. He was asked whether an infant ought to be baptized before the eighth ; because in the old law it was not lawful to circumcise an infant except on the eighth day. From this a question had arisen about the day for baptizing ; for there was no question concerning the origin of sin ; and therefore the question which had arisen was decided by that in regard to which there was no question. Among other things which occur previously to that which I am about to read, St. Cyprian said what follows : ' For which reason we think that no one should be hindered from obtaining grace by a law which was formerly enacted, and that carnal circumcision ought not to interfere with spiritual circumcision, but that every one, without exception, ought to be admitted to the grace of Christ ; since Peter, speaking in the Acts of the Apostles, says : *God hath shown me that no man is to be called common or unclean.* But if anything could hinder men from the reception of grace, it would be chiefly the more grievous sins in adults and persons of mature and advanced age. But if remission of sin is granted to the most grievous delinquents who have formerly committed a great deal of sin against the Lord, when they afterward believe, and no one is deprived of baptism and grace, how much less ought an infant to be deprived of it, who is just born, and has not sinned at all, except that, being carnally born of the race of Adam, he has contracted at the very source of his nativity the contagion of that ancient death? Who approaches so much the more easily to receive the remission of sins, because not his own but another's sins are remitted to him?'

" See how, having no doubt about this matter, he solved the other question about which a doubt had been raised. He took this from the foundation of the church, in order to wedge a loose stone.

" We therefore beseech our brethren, if our request avails anything, not to call us any more heretics, a name which we might perhaps apply to persons who dispute in the manner that they do, although we will abstain from calling them by that name. Let their mother bear with them with the bowels of compassion, in order to heal them, and tolerate them in order to instruct them, that she may not be obliged to lament them as dead. The point toward which they are advancing is beyond the limit of endurance, and that they have thus far been endured is an act of great patience, so much so that it is hardly to be borne with. Let them not abuse this patience of the church, but correct their errors, and it will turn out for the best. We exhort them as friends, we do not employ litigation as enemies. If they speak against us, we bear it; let them not speak against the canon, or against truth; let them not contradict the Holy

Church daily laboring for the remission of the original sin of infants. That matter is one that is settled. A disputer is to be tolerated who errs in some questions not thoroughly digested, and not yet settled by the full authority of the church ; but he ought not to go so far that he attempts to shake the very foundation of the church."*

Let us take but one more extract from a sermon on the Apostles' Creed, addressed to the candidates for baptism :

"'The remission of sins.' You have the symbol perfectly in you when you are baptized. Let no one say, I have done such a thing, perhaps it is not remitted to me. What have you done? How much have you done? Tell something enormous that you have done, so grievous and frightful that you shudder even to think of it ; let it be anything you please. Have you ever slain Christ? There can be no deed worse than that, because there cannot be anything better than Christ. How great a crime it is to kill Christ! Nevertheless, the Jews killed him, and afterward many of them believed in him, and drank his blood, and the sin which they had committed was forgiven them. When you have been baptized, maintain a good life in the commandments of God, that you may keep your baptism ever unto the end. . . . God does not remit sins except to the baptized. The very sins which he remits at first, he remits only to the baptized. When? When they

---

* *Serm.* 294, *in Natal. Mart. Guddentis.*

are baptized. . . . As long as they are catechumens, all their sins are upon them. If it is so with catechumens, how much more with pagans and heretics. But we do not change the baptism of heretics. Why not? Because they have baptism in the same way that a deserter has his military mark: in that way even they have baptism; they have it that they may be condemned by it, and not that they may be crowned for it. And, nevertheless, if a repentant deserter returns to his military duty, would any one dare to change his mark?"*

It is impossible that one should fail to see from these extracts that St. Augustine held the doctrine of baptismal regeneration. He clearly asserts that baptism is the only remedy for original sin, and actual sin before baptism. That in it remission of sins, the restoration to our primitive state, the grace of Christ, regeneration, and the right to eternal life are granted. That we are made by it Christians, children of God, and members of the faithful people of Jesus Christ, even if we receive it in infancy. The figment which Calvin attempted to substitute for the Catholic doctrine, and which had been long forgotten among his followers until it was recently revived—namely, that baptism is a sign of God's covenant with true believers to grant their children at some future period justifying faith—cannot stand for an instant before the fearful precision of St. Augustine. He declares most plainly that by baptism, and by baptism alone, the

* *De Symbolo, ad Catechumenos, Serm.* I.

infants of believers are saved, and that if they are not baptized they are lost.

Here, then, is a doctrine of the Catholic Church, which one small section of Protestants has partially adopted, but which all the rest have agreed in denouncing as totally subversive of evangelical religion, which is plainly taught by St. Augustine. This shows not only that they claim him falsely as the patron of their cause in regard to this one point, but that he could not possibly have held their system at all. The holding of this one doctrine necessarily includes the rejection of the Lutheran doctrine of justification and the whole system built on it, and the acceptance of the Catholic doctrine with its consequences. St. Augustine believed that baptism is the medium of justification, therefore he could not have believed that faith is the sole medium. If it is the grace of baptism which justifies, it is an indwelling and sanctifying grace of the Holy Ghost which makes a sinner just before God, and not an external, forensic imputation of righteousness. Besides this, as the sinner's "justification" is in consequence of his having been made holy and free from sin, when he ceases to be holy and relapses into sin, he loses his justification, which demolishes the doctrines of the inamissibility of grace and of final perseverance. The necessity of penance and the merit of good works follow closely behind. The principle of sacramental grace, contained in the doctrine of baptismal regeneration, brings in the entire sacramental system of the church, the sacerdotal office, the hierarchy, salvation in the true church alone, and the liturgical system. The positive evidence that St. Augustine actually held these and other parts of the Catholic system is given elsewhere in detail. His doctrine of baptism is, however, sufficient to show that he could not have held justification by faith alone, in the Lutheran sense, and therefore could not have held that system miscalled evangelical, of which it is the first principle. It is vain to say that he did hold it in spite of his holding also other doctrines contradictory to it, the full tendency of which he did not see. St. Augustine is too clear, too sagacious, too philosophical and consistent with himself, for such statements to be made about him. He did not take the doctrine of baptismal regeneration as a form of words, a tradition, an indistinct notion caught from others, a dead, an inert formula, neutralized by the more positive and living beliefs of his soul. It was one of his first principles, a fundamental dogma in his theology, a living, practical doctrine, which he had studied and thought out deeply, which he urged most vehemently, and on which he based his whole plan of religious instruction and education as a pastor.

CHAPTER VIII.

THE HOLY EUCHARIST—INVOCATION OF SAINTS—
PURGATORY—PENANCE.

IT does not enter in the scope of our work to give a minute and exhaustive statement of everything in the works of St. Augustine which throws light on the liturgical doctrine and practice of the church in his century. We presume no one who pretends to be well informed will question the fact, that in the fifth century the orders of bishop, priest, deacon, subdeacon, and minor clerics, were universally established. That Augustine himself was ordained priest by the Bishop of Hippo, afterward made principal preacher of the cathedral, then consecrated coadjutor bishop, and finally, on the death of Bishop Aurelian, succeeded to the see. That the principal liturgies now in use were at that time essentially the same that they are at present. That the churches had sanctuaries, altars, costly ornaments, and sacred vessels and baptisteries. That pontifical and sacerdotal vestments, solemn ceremonies in the celebration of divine service and the administration of the sacraments, frequent communion, fasts and festivals, religious vows and monastic orders, prayers for the dead, and public honors to the saints, were recognized parts of the Christian religion, not only in the Catholic Church, but in schismatical and heretical communions, such as the Donatists and Arians. Those who wish for more complete information in these matters must seek for it in books where they are treated *ex professo*. Our intention is merely to cite a sufficient number of passages from St. Augustine to show the place which the doctrine of the holy eucharist and its cognate doctrines held in his theology, so as to illustrate our main thesis of the general conformity of his spirit and teaching to those of the modern Catholic Church, and their entire opposition to the spirit and teaching of Evangelical Protestantism. The citations we shall make are merely a few specimens out of a great number of similar passages, and they show what is the tone pervading all his writings and giving character to his entire system of theology.

He says, in the first place, that bishops and presbyters are, in the proper sense of the word, priests.

"'*But they shall be priests of God and of Christ, and shall reign with him a thousand years*,' is not indeed said of bishops and presbyters alone, who are now called, in the proper sense, priests in the church."*

* *De Civ. Dei*, xx. 10.

He speaks also of the altar, of the priest offering at the altar, of the sacrifice, of the application of the sacrifice to individuals both living and dead, of the commemoration of the saints, and the special dedication of altars and shrines in their honor, and quotes from the preface and canon of the Mass some of the identical forms contained in them at the present time.

"That person, however, who says that the old things have passed away in such a sense, that in Christ the ara has given place to the altar, the sword to fasting, fire to prayers, the lamb to bread, blood to the cup, is ignorant that the name of altar is the one most commonly used in the writings of the law and the prophets, and that an altar was first placed in the tabernacle which was made by Moses; that the ara also is found in the apostolic writings, where the martyrs cry out under the ara Dei. . . . He says that the lamb has given place to bread, as if ignorant that loaves of proposition are wont now to be placed on the table of the Lord, and that now he takes a part of the body of the Immaculate Lamb. He says that blood has given place to the cup, not thinking that now he receives blood in the cup. How much better and more appropriately, therefore, would he have said that old things have passed away and new things have been made in Christ, in such a way that altar has yielded to altar, sword to sword, blood to blood."*

---

* *Ep.* xxxvi. *ad Casulanum.*

"Nor do we in those places erect altars on which we sacrifice to martyrs, but to the one God of the martyrs and also ours; at which sacrifice they are named in their own place and order, as men of God who by confession of him have conquered the world; nor are they invoked by the priest who sacrifices. For he sacrifices to God and not to them, although he sacrifices in their shrine, because he is the priest of God and not of them. But the sacrifice itself is the body of Christ, which is not offered to them, because they also are it."*

"Notwithstanding, my dearest brethren, we do not regard our martyrs as gods, we do not worship them as gods, we do not erect temples or altars to them, or offer sacrifice to them. Those things are offered to God himself, from whom we receive all things. Even when we offer at the shrines of the holy martyrs, do we not offer to God? The martyrs have an honorable place. Attend, holy brethren! In the recitation at the altar of Christ, they are recited in the most worthy place; but they are not therefore adored in the place of Christ. When have you heard it said by me, or by my brethren and colleagues, or by any presbyter at the shrine of St. Theognis, I offer to thee, St. Theognis? or, I offer to thee, Peter? or, I offer to thee, Paul? You have never heard it. It is not done; it is not lawful."†

Writing against Vincent Victor, who was unwilling to say distinctly that unbaptized infants go to

---

* *Civ. Dei*, xxii. 10.   † *Serm.* 273, *De S. Fructuos.*

heaven, and foolishly sought to evade the question by recommending that Masses should be offered for them, he says :

"But, as if sensible of the evil of what he had said, that the souls of children are redeemed unto eternal life and the kingdom of heaven, without any grace of Christ, and that they could be absolved from original sin without the baptism of Christ, in which remission of sins is given ; seeing, therefore, in what a deep whirlpool he had shipwrecked himself, 'Indeed,' he says, 'I think that assiduous oblations and sacrifices should be continually offered for them by holy priests.' Behold another dilemma out of which he will never be able to escape, unless he repents of what he has said. For who offers the body of Christ, except for those who are the members of Christ?

"But even let this be conceded to him, which cannot in any way be granted with safety to the Catholic faith and the ecclesiastical rule, that the SACRIFICE of the BODY and BLOOD of Christ can be offered for unbaptized men of any age," etc.*

"For neither are the souls of the pious dead separated from the church, which even now is the kingdom of Christ. Otherwise the commemoration of them would not be made at the altar of God, in the communication of the body of Christ."†

"She (Monica) desired that a memorial of her should be made at the altar at which she had served without the intermission of a single day, and from

* *De Animâ*, i. 10, 13.   † *Civ. Dei*, xx.

Studies in St. Augustine. 147

whence she knew the holy victim was dispensed, by which was abolished the handwriting which was against us."*

The commemoration of the saints and of the faithful departed in the Canon of the Mass having been mentioned in explaining the doctrine of the eucharistic sacrifice taught by St. Augustine, we will cite one or two passages respecting the intercession and invocation of saints and purgatory, now; and avoid the necessity of treating these separately. An attempt has often been made to show that the commemoration of the saints and of the other departed faithful in the Liturgy was the same; that there was no thought of recognizing the saints as advocates and intercessors by whose prayers we are aided, or the ordinary faithful as clients who are aided by our prayers.

This is completely refuted by the following from a sermon on St. Castus:

"The justice of the martyrs is perfect, since they are made perfect by their very passion. Therefore, prayer is not offered for them in the church. For the other faithful departed prayer is offered; for the martyrs, prayer is not offered, for they have departed this life so perfect, THAT THEY ARE NOT OUR CLIENTS, BUT OUR ADVOCATES."†

Whoever wishes to see more of St. Augustine's teaching concerning the power of the saints will find ample satisfaction, and probably feel no little astonishment, by perusing the eighth chapter of the twenty-second book of the *City of God*.

* *Conf.* ix. 36. † *Serm.* 285, *in Natal. S. Casti.*

In illustration of his meaning in calling the faithful departed our clients, and of the reason for which prayers were offered for them, a multitude of passages might be quoted. We will quote but one:

"The infantile age, if it has received the sacraments of the Mediator, although it should cease to live in those tender years, yet having been translated from the power of darkness into the kingdom of Christ, is not only not destined to eternal pains, but does not even suffer any purgatorial torments after death. . . . Whoever, therefore, desires to escape eternal pains, not only must be baptized, but also justified in Christ, and thus really pass from the devil to Christ. Let him believe, however, that there are no purgatorial pains, except before that last tremendous judgment."*

Returning now to our immediate subject, the holy eucharist, the following passage is from a sermon for Easter Sunday:

"I am mindful of my promise. For I promised to you who have been baptized a sermon, in which I would explain the sacrament of the Lord's table, which you now see, and of which you have on the preceding night been made partakers. You ought to know what you have received, what you are about to receive, what you ought to receive every day. That bread which you see on the altar, sanctified by the word of God, is the Body of Christ. That chalice, rather what the chalice contains, sanctified by the

---

* *Civ. Dei*, xxi. 16.

word of God, is the Blood of Christ. . . . When it is said, Sursum Corda, you answer, Habemus ad Dominum.

"The bishop or presbyter who offers continues and says, when the people have answered, We have lifted up our hearts unto the Lord, Gratias agamus Domino Deo Nostro, and you testify, Dignum et justum est. . . .

"Then after the sanctification of the sacrifice of God, because he willed that we also should be his sacrifice which was shown when that was first laid on the altar, which is both the sacrifice of God and is also we ourselves, that is, a sign of that thing which we are; behold, when the sanctification has been accomplished, we say the Lord's Prayer. . . . After that is said, Pax Vobiscum, and the Christians kiss one another with a holy kiss."*

Closely connected with the Catholic doctrine of the holy eucharist is that of the sacrament of penance, which involves the distinction between venial and mortal sins, and presupposes the whole doctrine of justification. A baptized Christian is in the state of grace, which is an infused habit or quality of the soul making it holy and just. So long as he keeps this holiness, he is a just man; when he loses it, he falls back into sin and the state of damnation. This essential holiness consists in freedom from mortal sin. A person in mortal sin cannot receive holy communion. He must be cleansed from mortal sin and re-

* *Serm.* 127, *in Die Pasch.*

conciled to God in the sacrament of penance before he can receive worthily. Venial sins do not destroy the life of grace; it is morally impossible wholly to avoid them, and they can be remitted without the sacrament of penance. Mortal sin can with due care and diligence be wholly avoided, during the entire period of life; and good Christians are expected to live habitually in the state of grace without committing any grievous sins.

Such, as every one knows, is the common, practical theology of the Catholic Church.

The following extracts will show that it was the doctrine of St. Augustine:

"The fourth petition is, *Give us this day our daily bread.* Upon which the blessed Cyprian shows how that also here we pray for perseverance. He says, among other things:

"'We pray that this bread may be given us daily, lest any of us who are in Christ and daily receive the eucharist as the food of salvation, through the means of some more grievous sin should be separated from the body of Christ, while abstaining and not communicating, we are forbidden the celestial bread.' These words of the holy man of God indicate that the saints demand perseverance entirely from the Lord, when with that intention they say, *Give us this day our daily bread*, in order that they may not be separated from the body of Christ, but may remain in that holiness in which they shall admit no crime on account of which they would deserve to be separated from it."*

* *De Dono Persev.* vii.

"I do not say to you that you will live here without sin; but there are venial sins, which our life here cannot be without. Baptism was appointed for all sins, and prayer for those light faults from which we cannot be altogether free. . . . But do not commit those on account of which it is necessary that you should be separated from the body of Christ, which misfortune I trust may not befall you. For those persons whom you see doing penance have committed crimes, either adultery or some other wicked action; therefore they are doing penance. For, if their sins were only light ones, daily prayer would suffice for their remission. Therefore, in three ways sins are remitted in the church, by baptism, by prayer, and BY THE GREATER HUMILIATION OF PENANCE; nevertheless, God does not remit sins except to the baptized."*

"Therefore all past sins are remitted to those who are converted; but there are certain grievous and deadly sins in this life which are not pardoned except through the most vehement grief of an humbled heart and a contrite spirit, together with the tribulation of penance. THESE SINS ARE REMITTED BY THE KEYS OF THE CHURCH."†

"Because usually the grief of one heart is hidden from another, and does not come to the knowledge of others except through words or some other signs; but is known only to him to whom it is said, *My groaning is not hidden from thee;* times of penance

---

* *Serm.* 1, *De Symbolo.* † *Serm.* 278, *De Voce Pauli.*

are rightly appointed by those who rule the church, that satisfaction may also be made to the church in which sins are remitted; for outside of her they are not remitted."*

"Do penance such as is done in the church. . . . Let no one say, I do it secretly, I do it before God. For then without reason it was said, *Whatsoever you shall loose on earth shall be loosed also in heaven;* for then without reason the keys were given to the Church of God: we frustrate the gospel of God: we frustrate the words of Christ; we promise what he denied."†

"We cannot forbid any one from communion, unless he has either voluntarily confessed, or has been denounced and convicted before some secular or ecclesiastical tribunal."‡

It is clear from these foregoing extracts, that, according to St. Augustine and the received theology of his time, only venial sins could be remitted without recourse to the keys of the church, and that those who committed mortal sin could not lawfully approach holy communion without undergoing a penance enjoined by ecclesiastical authority and receiving the remission of their sin through the absolving power left by Christ in the hands of the priesthood. There is no evidence that the faithful were in the habit of going to confession, as the present custom is, every time they went to communion, or at least very frequently; or that they were required to ask permission

---

* *De Fide, Spe, Char.* 65.   † *Serm.* 392.   ‡ *Serm.* 351.

in order to receive communion. The habit of confessing frequently, when one has only venial sins to confess, is no doubt salutary, and the law requiring the laity to regulate the number of their communions by the judgment of their director is a good one. But the divine law exacts only the confession of mortal sins as absolutely necessary, and forbids the reception of communion at any time only to those who are in mortal sin. In St. Augustine's time the faithful were left to judge for themselves whether they were worthy to receive communion or not, and how often they should receive it. So long as they lived a moral life, they were supposed to be good Christians, and permitted to receive communion as often as they wished. It was left to their conscience to decide whether they committed any mortal sin or not, and to confess it and submit themselves to penance if they did. It would seem from St. Augustine's language that this penance was always public. We know, however, from other sources that the penance for secret sins, which were known only through confession, was not public, unless the penitent consented to it, and the publicity of the penance was likely to give edification rather than scandal. In the case of open and public sins, the delinquents were publicly excluded from the communion of the faithful and obliged to perform long and severe penances in the face of the church. The publicity of the penance has never been regarded as an essential part of it, but as a peculiarity of discipline introduced in the third century as a check on immorality, and abolished subsequently on account of the abuse connected with it. The essential part of penance is the exclusion of the sinner from communion until he has been reconciled to God by the ministry of the keys which Christ has left to the church. To effect this reconciliation, it is necessary to have sincere contrition, to manifest this sorrow externally, and to submit to external humiliation by confessing the sins committed to the authorized minister of Christ and the church, who is empowered to judge the case and grant the absolution of sin; and to be disposed to perform penitential works. It is plain that St. Augustine teaches this doctrine. We have shown that he teaches that there are only two remedies for mortal sin, baptism and penance; that only venial sins are remitted by secret acts and prayers which are known to God alone, and that penance must be administered by virtue of that power of the keys, the power of binding and loosing, which Christ has left with the priests of his church.

It would be easy to multiply extracts from St. Augustine on the topics contained in this chapter, and in this way to treat of the doctrines of penance and the holy eucharist, with other doctrines incidentally touched upon, in a much more thorough and copious manner. It is not necessary, however, to do this. We have given a clew which any scholar disposed to study these and other doctrines in St. Augustine's works can easily follow for himself. In the present essay, we have not taken up these doctrines for their own sake, but in their bearing on St. Augustine's doctrine of justification. Taken in connection with all that has been cited and explained in foregoing chapters, it is easy to see that they establish the perfect contrariety of his teaching to that of the Evangelical system, and its perfect agreement with that of the Catholic Church. In the first part of the essay, we have shown that St. Augustine teaches the essential goodness of nature, the essential liberty of the will, the freedom of man in accepting and corresponding with grace, the possibility of keeping the commandments of God, and the merit of good works ; in contradiction to the Calvinistic doctrine of total depravity. In the second part, we have shown that he teaches the doctrine that the Catholic Church is the divinely appointed and necessary instrument for receiving the grace of God, which is dispensed through the sacraments ; in contradiction to the Calvinistic and Evangelical doctrine of justification by faith alone. This disposes of the whole subject matter of the controversy, which is completely included in these two doctrines. On the one hand, the Calvinistic and Evangelical partisans are deprived of every pretext for claiming St. Augustine as their champion : and on the other, the partisans of opposite opinions are deprived of all pretext for throwing the odium of Calvinistic distortions and exaggerations on St. Augustine, and on the Catholic Church, which venerates him as one of its chief doctors of theology.

We have not endeavored to establish these two points merely for the sake of controversy, or for throwing light on a curious question of history and criticism. Our object is higher than this. We have desired to show the sincere Calvinist those positive dogmas which he holds respecting the fall of man and his salvation by the grace of God in Christ, in a higher and more perfect ideal form; in which they can be reconciled with other revealed truths, and with the dictates of reason, as well as with the actual history of Christianity. We have desired to show the rational Christian and the philosopher that these dogmas do not contradict those truths to which they are the most attached. This is but clearing the way a little for the calm consideration of the positive evidence on which the whole system of Catholic dogma rests, as a divine revelation. It is a slight effort to help on that happy *connubium* between faith and science, which the illustrious Bishop of Augsburg has recently said should be at the present time the great object of our Christian aspirations.

As a collateral result, the evidence which has been cited from St. Augustine is available also, in proof of the general nature of the religion really bequeathed by the apostles to the Christian Church. So far as it goes, it establishes the truth of the assertion made in our own day, by a learned German Protestant, Julius Müller:

"This must be openly admitted by every unprejudiced historical investigation, that not merely the ecclesiastical theology of the middle ages, but even the patristic theology of the fourth, fifth, and sixth centuries, ARE UPON EVERY POINT THAT IS A MATTER OF DISPUTE BETWEEN CATHOLICISM AND PROTESTANTISM MORE ON THE SIDE OF THE FORMER THAN OF THE LATTER."*

---

* Quoted by Döllinger, *Church and Churches*, p. 298.

Glossary of Latin Words and Phrases

NOT TRANSLATED IN THE TEXT.

A parte Dei, . On the part of God.
A posteriori, Argument from effect to cause.
A priori, . Argument from cause to effect.
Ab æterno, From eternity.
Ab extra, . . From without.
Ab intra, . . From within.
Ad extra, . . Terminating in something without.
Ad infinitum, ... To infinity.
Æternitas a parte ante et a parte post, . Eternity of the past and of the future.
Amor entis, ... Love of being.
Bonâ fide, . . In good faith,
Causa altissima, . . Highest, that is, supreme cause.
Conditio sine quâ non, Indispensable condition.
Credenda, . . . Articles of faith.
Cultus, . Worship.
De fide, ... Pertaining to the faith.
De novo, ... Anew.
Durus pater infantium, . . A cruel father of children.
Ens a se, . . . Being from itself.
Ens ab alio, . . . Being from another.
Ens in actu, . Being in act.
Ens simpliciter, . Simple being.
Existentia, . Existence.

Glossary.

Fides quærens intellectum,	Faith in quest of understanding.
Figura substantiæ ejus,	The figure of his substance.
In se et ab intrinseco,	By its intrinsic force.
In se,	In itself.
In transitu,	In passing.
In potentiâ,	In a state of latent capacity.
Intelligo,	I understand.
Pace tantorum virorum,	With due respect for such great men.
Per speculum in ænigmate	Through a glass darkly.
Quid sit Deus,	What God is.
Ratione mali,	By reason or for the sake of evil; or, precisely as being evil.
Ratio peccati,	The quality which makes it sin.
Salvâ fide et auctoritate ecclesiæ,	Without injury to faith and the authority of the church.
Super omnem naturam creatam atque creabilem,	Above nature which has been and can be created.
Una res cum Deo,	One thing with God.
Ut Deus sit,	That God is.
Vis activa,	Active force.

LIST OF BOOKS

PUBLISHED BY

THE CATHOLIC PUBLICATION SOCIETY.

The Life and Sermons of the Rev. FRANCIS A. BAKER, Priest of the Congregation of St. Paul, edited by Rev. F. A. Hewit.
1 vol. crown 8vo, pp. 504, . . . $2 50
Half calf or morocco extra, . . . 4 00

Sermons of the Paulist Fathers, for 1865 and 1866. Price, . . . $1 50

May Carols and Hymns and POEMS. By Aubrey de Vere. Blue and gold, ... $1 25

Christine, and other Poems. By George H. Miles. Price, . . . $2 00
Gilt, extra, ... 2 50

Dr. Newman's Answer to Dr. Pusey's EIRENICON. Paper, ... 75

Three Phases of Christian Love: The Mother, the Maiden, and the Religious. By Lady Herbert.
1 vol. 12mo, ... $1 50
Gilt, extra, ... 2 00

Aspirations of Nature. By Rev. I. T. Hecker.
Fourth ed., revised, cloth, extra, . $1 50
Gilt extra, ... 2 00

The Clergy and the Pulpit, in THEIR RELATIONS TO THE PEOPLE. By M. L'Abbé Isidore Mullois, Chaplain to Napoleon III.
1 vol. 12mo, extra cloth, . . . $1 50
Half calf, extra, ... 2 50

The Inner Life of Very Rev. Pere LACORDAIRE, of the Order of Preachers. Translated from the French of the Rev. Père Chocarne, O.P. By a Father of the same Order, with a Preface by Father Aylward, Prior Provincial of England.
1 vol. 12mo, toned paper, . . . $3 00

Reason and Revelation. Lectures delivered in St. Ann's Church, New York, during Advent, 1867, by Rev. T. S. Preston. 1 vol. 12mo, . . . $1 50

Life and Letters of Madame Swetchine. Translated from the French of the Count Falloux. 1 vol. 12mo, . $2 00

The Comedy of Convocation in THE ENGLISH CHURCH. In Two Scenes. Edited by Archdeacon Chasuble, D.D., and dedicated to the Pan-Anglican Synod.
8vo, pamphlet, paper, ... $0 75
Bound in cloth, ... 1 00
People's Edition, paper, ... 25

The Catholic Crusoe; or, Adventures OF OWEN EVANS, Cast on a Desolate Island in the Caribbean Sea. By Rev. Dr. Anderdon.
1 vol. 12mo, illustrated, ... $1 00

The Life of the Blessed Virgin S. CATHARINE OF SIENNA.
1 vol. 12mo, ... $1 75

An Epistle of Jesus Christ to the FAITHFUL SOUL that is devoutly affected toward Him; wherein are contained certain Divine Inspirations, teaching a man to know himself, and instructing him in the Perfection of True Piety.
1 vol. 16mo, ... $1 00

Tales from the Diary of a Sister of MERCY. By C. M. Brame.
1 vol. 12mo, extra cloth, . . . $1 50
Extra gilt, ... 2 00

St. Columba, Apostle of Caledonia. By the Count de Montalembert.
1 vol. 12mo, toned paper, . . . $1 25
Cloth, gilt, ... 1 75

A Sister's Story. By Mrs. Augustus Craven. Translated from the French, by Emily Bowles. 1 vol. crown 8vo, pp. 528.
Cloth, extra, ... $2 50
Cloth, gilt, ... 3 00

The Illustrated Catholic Sunday- SCHOOL LIBRARY. First Series now ready. 12 vols. Handsomely bound, and put up in a box, cloth, extra, . $6 00
Cloth, gilt, ... 7 50
The following are the titles of the twelve volumes comprising the first series: Madeleine, the Rosière; Crusade of the Children; Tales of the Affections; Adventures of Travel; Truth and Trust; Select Popular Tales; The Rivals; The Battle of Lepanto, etc.; Scenes and Incidents at Sea; The Schoolboys, and the Boy and the Man; Beautiful Little Rose; Florestine. Any of the above volumes can be

List of Books.

had separately; price, 50 cents; gilt, 63 cents each.

Problems of the Age, with Studies in St. Augustine on Kindred Topics. By Rev. A. F. Hewit.
1 vol. 12mo, extra cloth, ... $2 00

Nellie Netterville; or, One of the Transplanted. A Tale of the Times of Cromwell in Ireland.
1 vol. 12mo, cloth, extra, . . . $1 50
Cloth, gilt, ... 2 00

Questions of the Soul. By Rev. I. T. Hecker. New edition, ... $1 50
Cloth, gilt, ... 2 00

Sermons of the Paulist Fathers for 1864. New edition, ... $1 50

Apologia Pro Vita Sua: Being a Reply to a Pamphlet entitled, "What, then, does Dr. Newman Mean?" By John Henry Newman, D.D. New edition. 1 vol. 12mo, ... $2 00

An Illustrated History of Ireland, from the Earliest Period to the Present Time; with first-class full-page Engravings of Historical Scenes, designed by Henry Doyle, and engraved by George Hanlon and George Pearson; together with upward of one hundred Woodcuts by eminent artists, illustrating Antiquities, Scenery, and Sites of Remarkable Events.
1 vol. 8vo, nearly 600 pages, only $5 00

Notes on the Rubrics of the Roman Ritual. By the Rev. James O'Kane, Senior Dean St. Patrick's College, Maynooth, Ireland.
1 vol. crown 8vo, cloth, ... $4 00

Symbolism; or, Exposition of the Doctrinal Differences between Catholics and Protestants, as evidenced by their Symbolical Writings. By John A. Moehler, D.D. Translated from the German, with a Memoir of the Author, preceded by an Historical Sketch of the State of Protestantism and Catholicism in Germany for the last Hundred Years, by J. B. Robertson, Esq., $4

The Works of the Most Rev. John Hughes, D.D., First Archbishop of New-York, containing Biography, Sermons, Letters, Lectures, Speeches, etc. Carefully compiled from the best sources, and edited by Lawrence Kehoe.
Cheap edition, 2 vols. 8vo, cloth, . $6 00
Fine edition, 2 vols., cloth, bev., . 8 00
2 vols., half morocco, bevelled, . 10 00
2 vols., half calf, extra, ... 12 00

The People's Pictorial Lives of the Saints, Scriptural and Historical. Abridged, for the most part, from those of the late Rev. Alban Butler. In packets of 12 each. One packet now ready, containing the lives of twelve different saints. Per packet, 25 cents.

Packets of Scripture Illustrations. Containing 50 Engravings of subjects from the Old and New Testament, after original designs by Elster.
Price, loose packages of fifty, . 75 cents.

Catholic Tracts. The Catholic Publication Society has issued the following Tracts:

1. Religious Indifferentism and its Remedy. 2. The Plea of Sincerity. 3. The Night before the Forlorn Hope; or, Prayer a Resource in all Danger. 4. The Prisoner of Cayenne: a True Narrative. 5. What Shall I do to be Saved? 6. The Plea of Uncertainty. 7. What my Uncle said about the Pope. 8. How Shall we Find True Christianity? 9. On Catholic Tradition. 10. What is to be Done in Such a Case? 11. The Senators of Sherburne; or, A Lawyer's Rule of Faith. 12. The Catholic Doctrine of the Real Presence Shown from Holy Scripture. 13. Union among Christians. 14. The Gospel-Door of Mercy. 15. What Shall I do to Become a Christian? 16. The Church and Children. 17. A Voice in the Night; or, Lessons of the Sick-Room. 18. The Gospel Church. 19. Who was Jesus Christ? 20. The Trinity. 21. Control your Passions. 22. Heroism in the Sick-Room. 23. Is the Sacrifice of the Mass of Human or of Divine Institution? 24. Why did God Become Man? 25. The Catholic Church. 26. Who Founded the Catholic Church? 27. The Exclusiveness of the Catholic Church. 28. Children and Protestantism. 29. How to Spend Lent. 30. Is it Honest? 31. What says the Bible?

All the above Tracts can be had at the Publication House, 126 Nassau Street, in packages of 100 each, or in packages of 100 assorted. Price, 50 cents per 100. To be had at all Catholic book-stores.

The Catholic Sunday-School Class-Book. New and improved edition, $1 per dozen.

All the American Catholic books kept in stock. A large and general assortment of English and Irish Catholic books always on hand. All the new English books received immediately after publication.

THE CATHOLIC PUBLICATION SOCIETY,

LAWRENCE KEHOE, *General Agent,*

126 Nassau Street, New York City.

www.ingramcontent.com/pod-product-compliance
Lightning Source LLC
Chambersburg PA
CBHW022134300426
44115CB00006B/183